COMMANDO

A BOER JOURNAL
OF THE BOER WAR

COMMANDO

A BOER JOURNAL OF THE BOER WAR

DENEYS REITZ

WITH A PREFACE BY

GENERAL THE RIGHT HONOURABLE

J.C. SMUTS

CruGuru

COMMANDO

Copyright © 2008 by CruGuru

ISBN: 978-1-920265-68-7

First published in 1929

This edition published in 2008 by CruGuru. Revised in 2009.

www.cruguru.com

THIS BOOK IS DEDICATED TO MY FATHER

FRANCIS WILLIAM REITZ

The only living President
of the old South African Republics

About the Author

Deneys Reitz (1882—1944) was a Boer Commando, South African soldier and politician. While still in his teens, Deneys Reitz served in the Boer forces during the Second Boer War. As a commando he fought in both the first conventional phase of the war and the second guerrilla phase. In the latter, he accompanied General Jan Smuts on raids deep into the Cape Province; he continued to fight to the "bitter end", and then went to live in Madagascar rather than sign the peace terms which every Boer soldier was called upon to sign.

While in exile in Madagascar, he wrote about his experience of the Boer War, so that, when it was eventually edited and published in 1929 as *Commando: A Boer Journal Of The Boer War*, it still had the freshness and detail of an account written soon after the war. Not only is the account very well written and an important source for the Second Boer War, his family connections (his father was State Secretary of the Transvaal) and sheer luck provides for a unique account, because he was present at virtually every major event of the war. For instance, while visiting his father at the start of the war and being too young to fight, the President of the Transvaal, Paul Kruger, gave him special permission to do so.

On the advice of his wartime commander, General Jan Smuts (later to become Field-Marshall and member of the British Imperial War Cabinet under Winston Churchill during World War II), he returned to South Africa in 1906. The malaria he had fought with in Madagascar had so severely affected his health that he collapsed unconscious upon his return to South Africa. He was nursed back to health over three years by Jan Smuts and his wife, Isie. He then returned to public life. In 1914 he helped Smuts suppress the Maritz Rebellion in the Free State, and he served on Smuts' army staff in the "German West campaign" (in the German colony of what today is called Namibia), and in the "German East campaign" (in German East Africa) where he rose to command a mounted regiment. On the Western Front during World War I he commanded the First Royal Scots Fusiliers until he was severely wounded early in 1918. He returned to active service to lead his men to the Rhine after the Armistice. He continued in public life as a Member of Parliament, Cabinet Minister, Deputy Prime Minister (1939-1943), and South African High Commissioner to London (1944).

Late in the Boer war, Reitz' Commando fought and won a sharp battle with men of the 17th Lancers, a crack regiment. One of the wounded British was Lord Vivian, who, noting how haggard and badly clothed Reitz was, advised him to take some of his possessions. Reitz declined, saying it was he who had wounded Vivian. Vivian replied that it had been the fortune of war and if Reitz did not take the clothing, others would. Vivian added that since he wanted to give his possessions to Reitz, it would be a gift, which is better than loot. Reitz took Vivian's Lee-Metford, bandoliers, a horse, trousers and tunic, and left behind his old Mauser. Just before his death in 1944, Deneys Reitz was in his London office when a visitor was ushered in, carrying a parcel. It was Lord Vivian, returning the Mauser Reitz had left behind.

COMMANDO

A BOER JOURNAL
OF THE BOER WAR

Victrix causa
Diis placuit
Sed victa Catoni

Preface

When Colonel Reitz asked me to write a preface to his book of Boer War memories, I at first hesitated, as I feared that I might be introducing a book in which I myself figured in some degree. However, on reading the manuscript, I find that I am only casually mentioned here and there and have therefore no reason not to comply with his request.

It is a pleasure and a privilege to introduce this book to the reading public. To me it is a wonderful book - wonderful in its simplicity and realism, its calm intensity and absorbing human interest. Here is the book of the Boer War for which I have been waiting for the last twenty-five years and more. Many military books have been written on the Boer War - books full of interest and of valuable material for the future historian; but something else was wanted. The Boer War was other than most wars. It was a vast tragedy in the life of a people, whose human interest far surpassed its military value. A book was wanted which would give us some insight into the human side of this epic struggle between the smallest and the greatest of peoples.

Here we have it at last. There is no strategy and little tactics in this plain unvarnished tale. Wars pass, but the human soul endures; the interest is not so much in the war as in the human experience behind it. This book tells the simple straightforward story of what the Boer War meant to one participant in it. Colonel Reitz entered the war as a stripling of seventeen years, fought right through it to the end, and immediately after its conclusion wrote down these memories. Of military adventures there is of course full measure. He passed through as varied a record of exciting experiences as have ever fallen to the lot of a young man. Indeed much of what is written in this book with such boyish simplicity may appear to the reader well-nigh incredible. But it is a true story, and the facts are often understated rather than exaggerated. The exciting incidents, the hair-breadth escapes, the daredevilry are literally true, and the dangers he passed through and courted are such as to make his unvarnished record read like one of pure romance. But there is here more than a record of war adventure. We have not only an unforgettable picture of mobile guerrilla warfare, but also an accurate description of life among the Boer forces. It is given, not in an abstract generalized form, but as the actual experience of one particular individual. As we read, we follow a true personal story which is often stranger than fiction. The interest of the story deepens as it moves on from the heavy fighting in the Natal campaign under Botha through the guerrilla warfare under Delarey in the Western Transvaal, to the climax of marching and privation under me in the Cape Colony. The intimate pictures give us the inner truth of the war. We see how human beings react under the most terrible stresses to the passion of patriotism. We see how, under the influence of an ideal - in this case the ideal of freedom - the most ordinary humans material rings true and rises superior to all danger and suffering and privation. And the effect is all the more striking because the story is so simple and unadorned and objective.

This book gives a wonderful personal record. But its wonder does not end with the book. The Boer boy who wrote this book was in the Wordsworthian sense the father of the man of after years. Let me add a few details to bring the account up to date. The boy left the country as an irreconcilable after the conclusion of the Boer War, as he and his family chose not to live under the British flag. He drifted to Madagascar, where these memories were written in the intervals of malaria and transport riding. There a letter from my wife found him, urged him to return and pointed out to him that he was no better than her husband, and if the latter could afford to serve his people under the Union Jack surely his young friend could do the same. The shaft went home; Reitz returned and was nursed back by her to health and peace of mind. He learnt to see Botha's great vision of a united South African people to whom the memories of the Boer War would mean no longer bitterness but only the richness and the inspiration of a spiritual experience. The loyalty of the Boer boy ripened into the broader loyalty of the South African. And I remember a night on the outbreak of the rebellion in 1914, when Reitz once more appeared before me, this time a fugitive, not from the British, but from his own people in the Free State who had gone into rebellion. Such tricks does high fate play upon us poor humans. He did his duty in helping to suppress the rebellion, and thereafter he served on my staff in the German West campaign, just as he had done in the Boer War; in the German East campaign he rose to command a mounted regiment, and in the later stages of the Great War he commanded the First Royal Scots Fusiliers, one of the oldest regiments in the British Army. He was severely wounded early in 1918, but returned to France in time to lead his battalion in the fierce battles that closed the great drama, and after the Armistice he led his men to the Rhine.

Since the War, he has taken an active part in the public life of his country. He has been a Cabinet Minister and still is a Member of Parliament in which capacity he is serving under me as loyally as he did in the sterner days of which he writes.

This book is a romance of truth; but behind it is a greater personal romance, and behind that again is the even more wonderful romance of South Africa, to whom much should be forgiven for the splendour of her record during a period as difficult as any young nation has ever passed through.

Pretoria,
16th August,
1929.
J.C. Smuts

Table of Contents

1. "MEM'RY'S TOWER"

We lived in the Orange Free State.

My father was Chief Justice in Sir John Brand's time and sub-sequently, in 1887, was himself elected President of the Republic. Our home was at Bloemfontein, the State capital, and here my brothers and I grew up. There were five of us, two older and two younger than myself, and we led a pleasant Tom sawyer-like existence such as falls to the lot of few boys nowadays. We learned to ride, shoot, and swim almost as soon as we could walk, and there was a string of hardy Basuto ponies in the stables, on which we were often away for weeks at a time, riding over the game-covered plains by day, and sleeping under the stars at night, hunting, fishing and camping to our heart's content, and clattering home again when we had had our fill.

Sometimes my father took us with him on his long tours into the remoter districts, where there was more hunting and more camping, and great wapin-shaws, held by the Boer commandos to do him honour. Our small country was a model one. There were no political parties, nor, until after the Jameson Raid of 1895, was there any bad blood between the Dutch and the English. We had no railways, and the noise of the outside world reached us but faintly, so that in our quiet way we were a contented community, isolated hundreds of miles from the seaboard.

In 1894, when I was twelve years old, we were taken to Europe. It was a wonderful experience for inland-bred boys to journey to the Coast, to cross the ocean in a ship, and to see the great crowds and cities of the old world. We went first of all to England, where we stayed for a while in London, marvelling at the things we saw. Thence to Amsterdam to visit the senior branch of our family, that had remained in Holland when our ancestors emigrated to South Africa long ago. The head of the old stock lived in a house on the Heerengracht; a wealthy man apparently, for he kept many servants and had fine paintings on his walls.

As our republic had taken its name from the House of Orange, my father was well received by the little Queen of the Netherlands, and the Court and people made much of us. Next, we travelled to Paris to meet Casimir-Perier, the newly elected President of the French. He took us to lay a wreath on the grave of Sadi

Carnot, his predecessor, lately assassinated by an anarchist at Lyons. From there we went to Brussels to see Monsieur Jesslein, our Consul. His house stood in the rue de la Blanchisserie, and he told us it was the one in which the Duchess of Richmond had given her famous ball on the eve of Waterloo. We were presented to King Leopold, an old man with a hooked nose and a long white beard, who extended only his little finger in greeting, perhaps because we belonged to a republic.

From Belgium we went to Hamburg to take ship across the North Sea to Edinburgh, and from there to visit the Cathcarts at Auchindrayne on the River Doon. My father had studied law in Scotland and my grandfather before him had studied agriculture, and they had both spent much time at Auchindrayne, so my father wished his sons in turn to carry on the tradition of friendship which for clearly a hundred years linked the two families.

My grandfather first went to Scotland in 1816. He met Walter Scott, to whom he took a lionskin which the poet Thomas Pringle had sent from Capetown, and he became intimate with the great writer. In later days in South Africa, he loved to tell of their meetings and of the banquet at which he was present when Scott for the first time admitted that he was the author of the Waverley Novels. Both my grandfather and my father had returned to South Africa with a deep love of Scotland and Scotch literature, and at our home scarcely a night passed without a reading from Burns or Scott, so that we felt as if we were among our own people.

From Auchindrayne we went to London to meet Sir George Grey, who, as Governor of the Cape, had been a friend of my father many years before. My father used to say that if the English had sent more men like him to South Africa our history would have been a happier one, and although I was only a boy, and Sir George Grey a very old man, he made a deep impression upon me - a something of inward beauty not easily described, but which I have not yet forgotten.

From London we sailed for South Africa. On our return my brothers and I were received by our less fortunate playfellows like pilgrims safely returned from Mecca, so hazardous an undertaking did our journey seem to them in those days.

We took up our old carefree life once more, all unaware of the storm that was brewing between the white races in the Transvaal.

The Jameson Raid had not yet brought matters to a head, but there was trouble in the air. President Kruger and the Commandant-General Piet Joubert, came frequently to Bloemfontein on official visits to my father, and we eagerly questioned them and listened to their stories of hunting and of the wars against the natives and the British long ago.

Sir Henry Loch, Governor of the Cape, also visited us, as did Cecil Rhodes, a big florid man who cracked jokes with us boys, but on whose political aims my father looked askance. These two tried to prevent the Free State from entering into an alliance with the Transvaal, but they did not succeed, and a treaty was made with President Kruger wherein we agreed to stand by the Transvaal in case of war with England, a promise which the Free State loyally fulfilled.

My brothers and I did not understand the import of all this coming and going of noted men, and life ran on pleasantly enough, until in 1895 my father's health failed and he had to resign. We went to live at Claremont, a cramped suburb of Capetown, greatly missing our horses and the freedom of our wide Northern uplands.

When my father recovered from his long illness we settled in the Transvaal, where he soon became Secretary of State under President Paul Kruger. My eldest brother, aged nineteen, was now sent to Europe to study law, and after a while the rest of us were put back to school at Bloemfontein until the middle of 1899.

During our absence at the Cape the ill-fated Jameson Raid had taken place, and we found on our return that feeling was running high between the English and the Dutch, and even in the Free State, where differences of this kind had hitherto been unknown, there was so much ill will that people openly talked of driving the English into the sea, whereas previously we had not given these matters a thought.

By July (1899) the situation had become so serious that my father ordered us up to Pretoria, as war with England seemed inevitable. We said goodbye to Bloemfontein the town where we had been born and bred and where we had spent such happy days, and journeyed north, leaving behind us the peace of boyhood, to face years of hardship, danger, and ultimate exile.

2.   ON THE BRINK

When we reached Pretoria, affairs were moving to a climax. Peremptory notes had been exchanged between the Transvaal and the British Government, and excitement was rising as each cable and its reply was published. Already the Transvaal capital was an armed camp. Batteries of artillery paraded the streets, commandos from the country districts rode through the town almost daily, bound for the Natal border, and the crack of rifles echoed from the surrounding hills where hundreds of men were having target practice. Crowded trains left for the coast with refugees flying from the coming storm, and business was at a standstill.

Looking back, I think that war was inevitable. I have no doubt that the British Government had made up its mind to force the issue, and was the chief culprit, but the Transvaalers were also spoiling for a fight, and, from what I saw in Pretoria during the few weeks that preceded the ultimatum, I feel sure that the Boers would in any case have insisted on a rupture.

I myself had no hatred of the British people; from my father's side I come of Dutch and French Huguenot blood, whilst my mother (dead for many years) was a pure-bred Norwegian from the North Cape, so one race was much like another to me. Yet, as a South African, one had to fight for one's country, and for the rest I did not concern myself overmuch with the merits or demerits of the quarrel. I looked on the prospect of war and adventure with the eyes of youth, seeing only the glamour, but knowing nothing of the horror and the misery.

I was seventeen years old and thus too young to be enrolled as a burgher. President Kruger himself solved this difficulty for me. One morning when I was at the Government buildings, I met him and my father in the corridor and I told the President that the Field-Cornet's office had refused to enrol me for active service. The old man looked me up and down for a moment and growled: 'Piet Joubert says the English are three to one - *Sal jij mij drie rooinekke lever?* (Will you stand me good for three of them?) I answered boldly: 'President, if I get close enough I'm good for three with one shot.' He gave a hoarse chuckle at my youthful conceit and, turning to my father, asked how old I was. When he heard my age he said: 'Well then, Mr State Secretary, the boy must go - I started fighting earlier than that', and he took me straight to the Commandant-General's room close by, where Piet Joubert in person handed me a new Mauser carbine, and a bandolier of ammunition, with which I returned home pleased and proud.

I saw a good deal of the President in these days as I used to go with my father to his house on the outskirts of the town, where they discussed State matters while I sat listening. The President had an uncouth, surly manner, and he was the ugliest man I have ever seen, but he had a strong rugged personality which impressed all with whom he came in contact. He was religious to a degree, and on Sundays he preached in the queer little Dopper church he had built across the street, where I sometimes heard him.

There was Mrs Kruger too, whom I often saw with her pails in the yard, for she kept dairy cows and sold milk to the neighbours. Once she brought us coffee while we were looking at a picture of the statue of her husband that was being set up on Church Square. The President was shown dressed like an elder of the Church in a top hat, and the old lady suggested that the hat should be hollowed out and filled with water, to serve as a drinking-fountain for the birds. My father and I laughed heartily on our way home at her simplicity, but we agreed that it was decent of her to have thought of such a thing.

I also knew Piet Joubert, the Commandant-General, for, apart from his visits to Bloemfontein, his son Jan and I were friends, and I sometimes went home with him to talk about the coming war, and his father was generally there. He was a kindly, well-meaning old man who had done useful service in the smaller campaigns of the past, but he gave me the impression of being bewildered at the heavy responsibility now resting upon him, and I felt that he was unequal to the burden.

One afternoon he showed me a cable which he had received from a Russian society offering to equip an ambulance in case of war, and when I expressed my pleasure I was astonished to hear him say that he had refused the gift. He said: 'You see, my boy, we Boers don't hold with these newfangled ideas; our herbal remedies (*bossie-middels*) are good enough.' Another time, when describing the festivities at the opening of the Delagoa Bay railway line, which he had attended as Commander-in-Chief, he told me that when the Portuguese paraded a thousand troops in his honour, he had gone down the ranks shaking hands with every one of the soldiers. I liked him very much personally, and to me he was always kind and fatherly, but I felt that he was unfit to lead armies, and it is a great pity that a younger man was not appointed in his place on the outbreak of the war.

And now the days were speeding by and in September of 1899 matters had come to such a pass that British troops were moving up to the western borders of the Transvaal and Free State, and other troops were on the water, while large Boer forces were mobilising on the various fronts. Committees and deputations from the Cape travelled up to make eleventh-hour attempts to avert the catastrophe of war, but it was clear that the die was cast and that neither side was in a mood for further parleying.

My eldest brother (named Hjalmar, after a Norwegian uncle) was away in Europe studying law, and my father had already cabled to him to return. My next brother, Joubert, named after the Commandant-General, was a year older than myself, and although he, too, was ineligible for burgher-rights, he intended volunteering for service, but the two younger ones were put back to school.

Joubert and I had made our preparations long before. Our horses were in good fettle and our saddlebags packed. My brother had a fine upstanding chestnut, and I had a strong little Basuto pony, and we were eager to be off.

Many of the country districts had been called up, but thus far no Pretoria men had gone forward. At last, on September fifth, the first batch from the town was ordered to entrain for the Natal border. The moment we heard of this we took our rifles, fetched our horses from the stable, and within ten minutes had saddled up and mounted.

We said goodbye to our stepmother and her children, for my father had re-married years before, and rode up through the town to the *Raadzaal* to take leave of him. We found him closeted with the President and members of the Executive Council, but we went in and, when we explained why we had come, all rose to shake us by the hand. The old President gave us a solemn blessing, and my father, who had not expected this sudden departure, bade us goodbye in a husky voice and said he knew we would do our best.

From the Government buildings we galloped to the station, where we found a great stir. Hundreds of friends and relatives had come to see the contingent leave, but, in spite of the crowd on the platform and the loading of baggage and batteries, we were able to truck our animals after which we lent a hand with the stowing of the ammunition and other work.

When all was ready the train pulled out to the sound of the Transvaal National Anthem. There were enthusiastic cheers and the waving of hats and umbrellas by those remaining behind, and we were off to the front in good earnest.

As for my brother and myself, we were not Transvaal burghers, nor had we been called out for service, but we automatically became soldiers of the Boer Army by virtue of having thrown our belongings through a carriage window and clambering aboard, little knowing on how long and difficult a trail this light-hearted enlistment was starting us.

3.   TO THE FRONTIER

Our officer, or Field-Cornet, as he was called, was Mr Zeederberg, a coach contractor, and the rank and file were mostly young fellows from the Civil Service and the legal offices and shops in the town. Few of them had ever seen war, or undergone military training, but they were full of ardour, and in spite of cramped quarters and rough fare, we were like school-boys as we clanked along.

After a monotonous journey of three days, often broken by interminable halts, we reached Sandspruit, a small station about ten miles from the Natal border, where we detrained. There were great numbers of burghers from the country districts already encamped on the plain, on either side of the railway line, and the veld on all sides was dotted with tents and wagon-laagers. On the left of the track stood a large marquee over which floated the *vier-kleur* flag of the Transvaal, indicating General Joubert's headquarters. Both he and his wife were thus early on the scene, it being her invariable custom to accompany her husband in the field.

When we had detrained our horses, and helped to ground the guns, we moved away to where a halting-ground was assigned us. We off-saddled in the tall grass, and after building fires, and preparing supper, spent our first night in the open. For the next ten days we lay here enjoying the novelty of our surroundings, as if we were on a pleasure jaunt, rather than seriously awaiting the coming of war. One evening my brother and I received a pleasant surprise, for there arrived in camp an old native servant of ours, grinning from ear to ear at having found us. His name was Charley, a grandson of the famous Basuto chief, Moshesh. He had been a family retainer ever since I can remember, first in the Free State and then in the Transvaal whither he had followed us. Latterly he had been on a visit to Umbandine, King of the Swazis, but, learning that there was to be a war, he returned at once to Pretoria, and my father sent him on to us. He was more than welcome, for we could now turn over to him our cooking and the care of the horses, duties which we had been performing ourselves up to then; moreover, he had brought me a splendid roan which my father had sent me, as he feared that the Basuto pony would not be up to my weight.

Every morning my brother and I had our horses fetched from the grazing-ground and rode out to visit neighbouring camps and laagers, eager to see all that we could. We saw the stream of fresh contingents arriving daily by rail, or riding in from the adjacent countryside, and watched with never-ending interest the long columns of shaggy men on shaggy horses passing by.

At the end of the week there must have been nearly 15,000 horsemen col-lected here, ready to invade Natal, and we told ourselves that nothing could stop us from reaching the sea.

Our military organization was a rough one. Each commando was divided into two or more field-cornetcies, and these again were subdivided into corporalships. A field-cornetcy was supposed to contain 150 to 200 men, and a corporalship nominally consisted of 25, but there was no fixed rule about this, and a popular field-cornet or corporal might have twice as many men as an unpopular one, for a burgher could elect which officer he wished to serve under, and could even choose his own commando, although generally he would belong to one represent-ing the town or district from which he came.

In the Pretoria commando, we divided ourselves into corporalships by a kind of selective process, friends from the same Government department or from the same part of the town pooling their resources in the way of cooking utensils, etc., and in this manner creating separate little groups that in course of time came to be recognized as military units. One of the number would be elected corporal, to act as the channel through which orders were transmitted from above, and much the same system held in all the other commandos. The commissariat arrange-ments were equally simple. Our Field-Cornet would know the approximate member of men under his command, and in order to maintain supplies all he needed to do was to send a party to the food depot, stacked beside the railway line, where they would break out as many bags of meal, sugar, and coffee as they considered necessary, load them on a wagon, and dump them in the middle of the camp for each corporalship to satisfy its requirements. The meat supply consisted of an immense herd of cattle on the hoof, from which every commando drew as many animals as wanted for slaughter purposes. This system, though somewhat wasteful, worked fairly well; the men were plainly but adequately fed on much the same diet as they were accustomed to at home, and there was little grumbling. Officers and men had to supply their own horses, rifles, clothing, and equipment, and nobody received any pay.

Ever since the Jameson Raid the Transvaal Government had been importing large quantities of Mauser rifles from Germany, which were sold to the burghers at a nominal figure, and as great stores of ammunition had likewise been accumulated, the commandos were very efficiently equipped. The two republics had mobilized between 60,000 and 70,000 horsemen, at this moment distributed west and east, ready to invade the Cape Colony and Natal at the given word. This great force, armed with modern weapons, was a formidable fighting machine which, had it been better led, might have made far other history than it did.

How many troops the British had in South Africa I do not know, but they were pouring reinforcements into the country, and I think our leaders underestimated the magnitude of the task on which they were embarked.

So far as our information went in regard to Natal, the nearest British troops lay at the town of Dundee, some fifty miles away. This force we subsequently found to be about 7,000 strong, and still farther south at Ladysmith they had another 6,000 or 7,000 men, but with fresh troops being landed every day it was difficult to say how soon the scales would dip against us.

On the 10th of October a great parade was held in honour of President Kruger's birthday. We mustered what was than probably the largest body of mounted men ever seen in South Africa. It was magnificent to see commando after commando file past the Commandant-General, each man brandishing hat or rifle according to his individual idea of a military salute. After the march-past we formed in mass, and galloped cheering up the slopes where Piet Joubert sat his horse beneath an embroidered banner. When we came to a halt he addressed us from the saddle. I was jammed among the horsemen, so could not get close enough to hear what he was saying, but soon word was passed that an ultimatum (written and signed by my father) had been sent to the British, giving them twenty-four hours in which to withdraw their troops from the borders of the Republic, failing which there was to be war.

The excitement that followed was immense. The great throng stood in its stirrups and shouted itself hoarse, and it was not until long after the Commandant-General and his retinue had fought their way through the crowd that the commandos began to disperse.

The jubilation continued far into the night, and as we sat around our fires discussing the coming struggle, we heard singing and shouting from the neighbouring camps until cock-crow.

Next day England accepted the challenge and the war began. Once more the excitement was unbounded. Fiery speeches were made, and General Joubert was received with tumultuous cheering as he rode through to address the men. Orders were issued for all commandos to be in readiness, and five days' rations of biltong and meal were issued. Flying columns were to invade Natal, and all transport was to be left behind, so my brother and I were obliged to send our native boy to the central laager where the wagons were being parked until they would follow later.

My brother and I had joined hands with some friends from our Pretoria suburb of Sunnyside, and after a few days we had become merged in a larger body, of which five brothers, named Malherbe, were the leading spirits. We chose Isaac Malherbe, the eldest of them, to be our Corporal, and a better man I never met. We soon came to be known as 'Isaac Malherbe's Corporalship'. He was about thirty-five years old, dark complexioned, silent and moody, but we looked up to him because of the confidence which he inspired. His brothers were brave men, too, but he stood head and shoulders above us all. After his death on the Tugela we found that he was a man of considerable means whose wife and two small daughters were left well provided for.

War was officially declared on October 11th. At dawn on the morning of the 12th, the assembled commandos moved off and we started on our first march.

As far as the eye could see the plain was alive with horsemen, guns, and cattle, all steadily going forward to the frontier. The scene was a stirring one, and I shall never forget riding to war with that great host.

It has all ended in disaster, and I am writing this in a strange country, but the memory of those first days will ever remain.

4. WE INVADE NATAL

We reached the border village of Volksrust before noon, and here the entire force was halted for the day, the Pretoria men camping beside the monument erected to commemorate the Battle of Majuba, fought on the mountain nearby in 1881.

The army was now split up to facilitate our passage through the mountainous country lying ahead. The Pretoria commando, about 300 strong, was attached to a larger force of 1,500 men under General Erasmus, nicknamed 'Maroola', with his brother, Commandant Erasmus, nick-named 'Swart Lawaai' (Black Noise) as second in command.

They were tall, swarthy men, clad in black claw-hammer coats, and semi-top hats, trimmed with crêpe, a style of dress and headgear affected by so many Boer officers as virtually to amount to insignia of rank. General Maroola had got his name during a recent native campaign in the Northern Transvaal, in the course of which he was said to have directed operations from behind a maroola tree, while Swart Lawaai's was a tribute to his dark complexion and quarrelsome temper.

Several other forces, more or less equal to ours, were carved out of the main body, and in the afternoon each of these new commandos was assigned its route. We spent an unhappy night in the rain. We had neither tents nor over-coats, so we sat on ant-heaps, or lay in the mud, snatching what sleep we could. It was our first introduction to the real hardships of war, and our martial feelings were considerably damped by the time the downpour ceased at daybreak. When it was light we moved out, shivering and hungry, for it was too wet to build fires.

Our road lay between high mountains, and the rain came down again in torrents. Far away to our right and left we caught an occasional glimpse of other forces marching through the mist, also making slow progress over the heavy country. We did not cross the border, but kept to a parallel road, and by dark we halted at a dismal spot, soon trampled into a quagmire by the multitude of horses. Again it rained all night, and again we could light no fires, and had to appease our hunger by munching biltong from our saddlebags.

It was a severe first test, for, in addition to the rain, a cold wind blew from the great Drakensberg range, cutting through us. Fortunately past troubles are soon forgotten, and when, towards sunrise, the weather lifted and we got under way, we were in good spirits again, with no thought of the unhappy night behind us.

After a long ride we emerged into open country and there, winding across the plain, ran the Buffalo River with the green hills and pleasant valleys of Natal stretching beyond. With one accord the long files of horsemen reined in, and we gazed silently on the land of promise. General Maroola, with a quick eye to the occasion, faced round and made a speech telling us that Natal was a heritage filched from our forefathers, which must now be recovered from the usurper. Amid enthusiastic cries we began to ford the stream. It took nearly an hour for all to cross, and during this time the cheering and singing of the 'Volkslied' were continuous, and we rode into the smiling land of Natal full of hope and courage.

As soon as we were through the river, we spread out on a front of several miles, and went forward. Far away, on either side, we could see the other forces moving abreast of us. There was not a man who did not believe that we were heading straight for the coast, and it was as well that the future was hidden from us, and that we did not know how our strength and enthusiasm were to be frittered away in meaningless siege, and in the holding of useless positions, when our only salvation lay in rapid advance. The nearest English soldiers were still many miles to the south, so that, beyond sending out vedettes, the men went as they pleased, riding hither and thither to forage for supplies at the farmhouses we passed.

By nightfall we reached the hills near the village of Newcastle, and here we halted, our camp fires glowing far and near like the lights of a great city. Next morning we moved in columns through the streets, such of the inhabitants as sympathized with us waving encouragement, and the rest looking on in sullen resentment, as the long lines of horse-men went by. Beyond the village, a halt was called to allow the other forces to come abreast, and then, at dusk, all commandos started on a forced march that lasted throughout the night, except for an occasional halt to rest the horses. By sunrise we had come within 15 miles of the flat-topped mountain behind which lay the town of Dundee and the nearest English forces.

Contrary to expectation, we halted for the greater part of the day, and again, at sunset, were ordered to prepare for another night march. The commandos had by now closed in, and our Natal army was assembled practically in one body, making a brave show as we rode out. General Joubert had passed among us during the day, and we knew from him that he planned to surround the English troops that night. General Maroola, with the 1,500 men of whom we of the Pretoria Commando formed part, was to occupy the mountain overlooking the enemy's camp at Dundee, while the other forces were to complete the pincers on the flanks and rear. There was much excitement at the prospect of fighting, and even the heavy rain that set in after we started could not depress our spirits. The night was black and our route seemed to lie chiefly over an open mud-bound plain, varied at times by more broken country in the passage of which there was a good deal of confusion and intermingling between the different commandos; but for all that, steady progress was made, and towards dawn Maroola succeeded in disentangling his commando from the other columns. Soon the frequent lightning revealed the steep side of a mountain, rising like a wall before us, and word was passed to commence the ascent, for this was the mountain from the top of which it was said one could look down on the English encampments on the other side. As there was almost certain to be a strong post holding the summit we climbed up in silence, expecting to be fired on at any moment, but when we reached the wide plateau above we found it deserted. This was so unlooked for that no one seemed to know what to do next, and, as it was still pitch dark, and the rain was coming down in torrents, we waited shivering in the cold for the coming of daybreak. When it grew light the rain ceased, but a mist enshrouded the mountain-top through which everything looked so ghostly and uncertain that we felt more at a loss than ever, and when Maroola was asked for orders he merely stood glowering into the fog without reply. We could not see 50 yards in any direction, but we knew that the English lines were immediately below us, for we could hear muffled shouts and the rumble of wagons, and we expected to be led down the face of the mountain to the attack. But General Maroola and his brother made no sign, and when President Kruger's son Caspar, who was serving with us as a private, and who for once in his life showed a little spirit, went up and implored them to march us to the enemy, Maroola curtly ordered him off.

He must have known what he was about though, for suddenly there came a violent cannonade, bringing us all to our feet as we listened to our first sound of battle.

We could see nothing, but heavy fighting had started close by, for the roar of the guns increased and at times we heard the rattle of small arms and Maxims. None of the fire, however, was directed at us, and so far as we were concerned nothing happened, and we fretted at the thought of standing passively by when others were striking the first blow of the war. After perhaps an hour the sound died down, indicating, although we did not know it at the time, that the English had driven the Vryheid men from Talana Hill with heavy losses. Towards midday the weather cleared somewhat, and while it still continued misty, patches of sunshine began to splash the plain behind us, across which we had approached the mountain overnight. And then, far down, into one of these sunlit spaces rode a troop of English horsemen about 300 strong. This was our first sight of the enemy, and we followed their course with close attention.

How this handful of men came to be right in the rear of the whole Boer Army I never heard, but they were on a desperate errand, for between them and their main body lay nearly 15,000 horsemen, and, now that the fog was lifting, their chance of regaining their base unobserved was gone. Already scattered Boer marksmen were appearing out of the mist, firing from the saddle as they came, and shepherding the soldiers still farther from their own people. Our men were by this time mostly crowding the forward edge of the mountain, hoping to catch sight of the English camp below, so that there were only a few of us who saw the troopers on the plain behind. Among these was our corporal, Isaac Malherbe, my brother and I, and five or six other Pretoria men, and, after watching the squadron below for a few seconds, we mounted our horses and rode down the mountain-side as fast as we could go. Arrived at the foot, we raced across the veld in the wake of the English troops, guided by the sound of dropping rifle-shots ahead of us, for we could no longer see our quarry, as they had disappeared for the time being among some low foot-hills. Following on, we soon came to the scene of action.

The English had gone to earth at a small homestead, and we were just in time to see the soldiers jumping from their horses, and running for cover to the walls of a stone cattle kraal, and among the rocks behind the farmhouse. Other burghers were flocking in, and soon the troops were completely surrounded. Across their front ran the dry bed of a spruit, and Isaac led us thither at once. This meant riding towards the enemy over the open, and now, for the first time in my life, I heard the sharp hiss of rifle-bullets about my ears, and for the first time I experienced the thrill of riding into action. My previous ideas of a battle had been different, for there was almost nothing to see here. The soldiers were hidden, and, except for an occasional helmet and the spurts of dust flicked up around us, there was nothing. We reached the spruit we were making for with one man wounded, and leaving him and our horses in the bed below, we climbed the bank and were soon blazing away our first shots in war.

The troops replied vigorously, but they were able to devote comparatively little attention to us, for by now the countryside was buzzing like an angry hive, with men arriving from every direction, and the end was but a question of time. After a few minutes a Creusot gun of the Transvaal Staats Artillery unlimbered and opened fire. The very first shell stampeded all the troop horses. The poor maddened brutes came tearing past us, and we leaped on our horses to head them off, but had to retreat to avoid being trampled down as they thundered by. I managed to hang on to the skirt of the mob, and, by seizing its flying reins, brought a fine black waler to a standstill. As I was looking over my prize I saw a white flag go up at the kraal and another from the farmhouse, so I hastened to be present at the surrender. By the time I got there the soldiers had thrown down their arms and were falling in under their officers. Their leader, Colonel Moller, stood on the stoep looking pretty crestfallen, but the private soldiers seemed to take the turn of events more cheerfully. Officers and men were dressed in drab khaki uniforms, instead of the scarlet I had seen in England, and this somewhat disappointed me as it seemed to detract from the glamour of war; but worse still was the sight of the dead soldiers. These were the first men I had seen killed in anger; and their ashen faces and staring eyeballs came as a great shock, for I had pictured the dignity of death in battle, but I now saw that it was horrible to look upon. I was too elated, however, at having taken part in our first success to be downcast for long, and I enjoyed the novelty of looking at the captured men and talk to such of them as were willing. After a final look round, those of us from Pretoria rode back towards the berg, where we had left the rest of our commando, leaving the wounded to make their way as best they could to the nearest medical assistance.

It fell dark before we reached the foot of the mountain on which our men were, and, heavy rain setting in, we made for a deserted farmhouse, and here we spent a comfortable night, pitying our companions out in such weather.

At dawn the rain stopped, and before long we saw Maroola's force winding down the mountain, so we saddled our horses and made haste to rejoin them as they came down.

The men were cold and wet and hungry, and they looked with envy on our dry clothes and on the trophies in the way of swords and bayonets which we had brought with us. The weather at last was clearing and the sun came shining warmly through so that all were soon in a more cheerful frame of mind in spite of Maroola's telling us that the encircling movement had failed and that the English forces in Dundee had got away towards Ladysmith. When his brother Swart Lawaai saw the horse I had captured the previous day, he made me hand it over to one of his Field-Cornets whose mount had gone lame, and I was fool enough to comply, for I still had some respect for authority, and that was the last I saw of my booty. This was the more unfortunate because the little Basuto pony that I had been using as a pack-animal had strayed during the night, and my brother and I were left without a led horse to carry our cooking-tins and supplies. We now felt our way round the corner of the mountain into Dundee town. As Maroola was not quite certain that the English evacuation was complete, he sent a patrol of ten men forward to investigate.

My brother and I were of the party, and, while we were riding ahead along the base of a kopje, we saw half a dozen English soldiers running up the slope about 500 yards off. We shouted to them to stop, but as they paid no heed, we sprang to the ground and fired, bringing two men down.

The others now halted, and, riding up, we found one dead and another badly wounded. The rest told us that they were a signalling party that had lost their way in the rains and mists of the preceding day, and they seemed greatly taken aback when they heard that their troops had evacuated Dundee.

We left the dead man lying where he fell and ordered the prisoners to carry their wounded companion into town, and as we were anxious to be first in, we left them and rode on.

By now Maroola's men were also making for Dundee, galloping hard behind us, but we were well in advance and easily got in before they came. They were not long, however, and soon 1,500 men were whooping through the streets, and behaving in a very undisciplined manner. Officers tried to stem the rush, but we were not to be denied, and we plundered shops and dwelling-houses, and did considerable damage before the Commandants and Field-Cornets were able to restore some semblance of order. It was not for what we got out of it, for we knew that we could carry little or nothing away with us, but the joy of ransacking other people's property is hard to resist, and we gave way to the impulse. My brother and I were hampered by the loss of our pony, but we brought away enough food for a royal feast, and after living on half-cured biltong for all these days, we made up for lost time.

There was not only the town to be looted, but there was a large military camp standing abandoned on the outskirts, and here were entire streets of tents, and great stacks of tinned and other foodstuffs, and, knowing the meagre way in which our men were fed and equipped, I was astonished at the numberless things an English army carried with it in the field. There were mountains of luxurious foods, comfortable camp stretchers and sleeping-bags, and there was even a gymnasium, and a profusion of other things too numerous to mention.

The looting of Dundee was the work of General Maroola's men, for the rest of the Boer forces were moving, east and west of the town in pursuit of the English garrison that was retreating to Ladysmith.

That afternoon Maroola managed to persuade his men to resume the advance, and he trekked off, but twenty men of our Pretoria commando were picked haphazard by him to remain behind to prevent further looting. I rode by just as he was making his selection and, his eye happening to fall on me, I was included in the party.

The old fellow probably thought he was doing me a good turn, but I was far from pleased, especially as my brother went on with the rest of the commando. After they were gone we searched around for one of the less-damaged houses, as we had no idea how long we might be marooned here and had decided to be comfortable. Towards evening I rode up again to the English camp to have another look at it and, wandering about, I came on the field hospital, flying the Geneva Cross. One of the tents was a large marquee for wounded officers, and here I saw General Penn-Symons, the Commander of the English troops. He was mortally wounded and the nurses told me that he could not last out the night. Next morning, as I was again on my way up to the camp, I met a bearer-party carrying his body, wrapped in a blanket, and I accompanied them to where they buried him behind the little English chapel. Now that the commandos were gone, and we were left in sole charge, we looked like settling down for some time, but that afternoon a dishevelled horseman rode into town with tidings of the disaster that had overtaken the Johannesburg men at Elandslaagte. He was in a state of great excitement and gave us such an exaggerated account of the fight, probably to excuse his presence so far to the rear, that I decided to go off in search of our commando, as I could see that there would be other fighting. The temporary Corporal in charge of us, one Paul de Villiers, forbade me to leave, as our instructions were to stay in Dundee until further orders, but I rode away within the hour. As it was late when I started, darkness came on before I had got very far, and I spent the night at Glencoe Junction, where I found other fugitives from the Elandslaagte battle, from whom I gathered that it had been a pretty serious affair, in which we had lost two guns and many men killed and wounded, besides some hundreds of prisoners.

At the station, too, I saw the wife of General Kock, who commanded the Johannesburg Commando. He had been badly wounded and taken into Ladysmith by the British, and the poor woman was hoping to get through their lines to see him. How she came to be here at all I do not know; probably she had accompanied the forces in the same way as the Commandant-General's wife, but I do not know whether she ever succeeded in reaching her husband, who died a few days later.

I rode on before daylight next morning, the memory of her tear-stained face giving me the first hint of what women suffer in time of war. I went down the Washbank Pass all by myself, and, although I was new to the country, I had no difficulty in finding my way, as the road was trampled and churned by the thousands of horsemen who had gone before.

During the two days while I was in Dundee, General Hubert had moved his whole army southwards, and was at this moment camped about ten miles from Ladysmith, where I rejoined after nightfall. As I approached I saw thousands of fires springing up on the hills, for the commandos were strung out over several miles, and it took me a long time to locate the Pretoria men in the dark. Stumbling about I came on General Maroola squatting by a fire, and, before I could slip away, he saw me, and testily demanded why I had left Dundee without his permission. I said I had come away to help him take Ladysmith, and, grinning sourly at my impudence, he packed me off. When at last I found my corporalship I was told that my brother had been missing since the day before, which troubled me, for we had promised my father to remain together if possible.

Next day our whole line moved forward, and a fine sight it was, as the masses of horsemen breasted the green slopes towards the final hills from which we could look down to Ladysmith. The English were standing on the defensive, for during the morning we had not come in contact with them and we could now see them building forts and redoubts in the low kopjes surrounding the town.

Neither side made any attempt to get to grips that day, but by night our men had occupied Bulwana and Lombaardskop, two prominent heights, and they were also holding a line that stretched around by Pepworth Hill and the ridges lying towards Nicholson's Nek. The following day was spent in preparation for the coming battle, but I was riding from commando to commando in fruitless search for my brother.

A collision with the British was imminent. They had 10,000 to 12,000 men, including those who had retired from Dundee, and we had 14,000 or 15,000, so that something was bound to happen.

That night the Pretoria Commando took up a suitable position to the right of Pepworth Hill, where we lay on our arms till morning, expecting an attack at any moment, but sunrise came and all remained quiet, from which we gathered that another day was to pass before the dash.

Towards eleven in the morning Piet Joubert, the Commandant-General, and his staff rode up to address us. He started by scolding the men for having looted a farm close by, and got so worked up that he forgot to tell us what the real object of his visit had been. We took his wigging in good part, but I am afraid no one treated our Commander-in-Chief very seriously. His staff was jocularly known as the 'Royal Family', mostly relations. There was a story going round of a burgher who saw a man ordering people about. The burgher asked him if he was an officer and the man replied: 'Of course I'm an officer, I am the Commandant-General's nephew.' This tale might have been true, for some of the 'Royal Family' put on airs, and we had no great love for any of them, although in fairness it must be said that none of the Commandant-General's own sons were on his staff, but were serving as ordinary privates.

After Piet Joubert had ridden off, Mr. Zeederberg, our Field-Cornet, set us to building breastworks in the line of hills forward of our halting-ground, and every man worked hard until sunset, for this was the position we were to hold when the enemy came against us.

5. A BATTLE

When the men returned to the camp that evening after finishing their work, I was left on outpost duty with seven others, at the place where we had been building *schanses* during the day.

The hill we were on formed the extreme right of the Boer line. From our station we looked over the plain leading towards Ladysmith, and to our right we looked across a broad valley, running between us and Nicholson's Nek, a flat-topped hill on the far side.

All remained quiet until three in the morning, when out of the darkness there came the sound of shots followed by confused shouting and trampling, but as the noise died down after a while we let things be. Shortly before daybreak, when it was growing light, two large mules came trotting up from below, their head-ropes trailing on the ground, and on bringing the animals to a halt we found that one of them carried on his back the barrel of a mountain gun, and the other a leathern box containing shell ammunition. They had obviously come from the British lines, and we only learned afterwards that a strong force of infantry had marched out of Ladysmith intending to get into our rear under cover of darkness, but that their battery mules had stampeded, throwing the troops into such disorder that instead of achieving their object, they were obliged to take up a position on our flanks on Nicholson's Nek where, later in the day, I took part in the fighting that led to their capture.

Meanwhile it was sunrise, and we could now make out this force on the level top of Nicholson's Nek across the valley. The soldiers were working like ants, building sangars of stone, and we could see a knot of officers, standing around what looked like an outspread map, while other men were pulling a tarpaulin over a tree for shade. At this time our commando, as well as the other commandos in the vicinity, was still peacefully at rest some 400 yards to the rear, out of sight behind a low ridge, and no alarm had yet been given, so we fired the first shots of the coming battle.

The range was too great for accurate shooting, but our volley had the effect of dispersing the officers, who hurriedly climbed up to join their troops on the hilltop above, where we could now no longer see any sign of life, as the men who had been working there had taken cover, and the plateau seemed deserted. Our shots had the further effect of arousing the commandos and, before long, horsemen came hurrying from the different camps to occupy the forward crest, and within twenty minutes there were hundreds of riflemen in position, facing the plain that runs to Ladysmith.

As for the English force on Nicholson's Nek, orders were sent to the Free State commandos, coming up from the west, to attack them, and by seven o'clock we heard the popping of rifle shots from that direction, but for the next hour or two we could spare them no thought, for tall pillars of dust were rising from Ladysmith, and soon long columns of infantry debouched into the plain before us.

The Transvaal Staats Artillery had dragged a 6-inch Creusot gun ('Long Tom') up Pepworth Hill, a mile to the left, and they had installed several smaller guns there as well, and all these now began to fire on the approaching troops. I expected to see the shells blow great gaps and lanes in the enemy ranks, but instead of this our first shots were spent in finding the range, and by that time the columns had opened out, and, in place of the havoc which I had expected, the firing only caused smoke and local disturbances of earth, while the infantry came steadily on.

And yet a great spectacle was developing.

From where we held the sweep of the hills, we looked down as from an amphitheatre at every movement of the troops on the plain below, infantry hurrying forward in successive waves; guns being galloped up, and all the bustle and activity of a battle shaping before our eyes.

The soldiers, paying little heed to the shells that dropped amongst them, advanced without a halt, although many now fell dead and wounded while in the rear, battery after battery unlimbered. We saw the horse teams ridden back, and then, to cover the progress of their troops, heavy fire was opened and there came the sound, once heard never forgotten, of shells tearing towards us and exploding around us, and overhead, with deafening concussions.

By now, what with the thunder of the British guns and of our own, the crash of bursting shells and the din of thousands of rifles, there was a volume of sound unheard in South Africa before. I was awed rather than frightened, and, once I had got over my first impression, I felt excited by all I saw and keenly joined in the firing. We were so successful that by the time the foremost infantrymen came within 1,200 yards of us, many fallen dotted the veld, and their advance wavered before the hail of bullets. They did not run away, but we saw them taking cover behind ant-heaps and such other shelter as the ground afforded. From there they directed a heavy fire on us, but their progress was definitely stayed, and our line held for the rest of the day.

Our casualties were not heavy, for we were well protected, but the guns on Pepworth Hill close by were being severely punished. The English batteries concentrated upon silencing our pieces there and we could see that the people were making heavy weather on the hill, for its summit was covered in smoke and flame, and the roar of the bursting shells shook the ground even where we lay.

For the past few days I had been without word of my brother, but now an artilleryman came racing up on horse-back with a message from General Maroola to say that most of the guns were out of action. I recognized the man as an old acquaintance, and, when he saw me, he said my brother was at that moment serving as a volunteer with the crew of the big Creusot on Pepworth Hill. Concerned to hear that he was there, I ran back for my horse, which was standing under cover with the rest, and rode for the hill as fast as I could go, through shell and bullet fire I reached the rear of the hill in safety, and certainly the dispatch-rider had not overstated the case. Six or seven dead artillerymen, some horribly mutilated, were laid out on a square of canvas to which they had been carried from above, and Ferdinand Holz, the German military doctor, was attending to a number of wounded also brought down from the emplacements.

An ambulance-van was standing nearby with several of its mule team dead in their traces, and in the distance the native drivers were running wildly to the rear. At the guns above twenty to thirty shells at a time were bursting with terrific noise. I tied my horse to a tree and, after an anxious glance at the dead and wounded, to make sure that my brother was not of their number, I began to work my way up, crawling from stone to stone, and running forward whenever there was a lull in the fire, until I reached the sand-bagged ramparts. Here I found my brother, and the surviving artillerymen, crouching behind the wall, unable to serve their guns under the storm that was lashing the position. It was mostly shrapnel, so that none of the guns were actually destroyed, but all were silenced.

More dead lay about and wounded men were sheltering with the rest in the lee of the parapet. I liked the spot so little that I tried to persuade my brother to return with me to our own commando, but, although he was somewhat shaken by this ordeal, he refused to come, and I had to admit that he was right. As there was no object in my remaining I bade him good-bye, and taking advantage of a slackening in the British gun-fire I made my way down. Below I found Dr. Holz, lying in a heap, struck dead by a shell while helping the wounded. A fresh ambulance wagon came up just then and I lent a hand at loading the casualties before I sought out my horse, fortunately unscratched, and made haste to get away. I found the Pretoria men still holding the ridge on which I had left them, and on the plain before them the situation had not materially altered. The English troops showed no signs of advancing, and our commandos lay inactive while the guns pounded away, the battle resolving itself into an artillery duel, except that on the right we could hear the continuous crackle of musketry from Nicholson's Nek, where the Freestaters were engaged with the force that had come out of Ladysmith during the night.

Our Corporal, Isaac Malherbe, now suggested to those of us lying near that we should accompany him across the valley to Nicholson's Nek. About a dozen of us followed him to the horses, dodging among the rocks and trees to escape the shrapnel, and we rode down into the broad valley on the opposite side of which rose Nicholson's Nek.

We came under plunging rifle-fire as we moved across the floor of the valley, but we got under cover at the foot of the hill without loss. Here there was a party of Indian dhoolie-bearers, who had brought down some wounded English soldiers, our unexpected appearance among them causing considerable consternation. Ignoring them, we tethered our horses and started to climb the hill, going warily for fear of blundering into the wrong side of the fighting which we could hear above. The top of Nicholson's Nek is a broad level plateau dotted with outcrops of loose boulders, and, on breasting the rim, we were for a moment or two unable to gauge the situation. Rifles were cracking and bullets were whizzing, but there was no one in sight. Crawling forward, however, we came on small parties of Free State burghers lying behind rocks and other shelter in a rough line across the hill, and when we joined one of these groups, they pointed out to us where the English troops lay posted, behind similar cover, 30 or 40 yards away.

Both sides were maintaining a vigorous short-range rifle contest, in which the soldiers were being badly worsted, for they were up against real old-fashioned Free State Boers for whom they were no match in sharpshooting of this kind. Time after time I saw soldiers looking over their defences to fire, and time after time I heard the thud of a bullet finding its mark, and could see the unfortunate man fall back out of sight, killed or wounded. We joined in the fight, and for the next hour we slowly but surely pressed the English to the far edge of the hill.

As we gained ground we began to come on their dead and wounded, and realized what heavy losses we were inflicting, for behind almost every rock lay a dead or wounded man, and we knew that we should have possession of the hill before long.

Towards noon, as we were increasingly hustling our opponents, we heard a bugle ring clear above the rifle-fire, and at the same time a white flag went up.

Hundreds of khaki-clad figures rose from among the rocks and walked towards us, their rifles at the trail. We stood up to wait for them. The haul was a good one, for there were 1,100 prisoners, mostly Dublin Fusiliers. The commando responsible for this came from the district at Heilbron in the Northern Free State. They were led by Commandant Mentz, but the man who had chiefly urged on the fight was Field-Cornet Christian de Wet, afterwards the redoubtable guerrilla leader. I saw him here for the first time as he made his way from point to point during the action, and I well remember his fierce eyes and keen determined face.

Shortly after the surrender I was talking to some of the captured officers when I heard one of them exclaim, 'My God; look there!' and turning round we saw the entire British force that had come out against us on the plain that morning in full retreat to Ladysmith. Great clouds of dust billowed over the veld as the troops withdrew, and the manner of their going had every appearance of a rout. There were about 10,000 soldiers, but General Joubert had far more than that number of horsemen ready to his hand, and we fully looked to see him unleash them on the enemy, but to our surprise there was no pursuit. I heard Christian de Wet mutter: *Los jou ruiters; Los jou ruiters'* (Loose your horsemen -

loose your horsemen), but the Commandant-General allowed this wonderful opportunity to go by, a failure that cost us dear in the days to come.

Judging by the disorderly appearance of the retreat, he could have driven the English clean through Ladysmith and out beyond, and he would have lost fewer men in the doing of it than we lost in the subsequent siege, but the English went hurrying back unmolested, save for an occasional shell from Pepworth Hill, where our guns had sprung into life again, and, with the whole Boer Army looking on, no attempt was made to exploit the victory that had been gained.

When we saw the troops falling back, and no chase given, we washed our hands of the business, and began to examine our own immediate surroundings on the hill-top. Dead and wounded soldiers lay all around, and the cries and groans of agony, and the dreadful sights haunted me for many a day, for though I had seen death by violence of late, there had been nothing to approach the horrors accumulated here.

Of our party under Isaac Malherbe not one had been hit, but the Free State men had eight or nine dead, and fifteen or twenty wounded. The English casualties were about two hundred killed and as many injured, the disparity being due to the fact that the English soldiers were no match for us in rifle-shooting. Whatever the defects of the commando system may be (and they are many) the Boer superiority in marksmanship was as great now as it had been in 1881. Having looked at the dreadful scenes on the plateau, we parted from the Freestaters and, returning down the hill to our horses, rode back through the valley to the Pretoria Commando, which we found in the same place in the line where we had left them, the men still holding the ridge, and their horses still under cover behind.

There was on this day, and for long after, much acrimonious discussion regarding the Commandant-General's failure to pursue when the English turned back, and I was told by old Maroola himself, that when officers came up to implore Piet Joubert to follow; he quoted the Dutch saying: 'When God holds out a finger, don't take the whole hand,' meaning that the Almighty had sufficiently aided us for one day, and that it did not behove us to presume upon His bounty, a view which Isaac Malherbe said might be sound theology but no good in making war.

With that lack of vision that marred most of our doings in the earlier stages, we hailed the Ladysmith battle as a great victory, and we acted as if we had a broken and defeated enemy before us. It certainly was a notable success, but in the end it would have been better for us had the British smashed our line that day, for our leaders would then have followed a better plan of campaign than sitting down to a prolonged and ruinous siege.

Had the Boers made for the coast, instead of tying up their horsemen around towns that were of no value to them, the outcome of the war might have been different, but they sacrificed their one great advantage of superior mobility, and allowed splendid guerrilla fighters to stagnate and demoralize in the monotony of siege warfare, at a time when our only salvation lay in pushing to the sea.

6. UPS AND DOWNS

We rested on our laurels for a few days, each commando camping immediately behind the position which it had held during the battle.

Ladysmith was soon completely invested; on every hill and kopje lay a force of riflemen, and there must have been nearly ten thousand thus tied down who could have been put to far better use.

The weather remained fine, and we divided our time between watching the beleaguered garrison build forts and breastworks against our ultimate reception, and riding about the rear foraging for supplies.

After a while we of Pretoria received orders to move forward to occupy a hill named Bell's Kop, facing a murderous-looking English construction that had gone up within the last few days. We rode out before light one morning to take up our new position, which, we were informed, was to be held by us as part of the cordon that was being drawn round the town. When we heard that this was to be our permanent abode, all hands turned to building shelters against the weather, and generally making our camp habitable. Neighbouring farms were laid under tribute and plundered of everything that could be turned to account. My brother rejoined us here. He had had enough of gunnery for the time being, and our native boy Charley also entered appearance, beaming with delight at having tracked us down. He travelled on foot all the way from the Transvaal border, and although several times arrested as a spy, he had talked and argued his way through until he found us. Needless to say, he was received with open arms, as we were once more able to turn over to him our duties of cooking, carrying water, horse-guard, etc., so my brother and I settled down to a life of ease, spending our time in sniping at the English outposts, or in riding to the neighbouring laagers.

Camp life was a pleasant existence. There were no drills or parades and, except for night picket and an occasional fatigue party to the railway depot to fetch supplies, there were no military duties. Our commando received many fresh drafts, and after a while varied from one thousand to fifteen hundred men, but discipline was slack, and there was a continual stream of burghers going home on self-granted leave, so that we never knew from day to day what strength we mustered.

Although we nominally stood under command of General Maroola and his brother, we seldom saw anything of them, for they lived at the head laager miles away, and to all intents and purposes we were a law unto ourselves.

Both Maroola and Swart Lawaai were incompetent as leaders, but they were true men nevertheless. They sacrificed all they possessed, and when, later in the war, they were deserted by their men and bereft of all authority, they remained in the field as private soldiers, until the end.

We settled down to a stationary life, and if occasionally time hung heavily on our hands, conditions were otherwise comfortable enough. Our boy Charley proved a capable freebooter, and thanks to his foraging expeditions into the hills among the Zulu kraals where he made play with his descent from Chief Moshesh, our larder flourished and our mess was the envy of the rest of the camp.

After a week or two, tents were served out, and my brother and I shared one with the five good friends of our corporalship with whom we had kept company ever since leaving home. They were Charles Jeppe, a mine-surveyor, Robert Reinecke, Walter de Vos, Frank Roos and Samuel van Zijl, Civil Servants, but they were all killed before long.

So quiet were things around Ladysmith, that, as time went on, many burghers got ox-wagons brought down from their farms, and some even had their wives and families with them, which tended further to increase the spirit of inactivity that was gaining on the commandos.

However, reports from all fronts were good, and we deluded ourselves into believing that everything was as it should be and, so far as my brother and I were concerned, we thoroughly enjoyed the business of besieging Ladysmith, and making regular excursions to see the guns fired into the town.

We went once every week to look up a Norwegian uncle of ours, named Theodor Thesell, serving with a Free State commando on the west side of the cordon. He had settled near the Vaal River many years before, and had been commandeered for service very much against the grain, as he held that we were bound to be defeated. I was surprised to see in what good part the burghers took his outspoken comment on their chances, but the real fighting Boer is ever a tolerant, good-natured fellow, and my uncle suffered no inconvenience for his views. Once, while we were chatting to him on a kopje occupied by a portion of the Kroonstad men beyond the Klip River, a considerable English mounted force moved forward to attack, or at any rate to demonstrate, before this position. Their guns unlimbered within range, and opened a cannonade, and their horsemen made as if to come at us. At the first alarm, the Kroonstad men ran from their tents, and directed such a hot fire that the cavalry wheeled round and galloped off; the guns were hooked up, and what looked like the promise of a lively battle fizzled out in a few minutes. Several shells had burst overhead, but as we were well sheltered behind rocks, we thought little of it until we found, when the affair was over, that three men had been killed and half a dozen wounded, quite close to us.

On another occasion, while my brother and I were returning from a call on the Commandant-General at the head laager, we were overtaken by darkness, and heavy rain coming on, we tied our horses in the shelter of some trees and, seeing a mule-wagon standing near with a canvas sheet drawn over it and pegged down on either side for a tent, we lifted a flap and crawled into a corner where we slept snug and warm all night. When we woke at daybreak a man on a camp stool with a mug of coffee in his hand was eyeing us appraisingly, so we unrolled ourselves and went forward to explain our use of his quarters. It was Mr Smuts, the State Attorney, my father's colleague on the Executive Council. He was here on some Government business, and, after a hearty laugh at our impudence, he ordered coffee and breakfast for the pair of us. Afterwards he became a fighting General, and I was to see much hard service under him in the Cape Colony nearly two years later.

I also recovered my little Basuto pony that had been lost near Dundee. I found him tethered to General Joubert's own wagon in the head laager, and I had an angry scuffle with some dispatch-riders, before I was able to undo the head-rope and take him away with me. The Commandant-General was absent and they promised me all sorts of pains and penalties when he returned, but I knew that among the Boers, ownership of a horse is almost sacrosanct, so I carried him off in triumph.

When next I met General Joubert and asked him how he came by my horse, he said that the pony was found straying on the void by one of his staff; and that he had kept the little animal more as a pet than anything else.

The British now and then shelled our camp, upon which we would take cover at the first sign of trouble, and the damage was generally confined to a riddled tent or two, and perhaps a few horses injured. During one of these squalls our native boy was hit, and for weeks afterwards he walked about proudly displaying a fragment of metal taken from his side.

At this time I was sent for to give evidence in Pretoria against a man who had stolen money and clothing, which my father had given him to take down to my brother and myself. I travelled up by goods train and the man was put in gaol. I was in Pretoria for only two days. Before returning to Natal, I walked with my father from his office in the morning and we touched at the State School where a number of captured British officers were confined, one of whom had asked for an interview. We passed through the sentries into a large classroom where he was playing games with his fellow-prisoners. His name was Winston Churchill, a son of Lord Randolph Churchill, of whom I had often heard. He said he was not a combatant but a war-correspondent, and asked to be released on that account. My father, however, replied that he was carrying a Mauser pistol when taken, and so must remain where he was. Winston Churchill said that all war-correspondents in the Sudan had carried weapons for self-protection, and the comparison annoyed my father, who told him that the Boers were not in the habit of killing non-combatants. In the end the young man asked my father to take with him some articles which he had written for a newspaper in England and if there was nothing wrong with them to send them on via Delagoa Bay. My father read portions of the articles to us at home that evening, and said that Churchill was a clever young man, in which he was not far wrong, for soon after the prisoner climbed over a wall and escaped out of the Transvaal - how, I never heard.

When I got back to Ladysmith all went on as before, and only once during the first month of the siege did we indulge in any military operation. This was a movement against the fort opposite us, the same work that the English had built at the time of our arrival while we stood looking on. It lay eleven hundred yards away, across a level plain, and was known as the Red Fort, and I had spent many moments sniping at it.

Towards the end of November some three hundred men were ordered to attack it at dawn.

Our commando had of late been receiving reinforcements of inferior quality, mostly poor-whites from the burgher-right 'erven', the slum quarters of Pretoria, a poverty-stricken class that had drifted in from the country districts after the great rinderpest epidemic of 1896. They had become debased by town life, and had so little stomach for fighting, that their presence among us was a source of weakness rather than strength. The attacking force was drawn chiefly from these newcomers with Isaac Malherbe's corporalship, and one other of our better corporalships added to stiffen them. We left camp before daybreak, and assembled in a dry watercourse at the foot of Bell's Kop. From there we were to cross the intervening thousand yards of open, and rush the Red Fort at dawn.

Owing to various delays it grew light before we emerged from the spruit, and the soldiers must have observed some movement, for they opened fire before we could make a start. Assistant Field-Cornet de Jager was in charge of the undertaking He was a poor-white himself, but a stout-hearted old warrior none the less, and seeing that we were discovered, he ordered us to advance, himself leading the way. Isaac Malherbe and his men followed, as did the other corporalship, but the remainder refused to budge from behind the safety of the bank. With de Jager at our head, about fifty of us ran forward, coming under heavy rifle-fire as we went. Visibility was still poor, so that we covered about four hundred yards without loss, until we reached a slight outcrop of rock, where we paused to take breath, and finding that we were not supported called the attack off. The net result of our efforts was that, having got thus far, we could go neither forward nor backward, as the sun was over the horizon by now, and to advance or retire over the level bullet-swept zone was too risky, so we made the best of it by lying in the blazing sun without food or water for the next ten hours.

The troops in the fort were very wide awake, forcing us to keep our noses glued to the ground to such an extent that we dared scarcely stir without bringing down a hail of bullets about our cars. A man named Anderson was shot through both legs, and Robert Reinecke of our tent pluckily carried him back to the spruit on his shoulders, the English firing all around him, until they realized that he was helping a wounded comrade, after which they left him to go in peace, and were even sporting enough to allow him to return to us without a shot fired.

We lay sweltering in the heat for the rest of the day, wishing ourselves well out of it, and the moment it began to get dusk we made a bolt, getting back over the plain without further casualties in spite of a hot fusillade. I had a lucky escape, for as we were nearing the dry course, I stopped for a moment to see whether anyone had been hit during the retirement, when a bullet grazed my throat, stinging like a hot poker and raising an angry weal. I was more startled that hurt, and quickly followed down into the spruit bed. Here we slaked our thirst from water-holes in the ground, after which we trudged home to find the balance of the assaulting column of that morning comfortably installed in camp, and I got the impression that they rather looked on us as fools for our pains.

The day after this typical piece of bungling I walked across to Surprise Hill, an isolated kopje standing about six hundred yards to the right of our camp. Here the State Artillery had a howitzer gun in position which I often visited, to watch it bombarding the town. On this morning as I was returning through the bush-covered valley, I saw a man named Mike Hands walking ahead of me, leading a horse. As I was going forward to join him I was astonished to see a tall English soldier appear through the trees, his rifle at the ready. The soldier instantly fired at Hands, but hit the horse instead. The animal dropped and Mike fired. The soldier threw out his arms and fell back, and I found him dead with a bullet through his brain. How he came to be behind our lines was a mystery; possibly he had been scouting during the night, and had lost his way in the dark.

I was to know Surprise Hill better before long, but, in the meanwhile, camp life continued uneventfully. The besieged garrison contented themselves with shelling us at intervals, and, as they made no serious attacks, we assumed that they were marking time, for there was great activity on the south bank of the Tugela, twenty miles away, where the English Commander-in-Chief, General Buller, was massing troops to attempt the relief of Ladysmith.

He was reported to have forty thousand men with great numbers of guns, and on our side reinforcements had been brought from the Transvaal and Free State, and there were about fifteen thousand Boers holding the north bank of the river, from a point below Colenso Bridge to Spion Kop, many miles upstream. As for us around Ladysmith, we felt secure in the belief that whatever might happen on the Tugela, the troops in the besieged town at any rate would make no move, so picket and other duties were carried out in a very perfunctory manner.

During the daytime no guards were set at all, as there was always a sufficient number of men on the hill above amusing themselves with sniping to make sure of an alarm being given in case of need; and at night, although we went on outpost so close to the English sentries that we could hear them challenge each other, and sometimes exchanged shouted pleasantries with them, we did not take our watches very seriously.

We used to go on foot after dark in parties of twenty or so, and, on reaching neutral ground on the plain between ourselves and the enemy line, two men at a time would walk forward a short distance. Here they stood or sat on sentry-go while the rest of us pulled off our boots, spread out blankets and went to sleep until it was the turn of the reliefs. At daybreak we collected our belongings, and tramped back to camp in time for morning coffee, and thus far no untoward incident had ever marred these tranquil doings.

But this happy state was disturbed on the night of December 9th, for a detachment of two or three hundred soldiers came out of Ladysmith and, scaling Lombaardskop, destroyed the big Creusot gun ('Long Tom') standing there. The kop lay six or seven miles from our camp, so we heard nothing till next morning, but when we did, it gave us food for reflection, for it looked as if the pleasant immunity of our night duties was a thing of the past.

Our fears were well founded.

The next night Isaac Malherbe was to take out his corporalship to the usual spot on the plain. We mustered only twelve men, the remainder having been sent to the railway for supplies, and, as they did not get back before we had to leave, we started off without them for an eventful night.

7. AN AFFAIR AT SURPRISE HILL

Two other corporalships went on duty at the same time. One, under Corporal Tossel, a former police detective, was posted at the foot of Surprise Hill and the other a long way to our left. My brother and myself and Samuel van Zijl were the only members of our tent who were present, the other four being absent with the carrying party. As we walked along in the dark behind Isaac Malherbe we discussed the previous night's attack on the Lombaardskop gun, and I remember poor Samuel saying he hoped our turn would not come next. But our turn did come next. When we reached the usual halting-place two men were sent forward according to custom, and the rest of us turned in. My time to go on duty was 1 a.m. At about half-past twelve I woke, and not thinking it worth while to fall asleep again, I lay on my blanket watching the stars.

After a while I distinctly heard the muffled sound of many footsteps in the direction of Surprise Hill, so I got up and walked forward to the two sentries to consult them. I found that they had also heard the noise, and the three of us listened for a few seconds to what were certainly men climbing the hill. We thought Corporal Tossel's men had taken fright at something, and were withdrawing up the slope towards the howitzer emplacement. This belief was rudely dispelled, for suddenly there broke from the summit of Surprise Hill a crash of musketry followed by wild bursts of cheering, and we realized that English troops were at the gun. As we stood undecidedly watching the hundreds of rifle flashes lighting up the hill-top, a vivid sheet of flame stabbed the darkness, followed by a tremendous roar, and we knew that our howitzer had been blown into the air. The two sentries and I rushed back to where our party were already on their feet. Isaac Malherbe now showed the stuff he was made of. Without a moment's hesitation he went straight for the danger-point, the continued cheering of the English soldiery and the volley-firing serving as a guide. His intention was to join hands with Tossel's corporalship if he could find them, and then to prevent or delay the troops from returning to Ladysmith, until the whole of the Pretoria commando could come from camp, and so destroy or capture the intruders.

As it turned out, Tossel's corporalship had bolted when they heard the English coming. They had not only given them a clear field but had fired no warning shot to alarm the unfortunate gunners up above, who were taken unawares and all bayoneted. And as for the remainder of our commando in camp, they stood to arms all night, but Field-Cornet Zeederberg refused to risk the confusion that he perhaps justly thought would ensue, if he tried to march his men in the dark to an unknown situation. So, the twelve of us were left to our own devices.

As we approached we could hear by the firing and shouting that the main body of the attackers were still on the hill, but they had posted a string of pickets at the foot to secure their line of withdrawal back to the town, and before we had gone very far we ran into one of these. Isaac and I were a few yards in advance when a 'Halt! Who goes there?' was shouted at us from a few paces away. We simultaneously fired a shot apiece and ran forward. We came on a dead soldier, a sergeant, as I saw next morning from his badge, but the rest of the picket had run into the night.

We went forward cautiously and soon we collided once more with another and stronger rearguard party. We were again challenged from dose quarters, and, a heavy fire being aimed at us, we took shelter in a dry spruit bed that runs along the base of Surprise Hill. From here we returned the fire, until this outpost too gave us right of way, and we now began to file along the bed in order to seek out a convenient point from which to make a stand against the troops on the hill when they descended.

As we were going, a soldier, lying concealed in the grass on the bank above us, thrust over the muzzle of his rifle and fired point-blank into us. My tent-mate, Samuel van Zijl, was walking immediately in front of me and I had my hand on his shoulder to steady myself on the uneven path. The bullet struck him full in the throat, and so near was the range that the discharge-scorched his face, and set fire to his beard, which flared up for a moment like a fusee. He staggered, and then dropped. He was still alive, but I could hear from his laboured breathing that he was badly wounded, so I made him as comfortable as I could by placing his blanket under his head, before hurrying up the spruit to rejoin the others. By now the troops were descending Surprise Hill, and we could hear them clattering down the slope towards us. Their officers were blowing whistles, and calling out: 'A Company here! ' 'This way B Company!' and so on, to collect their men. They seemed unaware that the road was to be disputed, for they made no attempt to conceal their progress, and there was laughter and repeated cries of 'Good old Rifle Brigade', and here and there we caught the gleam of matches being struck and the glow of cigarettes, to show how little they expected opposition.

In the meanwhile Isaac had selected a suitable spot on the bank, our faces towards Surprise Hill, our backs towards Ladysmith, and here we crouched, silently waiting for the oncoming troops.

From the sounds that reached us we judged them to be about three hundred strong and, with no sign of Tossel's men or of help from the commando, it dawned on us that we were in a pretty tight corner.

While the soldiers were still some distance away I ran down to see how Samuel van Zijl was faring. He was only just alive, and he asked me in a faint voice to turn him on his side to ease the pain, but as I did so I felt his body stiffen, and then go limp in my arms, and when I laid him down he was dead. I hurried back, for the laughter and talking were drawing very near. As I made up the course, a huge soldier, or he looked so in the dark, loomed up suddenly on the bank above. He lounged at me with his bayonet, but his insecure footing deflected the thrust and brought him stumbling against me. The man was at my mercy now, for I had my carbine against his side, but there came over me an aversion to shooting him down like a dog, so I ordered him to put up his hands instead, which he did at once, dropping his bayoneted rifle at my feet. I told him to sit down until I called him, a command which he so implicitly obeyed that I found him patiently waiting there next morning with a bullet through his leg from the cross-firing during the subsequent proceedings. This soldier must have come on ahead, for when I reached my companions, the main force was just reaching the foot of the hill and approaching us in a body.

Isaac whispered to us to hold our fire and each man peered into the darkness until, about fifteen yards away, we saw a black mass dimly outlined and then, at his word of command, we poured volley after volley into their closely packed ranks, shooting as fast as we could work the bolts of our rifles. When the blast struck them they thought they were being fired at by their own rearguard pickets, for there were cries of 'Rifle Brigade! Rifle Brigade, don't fire!' but discovering their error a commanding voice called out 'Bayonets, bayonets', and they came at us like a wall. In spite of our small number we delivered such a volume of fire that the head of the column swerved to the left and slanted across our front to make the spruit lower down, and, although we continued our volleys, we could not prevent their going by.

Several times, however, parties of soldiers who had lost their way in the dark walked in among us, and of these we shot some and took others prisoners.

A Captain named Geo. Paley came up to where my brother and I knelt, firing over the edge of the bank, and as he failed to halt when called out, we both loosed a round and brought him toppling between us. Another time one of our men, Jan Luttig, was seized by some soldiers within a few yards of us, and there was a hand-to-hand scuffle in which he was stabbed with a bayonet and clubbed on the head with a rifle-butt. In the dark we could not make out what was happening, but when we heard his cry for help and ran up, his assailants were gone. A moment later I made out three soldiers in the bed of the spruit behind me and slipped down towards them. One nearly spitted me with a vicious jab of his bayonet, which passed between my arm and body, but before he could repeat the thrust I had him covered and they surrendered. One was an army doctor with a bullet-wound in his foot, and the other two said they were helping him along. I ordered them to remain in the bed of the spruit, where I found them in the morning.

About this time we heard four or five shots in rapid succession, followed by groans, from the direction where the troops were still crossing the spruit twenty or thirty yards off. We did not know the meaning of this, and only at daybreak did we find that we had listened to the death-cry of some of our men who had come from the camp to our assistance.

It was now towards three in the morning, and we had nearly exhausted our ammunition, so we sat quietly watching the tail of the column vanish into the darkness beyond, on its way to Ladysmith.

When daylight came at last, a grim scene met our eyes. Before us, within a radius of less than twenty-five yards, lay over sixty dead and wounded English soldiers, and as we walked forward among them we came on the bodies of three of our men who had not been with us originally. Two were dead and dreadfully hacked with bayonets and the third was at his last gasp.

These had been away to the railway depot with the fatigue party, and on their return had gallantly attempted to make their way to us when they heard the firing. They nearly reached us, but ran into the withdrawing soldiers, and were bayoneted before they could fire more than a few shots. Behind us in the spruit bed lay poor Samuel van Zijl, and close by sat our prisoners, some twenty in number.

Dead, wounded, and prisoners, eleven of us had accounted for more than eighty opponents, an average of seven apiece.

Our work was now done, and shortly after sunrise Mr Zeederberg and a large escort of men came scouting through the bush to see what was left of us, and they were surprised to find so many of us still alive.

We stood among the dead and wounded soldiers, the centre of an admiring crowd, and from now onwards Isaac Malherbe's corporalship was spoken of as the best in the commando.[1]

---

[1] *See Conan Doyle's 'History of The Great Boer War', where he refers to me by name in connection with this affair. The Times Story of The War gives the following account: -*
The soldiers scrambled down Surprise Hill.... Suddenly a ring of flame blazed forth at their very feet. A party of some twenty Pretorians, mostly young lawyers and business men, had boldly come round the side of the hill and, regardless of the heavy fire, had lain down in a line across the slope to intercept the storming party of whose numbers they probably had no idea. Disregarding the misleading orders shouted by the Boers, the men charged in grim silence. The gallant Pretorians emptied their magazines in a vain endeavour to stem the rush, and then the riflemen surged over them, killing or wounding several as they passed. The British casualties were fourteen killed and fifty wounded, not an excessive price to pay for so successful a feat.

8. A VISIT TO THE TUGELA LINE – TRAGEDY OF THE RED FORT

A few days after our fight at Surprise Hill we woke one morning to the rumble of distant gun-fire from the direction of the Tugela River and there was a buzz of excitement in the camps around Ladysmith when it became known that General Buller was launching his long-expected attempt to break through to the relief of the town. For a while there was no definite news, and we waited until sunset when word came that the British had been repulsed with heavy losses and that a number of guns had been taken.

Hard on the success at Colenso arrived the news of victories on the other fronts. Piet Cronje had defeated and killed General Wauchope at Magersfontein, and General Gatacre was beaten at Colesberg. These tidings caused universal rejoicing, and there were few of us who did not believe that peace would soon follow, as it had after the Battle of Amajuba in 1881.

This time, however, their reverses seemed only to render the British more determined, but, the future being mercifully hidden from us, we confidently awaited the opening of peace negotiations and the surrender of Ladysmith, both of which events were expected to take place at any moment, and meanwhile camp life once more fell into the usual rut.

On Christmas Day another uncle of ours, Jan Mulder, paid us a visit. He was a Hollander by birth and a rolling stone by nature. After filling varied posts, and taking part in many native campaigns, he was Registrar of the Supreme Court in Swaziland when the war broke out and he enlisted as a private in the Swaziland Police, with which force he was now serving on the Tugela.

As I was anxious to see the entrenchments there of which we had heard so much, I accompanied him on his return two days later.

We left the Pretoria camp at daybreak and rode round the east side of Lady-smith, touching at the laagers en route for a talk or a meal, and reaching the Tugela opposite Colenso by four in the afternoon. The Boer line roughly followed the ragged hills that fringe the north bank of the river, though here and there they were dug in forward of the hills on the edge of the stream itself, and it was in one of these trench-lengths that we found the Swaziland Police, a small body of about one hundred strong.

The British Army lay across the river where their great tented camps were spread out on the plain. Judging by these and by the large numbers of troops being exercised every day, it was reckoned that there were forty thousand men facing us. I spent an interesting time riding up and down the line, and as things were quiet a party of us even rode through the river one morning to inspect the spot where the British guns had been captured and Lord Roberts's son killed in the recent battle. There were only decomposing horses and broken rifles lying about, and as the English gunners presently sent a brace of shrapnel over us we made haste to regain our own side.

Our trench was shelled at intervals by a sixty-pound naval gun standing at Chievely, seven miles away, but although some of the huge projectiles fell within a few feet of us, we suffered no damage. This was my first experience of lyddite, a newly invented explosive which went off with an appalling bang, emitting acrid green and yellow fumes that gave one a burning sensation in throat, and chest. I had read of its effect on the Dervishes at Omdurman, and the English newspapers had predicted equally terrible results for us; but the men made light of it and dubbed the shells 'little niggers'. Whenever one of them came through the air there was a warning cry: 'Look out — a little nigger', and everyone dived for cover behind the sandbags.

I saw the New Year (1900) in with the Swazilanders, who held a sing-song in celebration, and three days later I said good-bye to my uncle, and started home.

This time I rode round the western circle of Ladysmith in order to visit the Free State commandos guarding that side of the cordon, as I had many friends and acquaintances there, and, after spending a pleasant day among them, I timed my journey to reach the Kroonstad camp by sunset, as I wished to put in a night with my Norwegian uncle. I found him making ready to accompany a picket to the plain towards the English lines. His preparations for going on duty were unusual, for he inspanned an American buck-board on which he piled a feather bed, blankets and pillows, and as soon as the rest of the picket moved out after dark he told me to leave my roan horse in camp, and he and I drove in state to the place where we had to do guard for the night. The spot was not more than four hundred yards from the nearest English sentries, but this in no way disturbed my uncle's serenity. He unharnessed his two animals, hitched them to the wheels of the buggy, and giving one of the younger fry half-a-crown to do his sentry-go, he spread his bedding and was soon comfortably snoring within earshot of the British. I shared his couch, and we both slept soundly until awakened shortly before daybreak in time to harness the horses and get back to camp before it grow light. I spent the day with the Kroonstad people and listened to a council-of-war.

For weeks there had been talk of an attack by the Free State forces against a loose-standing kop called Wagon Hill, considered to be the key of the Ladysmith defences. We had so often heard of the proposed attempt that by now we had ceased to believe in it, but this time it looked as if something was on foot at last, for Commandants and Field-Cornets came riding in from the neighbouring camps to attend the meeting. Here I learned that it had been decided to storm the hill within the next day or two. It was said that Piet Joubert was growing impatient at the delay of the Ladysmith garrison in surrendering, and hoped to help them to make up their minds by the capture of this commanding position. I had a good look at Wagon Hill, but I came away somewhat dubious of success, although the Freestaters were eager to have a shot at it.

Next morning I rode through the Klip River and past Nicholson's Nek back to the Pretoria camp, still wondering whether the attack would materialize. When I arrived at our tent I was told that it was in fact due for the very next morning, and that four hundred Pretoria men were to create a diversion by falling upon our old friend the Red Fort in order to draw off the enemy's attention from the main objective while the Freestaters attacked Wagon Hill.

Our corporalship was to take part, and Isaac Malherbe had already given the necessary orders.

At 3 a.m. on the morning of January 6th, the whistles blew for the attacking force to assemble, and soon we were marched off on foot, headed by Mr Zeederberg and Assistant Field-Cornet de Jager. We collected in the same dry spruit below Bell's Kop from which we had started on our previous abortive expedition. Our experience on that occasion did not tend to reassure us, for once more there was a strong dilution of burgher-right *erven* men in our ranks, and we shook our heads when we saw them dejectedly standing behind the bank of the spruit, showing little inclination for the work in hand.

However, nearly half our forces were of better calibre, and when, shortly before sunrise, the two Field-Cornets led the way, about two hundred men responded, the rest refusing to follow. There was no time to argue, so, leaving the shirkers behind, we made over the plain towards the enemy works. It was still dark and we went along unobserved until we reached the outcrop of rock halfway across, where some of us had spent such evil hours during the former demonstration six weeks ago. Here the English in the fort observed us, and although the dawn was just breaking, they opened a heavy fire in our direction. This brought us to a standstill, and for a few moments we were uncertain whether to go forward or to fall back. The Field-Cornets seemed equally undecided, but, while they were debating, a man named Willemse intervened. He was a member of President Kruger's bodyguard, a fine tall fellow in police uniform. He was a stranger to us, for he had been on a chance visit to a relative at our camp, and had volunteered when he heard of the attack. He made an eloquent appeal to them to proceed, his words creating such an impression that we started for the fort at a run. The place was built on the brow of a low stony kopje immediately beyond the Harrismith railway line and, except where its earthworks formed an embankment, there was no cover. We had about four hundred yards to go, but the light was still uncertain, so we gained the safety of the ramp with the loss of only one man. This railway causeway proved our undoing, for had it not been there the chances are we should have gone straight on into the fort, but the sheltering bank was too tempting, and with one accord the men halted behind it to recover their breath. In the circumstances the delay was fatal, for we lost the original impulse that had carried us thus far, and as the light was increasing and with it the fierce volleying, we became disinclined to leave cover, and, instead of resuming our advance, stayed where we were.

We were now close in under the walls of the fort and could plainly see the muzzles of the defenders' rifles as they stuck them through the loopholes to fire at us. Other soldiers were standing by to repel boarders, for above the breast-works their bayonets glinted in the rising sun and gave us still further food for thought.

After a while, Isaac Malherbe, my brother, and a few more of us crawled along the track and, jumping across the metals, ran up the slope to where fair-sized boulders gave good cover within twenty-five yards of the work. Our inten-tion was to have a quick jumping-off point should the Field-Cornet give the order for a final rush, and from here we lay firing into the loopholes, waiting for the command to advance.

As we were now well ahead of where the rest of our force lay crouching be-hind the railway embankment, we were out of touch with them, although we kept looking back to see whether there was any sign of their coming on. Just as we were beginning to think that the attack had been called off we heard a shout, and saw Willemse leap out on to the track with about a dozen or fifteen men at his heels. At this we, too, sprang up to join in the charge, but almost as we rose, swift destruction overtook the storming party. A single volley flamed along the portholes, and before we had time to think the attack had withered away. We saw the men go down in a heap, leaving only one man erect. The rest were either dead or wounded or had flung themselves headlong for such cover as they could find.

Those of us with Isaac escaped annihilation because we were out of the direct line of fire and were able to regain protection before the soldiers had time to turn their attention to us, but we did not go quite unharmed, for Frank Roos, my tent-mate, fell dead among us with a bullet through his heart. The man who still faced the enemy was Willemse, and he, undeterred, ran up to the fort and tried to scale the wall. Bayonets were thrust at him which he parried with his rifle until a revolver was fired point-blank into him. He sank below the wall where he sat rocking to and fro, his head resting on his knees as if in great pain, and then another bullet found him, for he suddenly pitched forward on his face. We were so bewildered by the suddenness of everything that before we could collect our thoughts it was all over.

Willemse and six of his band lay dead, the survivors crouched behind cover against the driving bullets. Several of them were wounded, for they lay trying to bandage their injuries without exposing themselves from behind their scant shelter, and it was painful to see their efforts without being able to assist; but it was suicide to venture out under the wall in the teeth of such heavy fire.

We did not know why this piecemeal sally had been made, but after waiting for some time we were satisfied that there was to be no further attempt on the fort, so we recrossed the railway line, one at a time, crawling over until we were all back behind the bank where the rest of the men were gathered. Mr Zeederberg told me that the sortie had been made without his orders. Before he could stop them Willemse and the men were climbing up the slope to the disastrous end which we had witnessed.

There was now nothing else for us to do but to repeat our previous experience by staying where we were until the coming of night would enable us to retire. To renew the attack after what had happened was out of the question, nor was it feasible to withdraw in broad daylight from under the walls of the fort across a thousand yards of open veld.

It was as yet before eight in the morning, but we heard the sound of violent gun and rifle-fire from Wagon Hill, three or four miles away, where the main battle was being joined. How the Freestaters were prospering we had no means of knowing, but we guessed that heavy fighting was in progress, for the throbbing of the guns increased, and the rattle of thousands of rifles. Our share in the proceedings, however, was over: caught like rats in a trap we had to confine ourselves to loosing an occasional shot, and gazing longingly at the hill far to rearward where the balance of the Pretoria Commando looked on comfortably at our plight.

As the hours dragged by, the sun blazed down unbearably, and the wounded moaned and cried for water; of which we had none. By scrambling across the track and crawling from rock to rock we managed to pull most of them into the shelter of the embankment until we had brought in all except a few who were lying too far up. While busy at this I took a hurried glance at the dead. One of them was Assistant Field-Cornet de Jager, the others were men I had seen about camp, but did not know personally. Then I lay reading an old newspaper I had in my pocket, and slept at intervals to pass the time. This brought me subsequent notoriety, for when I unfolded the paper those watching us from the rear thought that it was a white flag, and some busybody rushed down into the laager to spread the news that we were surrendering to the enemy. Before field-glasses could be procured to verify the report it was too late to overtake the rumour, and by nightfall every commando around Ladysmith had heard that we had been marched into the town.

In this manner the day wore through. Occasionally we put a shot into the loopholes above us, but otherwise we lay inactive behind the railway earthwork counting the hours still to elapse before darkness. Through it all we heard the battle on Wagon Hill ebb and flow. At times it flared up and then died away, until some new turn caused a further eruption. The condition of our wounded grew worse and worse as the heat increased, and there was nothing we could do for them. It was bad enough to be thirsty ourselves, but to hear them beg for water and to sit helpless by was terrible, so we averted our eyes and pretended not to hear them.

At length, towards five in the afternoon, when things were getting unbearable, relief came from an unexpected quarter. Almost without warning, black clouds raced across the sky and there broke upon us the most violent storm that I have over experienced. It leapt at us with a roar, and there fell a deluge which in an instant blotted all from view. The rolling thunder and the drumming of the waters were deafening. For perhaps a minute we waited and then we abandoned our dead and wounded and fled blindly through the hurricane in the direction of our camp, a mile away.

We found the whole place thrown into confusion by the storm. Our tents were down and our belongings were littered a mile and more along the valley, washed away by the flood. As we could neither light a fire nor dry our clothing, we spent a miserable night, made the more unhappy by the knowledge that we had selfishly left our wounded in the dark and rain and, to add to our discomfiture, came the tidings next morning that the Freestaters, despite magnificent courage, had failed to take Wagon Hill, and had lost three hundred men in the attempt.

Later in the day our dead were fetched in by wagon under flag of truce.

We carried poor Frank Roos to our tent, and for the second time in three weeks my companions and I sat by the body of a messmate, wondering whose turn was next.

9. THE BATTLE OF SPION KOP

About a week later, Mr Zeederberg said I could go to Pretoria for a fortnight, so leaving my brother in charge of my horses, I once again boarded a north-bound goods train and travelled home in a cattle-truck, getting there in three days time. My father did not know I was coming, and although he gave me a warm welcome, he insisted on my returning at once, as he said the British were on the eve of delivering another great blow on the Tugela, and that my place was in Natal. I told him that the burghers thought there would be no more serious fighting, but he shook his head and said he only wished he could share our optimism.

I was disappointed, as I had been looking forward to the luxury of home life and good food for a little while, but I saw his point and started back on the second day.

I reached our camp at Ladysmith on January 23rd (1900) to find that volunteers were being called for to go to the Tugela, and I now heard that General Buller had moved the English army twenty-five miles upstream from Colenso in preparation for another big-scale attack in the vicinity of Spion Kop, a prominent hill forming part of the Boer line on the north bank of the Tugela. Already they were hammering away at different points, seeking a weak spot at which to thrust; so my father had been right, and, indeed, the situation was so critical that reinforcements were being sent from every commando lying around Lady-smith.

From the Pretoria laager fifty volunteers were asked for, and more than three times that number immediately offered themselves. The Field-Cornet made a selection which included Isaac Malherbe, my brother and myself and our three remaining tent-mates, Charles Jeppe, de Vos and Heinecke, as well as several more of our corporalship.

We set out within an hour of my arrival from Pretoria, and crossed the Klip River after dark, riding all night round by the west until we reached the rear of Spion Kop at day-break. As we rode, we could hear the sound of heavy gun-fire from the forward hills, and it never ceased for any length of time although we were still too far back to be in danger.

After a short halt to rest our horses and cook breakfast, we were ordered to the top of a steep ridge lying about a mile to the right, where we had to dig a reserve trench. A mule-wagon had accompanied us from Ladysmith carrying provisions, ammunition and a supply of pick-axes and shovels, with which unaccustomed tools we started up the slope, horses and all.

When we had dug for some time, Field-Cornet Zeederberg, who was always very kind to me, said that as I was the youngest I need not dig any more and could go down to where the wagon had been left for a rest. Nothing loath, I made haste to reach the halting-place, and, leaving my horse in charge of the mule-drivers, I started out to see what was going on in the front positions, which were out of sight from where we had been digging.

Ever since sunrise there had come the unbroken boom of guns and the rattle of small arms, and now that I was free I decided to walk across the intervening hills to the firing-line. As I went, the gun and rifle-fire grew louder, and before long I reached a point from which I could see the Boer front strung out along the top of the next rise.

Black mushrooms of earth and smoke hung along the course of the positions from the heavy shells flung across the Tugela, and puffs of shrapnel flecked the air above. From the noise I judged that a battle was in full progress and, after some hesitation, I hurried on and reached the line in safety. The spectacle from here was a fine one. Far below on the plain the Tugela wound shining in the sun, and the bank beyond was alive with English foot and horse. From the wooded hills farther back came the flashes of the British guns, and in the din I asked myself more than once why I had been foolish enough to come.

During the preceding days the English had effected a lodgement at numerous points on our side of the river, and their troops were occupying such spurs and ridges running up from the water's edge as they had been able to seize. The Boers, on being pushed back, had reformed along the crest of the height, where they were now holding a series of hastily dug trenches and whatever natural cover they could find, and were stoutly resisting any further encroachments of the enemy, who in places were lying within a few hundred yards of us.

The positions here were held by Free State commandos while downstream lay the Transvaalers. There were probably ten or twelve thousand burghers in all on these hills, with the bastion of Spion Kop standing like a pivot in the centre. For the most part the men made slight reply to the fire in order to husband their ammunition, and our artillery kept silent for the same reason, although it was estimated that there were over two hundred guns firing at us, and I have heard that this was the heaviest concentration of gun fire that has been seen in any war up to the present.

The casualties were considerable and I saw some men fearfully mutilated, including a father and son of the Frankfort commando who were torn to pieces by a howitzer shell, their rifles being sent spinning down the incline at the back of us.

It was a day of strain. Not only was there the horror of seeing men killed and maimed, but there was the long-drawn tension and fear of the approaching shells.

This tremendous volume of fire indicated an early attack, and throughout the day we looked to see the storm break at any moment, but, as it turned out, the bombardment was a feint, the real blow being delivered after midnight at a different point.

I was entitled to quit the line as my unit lay in the rear, but I did not like to go, and remained until things died down towards sunset, when I could return without loss of face. I found the Pretoria volunteers where I had left them digging that morning. They must have worked well, for they had completed quite a long trench.

I joined Isaac Malherbe and others sitting round the fires cooking their supper, and, watching the light fade away over the distant Drakensbergen, I chatted for a quiet hour with men who were mostly dead next morning.

Field-Cornet Zeederberg now ordered me down with him to the supply wagon. He said he was going to spend the night there, and, as he might require to send a message up to the trench, I was to come with him for I had good climbing legs.

When we got below, a tent had been pitched for him which I was allowed to share, and I was soon fast asleep. It rained at intervals during the night, and towards three in the morning we were waked by an angry stutter of rifle-fire coming from Spion Kop. We sat up listening, but as there was nothing we could do in the rain and darkness, and as after a while the firing died down, we fell asleep again.

At sunrise loud gun and rifle-fire broke out along the front on which I had been the day before; but, as it was no worse than it had then been, Mr Zeederberg and I were not unduly perturbed and sat sipping our morning coffee in the lee of the wagon out of the way of the spent bullets that whined over our heads.

As we breakfasted one of our Pretoria men galloped up with a message from; Isaac Malherbe to say that the British had made a night attack and had captured Spion Kop. This was most serious, for if the hill went, the entire Tugela line would go with it, and we could hardly bring ourselves to believe the news. The man, however, assured us that it was true, but he said that a strong force of burghers was assembling below the hill and that Isaac Malherbe had ridden down by a short cut with all the men who were with him, so we shouted to the mule-drivers to saddle our horses, and filling up with ammunition from a box on the wagon we followed on the heels of our guide.

Heavy shells were lobbing over as we went but we had not far to go and in less than fifteen minutes reached the bottom of Spion Kop. Here stood hundreds of saddled horses in long rows, and we looked up at an arresting sight.

The Boer counter-attack had started shortly before. Eight or nine hundred riflemen were climbing up the steep side of the hill in face of a close-range fire from the English troops who had established themselves on the flat summit overnight. Many of our men dropped, but already the foremost were within a few yards of the rocky edge which marked the crest, and soldiers were rising from behind their cover to meet the final rush. For a moment or two there was confused hand-to-hand fighting, then the combatants surged over the rim on to the plateau beyond, where we could no longer see them. Spellbound, we watched until our men passed out of view, and then, recovering ourselves, dismounted, and tying our horses with the rest, hurried up in the wake of the attack.

Dead and dying men lay all along the way, and there was proof that the Pretoria men had gone by, for I soon came on the body of John Malherbe, our Corporal's brother, with a bullet between his eyes; a few paces farther lay two more dead men of our commando. Farther on I found my tent-mate, poor Robert Reinecke, shot through the head, and not far off L. de Villiers of our corporalship lay dead. Yet higher up was Krige, another of Isaac's men, with a bullet through both lungs, still alive, and beyond him Walter de Vos of my tent, shot through the chest, but smiling cheerfully as we passed. Apart from the Pretoria men there were many other dead and wounded, mostly Carolina burghers from the eastern Transvaal, who formed the bulk of the assaulting column. Spion Kop, although steep, is not very high on the northern slope where we went up, and it did not take us long to reach the top. Here we found that the advance had got no farther than the fringe of loose rocks that runs like a girdle around the upper tableland. For the rest of the flat stretch beyond was still wholly in the hands of the British, who lay in a shallow trench behind a long low wall of stone about twenty yards away. From here came a vicious rifle-fire that made further progress impossible. It was marvellous that the Boers had got even thus far, for they had swarmed up the bare hillside in the face of a devastating fire, and they had pushed home the attack with such vigour that the narrow belt of rocks was thickly strewn with their dead.

I met my brother coming down in charge of captured soldiers and did not see him again as he had orders to escort them to Ladysmith, and he took no further part in the battle.

Giving him a hurried handshake, I went forward to the firing-line a few yards farther on. During the short delay I lost touch with Mr Zeederberg, and when I inquired from the men crouching behind the rocks for Isaac Malherbe, I was told by Red Daniel Opperman, the officer in command, that he had sent the Pretorians round to the ledge a few minutes earlier to rake the English flank. Working my way in that direction, I reached a spot where the outcrop of rocks came to a dead end. From here spread a patch of open ground until the ledge reappeared a hundred yards beyond.

One of the men holding this point told me that the Pretoria men had doubled across the gap shortly before and were now lying among the rocks on the far side, so I decided to follow; but the moment I left cover I drew so hot a fire that I was thankful to dive back for shelter and give up the attempt. Halfway across lay the huddled body of a dead man, and now that I had time to look more carefully at him, I recognized Charles Jeppe, the last of my tent-mates. His death affected me keenly, for we had been particularly good friends. Outwardly he was a surly man, but he had shown me many a kindness since first we messed together on the Natal border. As I was unable to find my Corporal, I now returned to where I had first reached the top and took my place in the firing-line.

During my absence about fifty soldiers had run forward to surrender, but otherwise things were going none too well. We were sustaining heavy casualties from the English *schans* immediately in front of us, and the men grew restive under the galling point-blank fire, a thing not to be wondered at, for the moral effect of Lee-Metford volleys at twenty yards must be experienced to be appreciated. The English troops lay so near that one could have tossed a biscuit among them, and whilst the losses which they were causing us were only too evident, we on our side did not know that we were inflicting even greater damage upon them. Our own casualties lay hideously among us, but theirs were screened from view behind the breastwork, so that the comfort of knowing that we were giving worse than we received was denied us.

Fortunately, towards nine o'clock the situation eased, for the Transvaal artillerists got their guns into action on a commanding spur a mile away, and they began to fire over our heads into the troops crowded on the restricted space on the plateau before us. As the guns searched the hill-top the English fire slackened, and from then onward our losses were less. The position, however, remained unsatisfactory. The sun became hotter and hotter, and we had neither food nor water. Around us lay scores of dead and wounded men, a depressing sight, and by midday a feeling of discouragement had gained ground that was only kept in check by Commandant Opperman's forceful personality and vigorous language to any man who seemed to be wavering. Had it not been for him the majority would have gone far sooner than they did, for the belief spread that we were being left in the lurch. We could see large numbers of horsemen collecting at the laagers on the plain behind, but no reinforcements reached us throughout the day. I repeatedly heard old Red Daniel assure the men that help would be forthcoming, but from the way he kept scanning the country below I could see that he was getting uneasy himself.

As the hours dragged on a trickle of men slipped down the hill, and in spite of his watchful eye this gradual wastage so depleted our strength that long before nightfall we were holding the blood-spattered ledge with a mere handful of rifles. I wanted to go too, but the thought of Isaac and my other friends saved me from deserting. No further attempt was made to press forward, and for the rest of this terrible day both sides stubbornly held their ground, and, although the battle remained stationary, the heavy close-range rifle-fire continued hours after hour, and the tale of losses mounted while we lay in the blazing heat.

I saw a strange incident during the morning. Near me was a German named von Brusewitz. He had been an officer in the German army, but the year before he had run a civilian through with his sword during some scuffle in a Berlin café. There was a great outcry over the incident, and to allay popular clamour the German Emperor broke him from his regiment. They say that in Germany the word 'Brusewitzerei' is still used to denote the arrogance of the officer-caste. However that may be, von Brusewitz was now on top of Spion Kop, where he seemed bent on getting killed, for although we warned him not to expose himself

too recklessly, he paid no heed, and repeatedly stood out from among the rocks
to fire.

As the English soldier were so close to us this was sheer folly, and after he
had tempted providence several times the inevitable happened. I saw him rise
once more, and, lighting a cigarette, puff away careless of the flying bullets until
we heard a thud, and he fell dead within a few feet of me, shot through the head.
Not long after this something similar happened. An old native servant came
whimpering up among us from below, looking for his master's body. I advised
him to be careful as he went from rock to rock peering over to examine the dead
men lying in the open, but he would not listen, and soon he too had a bullet
through his brain.

The hours went by; we kept watch, peering over and firing whenever a helmet
showed itself, and in reply the soldiers volleyed unremittingly. We were hungry,
thirsty and tired; around us were the dead men covered with swarms of flies
attracted by the smell of blood. We did not know the cruel losses that the English
were suffering, and we believed that they were easily holding their own, so
discouragement spread as the shadows lengthened.

Batches of men left the line, openly defying Red Daniel, who was impotent in
the face of this wholesale defection, and when at last the sun set I do not think
there were sixty men left on the ledge.

Darkness fell swiftly; the firing died away, and there was silence, save for a
rare shot and the moans of the wounded. For a long time I remained at my post,
staring into the night to whew the enemy lay, so close that I could hear the cries
of their wounded and the murmur of voices from behind their breastwork.

Afterwards my nerve began to go, and I thought I saw figures with bayonets
stealing forward. When I tried to find the men who earlier in the evening had
been beside me, they were gone. Almost in a panic I left my place and hastened
along the fringe of rocks in search of company, and to my immense relief heard a
gruff 'Werda?' It was Commandant Opperman still in his place with about two
dozen men. He told me to stay beside him, and we remained here until after ten
o'clock, listening to the enemy who were talking and stumbling about in the
darkness beyond.

At last Opperman decided to retreat, and we descended the hill by the way
which he had climbed up nearly sixteen hours before, our feet striking sicken-
ingly at times against the dead bodies in our path. When we reached the bottom
most of the horses were gone, the men who had retired having taken their
mounts and ridden away, but our own animals, and those belonging to the dead
or wounded were still standing without food or water where they had been left at
daybreak.

The first thing to do was to quench our raging thirst and that of our horses at
a spring near by. We then consulted as to our next move. Most of the wounded
had been taken off in the course of the day, but we found a few serious cases
that would not bear transport collected in charge of an old man, who, by the dim
light of a lantern, was attending to their wants. We could get no coherent
information and stood discussing what to do next, for we did not know that the

English had also been fought to a standstill, and that they in turn were at that very moment retreating down their own side of Spion Kop. We fully believed that the morning would see them streaming through the breach to the relief of Ladysmith, and the rolling up of all our Tugela line.

While we were talking, Mr Zeederberg came out of the dark. I had lost sight of him during most of the day, but he had been on the hill all the time, and had only come down shortly before us. He had seen nothing of Isaac Malherbe and the rest of our Pretoria men, and had no idea of what had become of them. A few more stragglers joined us and we agreed to lead our horses to the Carolina wagon-laager that, as we knew, lay not far off. We foraged for food in the saddle-bags of such horses as were left, and then went off. When we reached the laager we found everything in a state of chaos. The wagons were being hurriedly packed, and the entire Carolina commando was making ready to retire. They had borne the brunt of the day's battle and had fought bravely, but, now that the struggle was over, a reaction had set in and there was panic in the camp. Fortunately, just as the foremost wagons moved away and the horsemen were getting ready to follow, there came the sound of galloping hoofs, and a man rode into our midst who shouted to them to halt. I could not see his face in the dark, but word went round that it was Louis Botha, the new Commandant-General, appointed in place of Piet Joubert who was seriously ill. He addressed the men from the saddle, telling them of the shame that would be theirs if they deserted their posts in this hour of danger; and so eloquent was his appeal that in a few minutes the men were filing off into the dark to reoccupy their positions on either side of the Spion Kop gap. I believe that he spent the rest of the night riding from commando to commando exhorting and threatening, until he persuaded the men to return to the line, thus averting a great disaster.

As for Commandant Opperman and our party, now that the Carolina burghers were returning we led our horses back to the foot of Spion Kop, to wait there.

We woke with the falling of the dew and, as the sky lightened, gazed eagerly at the dim outline of the hill above, but could make out no sign of life.

Gradually the dawn came and still there was no movement. Then to our utter surprise we saw two men on the top triumphantly waving their hats and holding their rifles aloft. They were Boers, and their presence there was proof that, almost unbelievably, defeat had turned to victory—the English were gone and the hill was still ours.

Leaving our horses to fend for themselves, We were soon hastening up the slope past the dead until we reached yesterday's bloody ledge. From here we hurried across to the English breastworks, to find them abandoned. On our side of the fighting-line there had been many casualties, but a worse sight met our eyes behind the English schanses.

In the shallow trenches where they had fought the soldiers lay dead in swathes, and in places they were piled three deep.

The Boer guns in particular had wrought terrible havoc and some of the bodies were shockingly mutilated. There must have been six hundred dead men on this strip of earth, and there cannot have been many battlefields where there was such an accumulation of horrors within so small a compass.

Shortly after I reached the top, Isaac Malherbe and the remaining Pretoria men came up. They had spent the night somewhere below the kop, and like ourselves had come up the moment they realized that the English were gone. Isaac looked grim and worn, grieved at the death of his brother and of our other companions, but he was full of courage, and so were we all, for from where we stood we could look down on the Tugela River, and we were now able to grasp the full significance of our unexpected success.

Long columns of troops and long convoys of transport were re-crossing to the south bank, and everywhere the British were in full retreat from the positions which they had captured on this side of the streams and the clouds of dust rising on the Colenso road told us that General Buller's second great attempt to pierce the Tugela defences had failed. We spent the next hour or two helping the English Red Cross doctors and bearer parties that came up to bury their dead and carry away their wounded. By now hundreds of other burghers had arrived, mostly men who had retreated the day before, but like ourselves had loitered in neighbouring kloofs and gullies to see if they could renew the fight.

Towards midday Isaac Malherbe ordered us to collect our Pretoria dead. We carried them down in blankets, and when the commando wagon came up we placed the bodies on board and escorted them to Ladysmith, whence they were sent to Pretoria for burial. So we rode behind the wagon which carried all that was left of our friends and companions, their horses trotting alongside with empty saddles.

I personally came home to a deserted tent, for within a few weeks four good friends had gone from it to their death, and our fifth messmate, de Vos, was lying dangerously wounded at some laager below Spion Kop. Only my brother and I were left, and he had been sent to Pretoria with the prisoners, so I was all alone, except for our faithful old native retainer, who did what he could to cheer me up.

10. THE REST OF OUR CORPORALSHIP IS DESTROYED

For a while the success at Spion Kop went to our heads, and we thought that the English would be sure to make peace, but again the days came and went with no sign.

Indeed, we presently heard that General Buller was back at Colenso collecting an ever larger army to attack again, but we were confident that the Tugela defences would hold and we saw no shadow of the disasters that were soon to overtake us. After a week my brother Joubert returned from Pretoria. He said that he and the escort had been made much of by the townspeople, for, coming straight from the battle on the hill, they were the heroes of the hour, and they were marched down to shake hands with President Kruger, the nearest approach to battle honours that we ever attained.

He arrived in camp with my three remaining brothers. The eldest, Hjalmar, aged twenty, was studying law in Holland when the war broke out, and he had after considerable difficulty succeeded in reaching the Transvaal through Portuguese territory. The other two, Amt and Jack, aged sixteen and twelve respectively, had been at school up to now; but they had at last persuaded my father to let them come to the war. Jack only remained for a few days, as old Maroola on one of his visits to our laager caught sight of him and ordered him to be sent home, but at any rate from now onward there were four of us in our tent.

About the middle of February, a force of eight hundred mounted men was drawn from different commandos for the purpose of carrying out a raid into Zululand. The exact object of this expedition I never heard, but I think that it was intended to create a diversion, for the British were massing heavily at Colenso. My two newly arrived brothers were absent on a visit to the Tugela, for commando life was a novelty to them, and they spent much of their time riding about, but my brother Joubert and I joined the Zululand column. It assembled at the Commandant-General's headquarters behind Bulwana Hill, and we started the same morning under old Maroola. For several days we travelled due east through lovely mountain country everywhere dotted with picturesque native kraals. The Zulus showed no fear of us and refused to serve as guides, for they sided with the British, as they have always done.

Of English troops we saw no sign, and our journey was a restful interlude after the excitement of the past few weeks. Unfortunately it soon came to an end, for about the fifth day out a messenger came riding post-haste with orders for Maroola to return to Ladysmith at once.

We retraced our steps by forced marches, arriving back at the head laager on about the eighth day after leaving. During the last two days of the journey we heard a constant rumble of gun-fire coming from the direction of Colenso, and, on reaching our Pretoria camp, we were met with the disturbing news that the English had broken into our defences there to the extent of capturing Hlangwane Hill, a commanding position that was considered the key to the Tugela line. Once more volunteers from every commando around the town were called for. My two brothers Hjalmar and Arnt had returned and gone off again on some jaunt, so Joubert and I, with the rest of Isaac Malherbe's corporalship, handed in our names. There was no difficulty in getting the required fifty men, and at dusk on the day after our return from Zululand we set out on a journey from which few were to come back.

We rode through most of the night in company with other units hurrying to the danger-point. Farther on we fell in with small parties riding in the contrary direction, who made no secret of having quitted the Tugela firing-line, and when we neared the river at daybreak we found a critical situation. Not only had Hlangwane been taken, but every Boer trench on the north bank for a distance of several miles had been evacuated, and, what was far more serious, there was a feeling of discouragement in the air that dismayed us.

Up to now, the prevailing note in Natal had been one of confidence in an early peace, but, almost in a night and without apparent cause, a wave of pessimism had set in and the nearer we came the more evidence was there of growing demoralization.

Hundreds of men were leaving the new line that had been formed in the hills behind the abandoned trenches. They were dispersing about the back area, some holding meetings, others making for the wagon-laagers in the rear, and from their talk and attitude we sniffed disaster, for though we knew before starting that Hlangwane had been taken, we did not know that the fighting spirit of the men had gone with it.

Bad as it looked, however, things were not yet quite hopeless, for General Botha had taken up a new lane to the rear of the old one and was once more standing on the defensive with eight or nine thousand men. We were met by one of his officers, who allotted different points to the various fresh detachments. We of the Pretoria commando were told to leave our horses in charge of guards and march on foot down a rocky gorge which led towards the Tugela. Heavy lyddite shells crashed against the cliffs on either side as we went down, but we emerged without loss at the lower exit of the canyon, to find ourselves in the bed of a dry spruit which ran across an open plain to where it joined the Tugela River about a mile and a half away. This dry bed skirted along the base of the foothills for some distance before bending away across the plain, and, from the exit of the gorge to the point where it curved away, its bank had been converted into a sector of the new line. We were assigned a position near the top end, not far from where we had come out of the gorge, and we fell to at once, hacking firing steps, with pocket-knives and any other implements on which we could lay our hands.

The English infantry were eight hundred yards off, approximately along the line of our former trenches that had been abandoned two days before. From here they were maintaining a continuous rifle-fire, a multitude of bullets whizzing overhead or plugging into the ground in front.

They were also methodically shelling the course of the spruit with many guns, including high-angle howitzers, so that we were in a very warm and unpleasant locality.

The casualties were few, owing to the height of the bank, and not one of the Pretoria men was hit, although I got a shell splinter through my hat before I had been there ten minutes, and one or two of our men had scratches from flying earth as the shells exploded in the bed of the spruit below.

The British did not attack on our front, but later in the morning made a determined attempt to our left against some hills known as Pieters Heights, where the Bethal Commando was posted.

We saw waves of infantry going forward, but it was too far off for us to participate. At first the soldiers advanced in regular lines, but gradually their progress was stayed, and we could see the survivors crouching behind rocks and stones. They lost heavily, and it was soon evident that the attack had been repulsed.

Nothing further happened that day and by dark all was quiet. We spent an undisturbed night, and next morning (February 26th, 1900) the English sent in under flag of truce to fetch away their dead and wounded, so that there was no firing at all.

Having nothing to do, my brother and I walked down to watch the removal of the fallen soldiers and we spent some hours going over the ground discussing events with the English doctors and stretcher-bearers.

Returning, up the spruit on the way to our own quarters, we met my Hollander uncle, still serving with the Swaziland Police, a chance encounter which probably saved the lives of both of us. My uncle, seeing us pass, asked us to spend a day or two with him, and, fading in with his suggestion, we went to get our things and to tell Isaac Malherbe where we were going. He made no objection to our visiting the Swazilanders, seeing that they were close by, and he promised to send for us should we be wanted. As we were going off he looked at us with his quiet smile and said: 'Be sure and come quickly should I send word, for how shall I hold this bank without you two boys beside me ?' He was referring to the night below Surprise Hill, but we never again saw him alive, nor any of the others.

Carrying our cooking-tins and blankets, we returned to the Swaziland Police. At sunrise next morning the English started in real earnest to bombard the spruit. All day long they shelled us with light and heavy guns, while we hugged the sheltering bank. Shrapnel and lyddite crashed upon us, causing a great many casualties, and we suffered a terrible ordeal.

Considering the demoralisation that had set in, the men stood the bombardment well. There were some who retreated up the gorge, but there was no general desertion, and, when at sunset the fire died down, our forces were holding firm after one of the worst days of the war. This heavy shelling was the obvious preparation for an attack next day, so my brother and I, when the fire slackened, went up to find the Pretoria men. In the dusk we made our way along the bed of the spruit, past groups of burghers standing around their dead or wounded and other groups discussing the incidents of the day, but when we came to where we had left our companions the evening before, they were gone, and we were told by those near by that they had marched up the gorge an hour ago for some other point of the line. We could not understand why Isaac had not let us know, but thought that his messenger had missed us in the failing light. We were upset by his departure and decided to follow after at once, so we went back to tell my uncle of our intention. He said he was coming with us, too, as he had been thinking of a change for some time, and would like to join the Pretoria Commando. Accordingly he told his Field-Cornet of his plans and the three of us set off through the gorge. It was pitch-dark by now, and we had a difficult climb up the boulder-strewn bed, stumbling and groping our way as best we could.

When at last we reached the top entrance, we were so weary with the heavy loads we were carrying, and there was so little chance of finding our corporalship at that time of night, that we flung ourselves down on the first piece of level ground and slept until daybreak. As soon as it was light we made out the tents of the horse-guards, where we found our saddles just as we had left them, and our horses grazing not far away. These guards were here on permanent duty to look after the animals of the burghers in the firing-line, and they told us that Isaac Malherbe and his party had spent the night with them, and had ridden off before dawn to join the Bethal commando at Pieters Heights some miles east of this, so we hurriedly cooked a meal and, saddling our horses, rode after him, following behind the range of hills that formed the Boer line.

As we went along, a bombardment more violent than that of yesterday broke out ahead of us, and, when we came to the rear of Pieters Heights, we saw the ridge on which lay the Bethal men (and our own) going up in smoke and flame. It was an alarming sight. The English batteries were so concentrating on the crest that it was almost invisible under the clouds of flying earth and fumes, while the volume of sound was beyond anything that I have ever heard. At intervals the curtain lifted, letting us catch a glimpse of the trenches above, but we could see no sign of movement, nor could we hear whether the men up there were still firing, for the din of the guns drowned all lesser sounds.

We reined in about four hundred yards from the foot of the hill, at a loss what to do. To approach our men through that inferno was to court destruction, while not to try seemed like desertion. For a minute or two we debated and then, suddenly, the gun-fire ceased, and for a space we caught the fierce rattle of Mauser rifles followed by British infantry swamping over the skyline, their bayonets flashing in the sun. Shouts and cries reached us, and we could see men desperately thrusting and clubbing. Then a rout of burghers broke back from the hill, streaming towards us in disorderly flight. The soldiers fired into them, bringing many down as they made blindly past us, not looking to right or left. We went, too, for the troops, cheering loudly, came shooting and running down the slope.

Of our Pretoria men who had been on the ridge not one came back. They had been holding an advanced position to the right of the Bethal section, and had been overwhelmed there. They stood their ground until the enemy was on them, and they were bayoneted or taken to the last man. Thus our corporalship was wiped out, with its leader, Isaac Malherbe, the bravest of them all, and their going at this calamitous time was scarcely noticed. For this day marked the beginning of the end in Natal. The British had blasted a gap through which the victorious soldiery came pouring and, wherever we looked, Boer horsemen, wagons and guns went streaming to the rear in headlong retreat.

We followed the current, hemmed in by a great throng, all making for the various fords of the Klip River, and it was lucky indeed that the English sent no cavalry in pursuit, for the passages across the river were steep and narrow, and there was frightful confusion of men and wagons struggling to get past.

By nightfall my uncle and my brother and I had managed to cross, and as it started to rain we annexed a deserted tent behind Lombaardskop, picketed and fed our tired horses, and slept there till morning. We now resumed our journey as far as the head laager, where we spent a dismal hour or two watching the tide of defeat roll northward.

We knew that the siege of Ladysmith would have to be raised, and now came the news, while we were halted here, that Kimberley had also been relieved, and that General Cronje had been captured at Paardeberg with four thousand men, so that the whole universe seemed to be toppling about our cars.

From the way in which the commandos were hurrying past, it looked that morning as if the Boer cause was going to pieces before our eyes, and it would have taken a bold man to prophesy that the war had still more than two long years to run.

We hung about the dismantled head laager till midday, after which the three of us rode on gloomily to the Pretoria camp, arriving towards five in the after-noon. word of the disaster to our men on the Tugela had already preceded us, as is the way with evil tidings, and, as it was not known that my brother and I had escaped, our unexpected appearance caused a sensation, men running up from all sides to hear the truth. My other brothers had returned and their welcome was a warm one.

It was by now clear enough that the siege could no longer be maintained and, indeed, orders had already been received that all commandos were to evacuate their positions around Ladysmith after dark. Our wagons were standing packed, but at the last moment it was found that someone had levanted with the trans-port mules, so everything had to be burned. It came on to rain heavily by nightfall. Peals of thunder growled across the sky, and, wet to the skin, we stood huddled against the storm in depressed groups, awaiting our final orders. At last, long after dark, Field-Cornet Zeederberg gave the word that we were to move off to Elandslaagte some twenty miles to the rear. It was an inky night, with rain in torrents, through which we had to feel our way, and thus we turned our backs on Ladysmith for good and all.

No march order was attempted; we were simply told to go, and it was left to each man to carry out his own retirement.

At the outset we travelled in company with many others, but, as I knew a short cut, threading the hills to the railway depot at Modderspruit, my brothers and I decided to go thither, for we saw no use in floundering about in mud and water, and the four of us, with my uncle and our native boy Charley, branched away by ourselves.

We reached the depot after two hours and found shelter until daybreak, after which we rode on.

The rain now stopped and the sun rose warm and bright, but it looked on a dismal scene. In all directions the plain was covered with a multitude of men, wagons, and guns ploughing across the sodden veld in the greatest disorder. Wherever a spruit or nullah barred the way there arose fierce quarrels between the frightened teamsters, each wanting to cross first, with the result that whole parks of vehicles got their wheels so interlocked that at times it seemed as if the bulk of the transport and artillery would have to be abandoned, for the mounted men pressed steadily on without concerning themselves with the convoys. Had the British fired a single gun at this surging mob everything on wheels would have fallen into their hands, but by great good luck there was no pursuit and towards afternoon the tangle gradually straightened itself out.

Our little family party remained behind with a number of others as a rear-guard and we did not reach Elandslaagte until late that night. This place had been the chief supply centre for the Natal forces, and there were still huge quantities of stores that had been left to the enemy. These we burnt, lighting a conflagration that must have been visible for fifty miles around.

By now the bulk of the retreat had passed on, and next day we rode along leisurely, climbing up the Washbank valley to Glencoe near Dundee by the following evening. Here were stray remnants of almost every commando that had been in Natal, but things were in such confusion that most of the army had continued straight on, and there was scarcely a man who could tell us what had become of his officers, or what we were supposed to do next.

Mr. Zeederberg, however, was at Glencoe when we got there, and during the next few days he succeeded in collecting about three hundred Pretoria men, while more drifted back later on, as did stragglers from the other commandos, until after a week or ten days there was quite a respectable body of men numbering well over five thousand.

During this time my brothers and I with our uncle subsisted on what we could loot from the supply trains at the station, for there were practically no commissariat arrangements, but by raiding the trucks at night we did not do badly.

After a while General Botha reorganized everything, and a new line of defence was established along the forward slopes of the Biggarsbergen, to which all available men were marched. We of the Pretoria commando were assigned a post on the shoulder of the mountain to the right of where the Washbank valley reaches the plain below, and here we lay amongst pleasant scenery, from which we looked regretfully over the wide sweep of country to the south from which we had been driven, but we enjoyed the spell of peace and quiet after the turmoil of the past weeks.

11. A CAMPAIGN IN THE FREE STATE

The English Army, having forced the Tugela and relieved Ladysmith, was also resting.

Far down on the plain, large camps were springing up, but all through the month of March and half of April they made no move at all and the weeks went by unbroken, except for an occasional patrol when we would leave over horses below some kopje and climb up to watch the troops at exercise in the distance.

While matters went this easily in Natal, grave rumours reached us as to the situation in the Free State. Reliable information was scarce, but it was freely said that a powerful army under Lord Roberts had crossed the Free State border and was marching on Bloemfontein.

When my brothers and I heard this we felt we ought to go to our own country. We decided to go to Pretoria first and thence south by rail, for since the destruction of our corporalship we considered ourselves free to go where we pleased.

The day before we meant to leave we were ordered to take part in an attack on the English camps lying at Elandslaagte, halfway back to Ladysmith.

This much-criticized affair was to have been carried out by three thousand Transvaalers in conjunction with an equal force of Freestaters from the Drakensbergen. We assembled after midnight at the exit of the Washbank valley and reached the Elandslaagte hills as it grew light, but we looked in vain for the Free State commandos.

The Free State Commandant-General, Prinsloo (the same who surrendered so ignominiously with three thousand men a few months later), had telegraphed to General Botha at the last moment to say that he and his officers were attending a cattle sale at Harrismith on the day set for the attack, and were therefore unable to be present.

In view of this, General Botha had to change his plans and content himself with a mere demonstration instead of serious business and the whole thing fizzled out in an artillery duel with heavy expenditure of ammunition and very little damage done. To me it was memorable only for the fact that while I was watching one of our Creusot guns being fired, the wind of a shell from the English batteries sent me spinning yards away. It must have passed within a few inches of me and I shall not soon forget being blown head over heels.

We remained before the camps all day, subjected to severe shell-fire at times, and after dark we rode back to our stations in the Biggarsbergen, none the better for our outing.

The next day my brothers and I took leave of the Pretoria commando with which we had served for so long.

We rode up the valley to the train at Glencoe Junction, and it was months before we saw our old force again.

At the railway station we held up the first north-bound train, loaded our horses in one truck and ourselves in another, and steamed off, leaving Natal behind us for ever.

After the usual three days' journey and the usual delays at halts and stations, we arrived at Pretoria. My uncle, Jan Mulder, was not of our party, for he had remained with the Irish Brigade, a band of two hundred adventurers commanded by an American Colonel named Blake, whose roistering habits and devil-may-care methods suited his own, so that we four brothers and Charley, our boy, formed our party.

My father did not know of our arrival until we came riding up to the front door, but when we told him we were for the Free State he approved. We gathered that the position was very bad, and he himself seemed aged and worn, for he bore great responsibilities upon his shoulders. He had signed the ultimatum to Great Britain, and in a large measure the policy which had led to the war had been his, so the gloomy military situation lay heavily upon his mind, as well as the personal anxiety of having four sons at the front. We spent the next few days in the luxury and comfort of home life, the last we were ever to enjoy.

I even visited Johannesburg for the first time. The city was practically deserted; the shops were boarded up and there was little or no life in the streets, but I remember the visit because that afternoon there came the roar of a great explosion and a column of smoke shot up into the sky a mile high. It was the Begbie foundry, where the Government was manufacturing shells and ammunition, that had gone into the air, by treachery it was said.

About thirty people were killed, but so fierce was the blaze that we could give no assistance and we had to look on helplessly while the fire burnt itself out.

On April 30th (1900) my three brothers and I, with our boy Charley, entrained for the Free State. We knew that the British had occupied Bloemfontein by now and were advancing towards the Transvaal, but no one seemed certain how far they had got, or for how far the railway line to the south was still open. We crossed the Vaal River that night, and, after a slow journey over the rolling plains of the northern Free State, we reached a small station near the banks of the Vet River by eleven o'clock next night. We were now within fifty miles of Bloemfontein and the train was going no farther, as the engine-driver told us that the British advance was at the next station but one down the line. On hearing this, we unslipped our horses and camped beside the track until daybreak, intending then to ride forward in search of the Boer forces that we knew must be somewhere ahead.

As we were preparing to start next morning, another train steamed in from the north, carrying a hundred and fifty men under Commandant Malan, a brother-in-law of the Commandant-General Piet Joubert, who had recently died. Malan had collected a lot of young fellows whom he had formed into a flying column, the 'Africander Cavalry Corps', and they were on their way to the nearest fighting.

They detrained here and we lost no time in enrolling ourselves as members of the 'A.C.C.' as it was called for short. Among them was my old schoolfellow Jan Joubert, the Commandant General's son, with other friends and acquaintances.

We spent the morning getting ready and that afternoon we trekked off, riding south through the Vet River towards the sound of the distant gun-fire that we could now hear on the wind.

Darkness found us on the wide plain beyond the river, where we met hundreds of horsemen withdrawing, so they told us, to fresh positions, but whom we suspected of being on their way home for good. They said that great swarms of British troops were on the move, and that it was useless to think of fighting them in the open.

Nevertheless we rode on until midnight, when we came to where General de la Rey was halted with the Transvaal commandos. We found him squatted by a small fire, a splendid-looking old man with a hawk-like nose and fierce black eyes. Beside him was his brother, nursing an arm shattered by a bullet that afternoon. He gave us a hurried account of the situation, which was very black. The British Army, after capturing Cronje and taking Bloemfontein, was now advancing on the Transvaal and, owing to the demoralized state of the commandos and the lack of defensive cover in this bare region, he saw little or no hope of stopping them.

He said he had about four thousand Transvaalers who had escaped the debacle at Paardeberg, but they were discouraged and were making the merest show of opposition.

The Free State commandos had disappeared altogether, although he believed that President Steyn and Christian de Wet were trying to reorganize them somewhere in the mountain country to the east, but for the time being they were out of action. The British were within a few miles of us, and would doubtless resume their advance in the morning.

So far as the 'A.C.C.' was concerned, he ordered us to ride forward for half an hour and halt till daybreak, after which we were to fit ourselves into the firing-line and act according to circumstances. We took leave of him and, mounting our horses, rode on for three or four miles.

Since we had come south the weather had turned bitterly cold, and we felt the change from the warmer climate of Natal.

For months we were not to spend one really comfortable night until summer came round again, and on this particular night we sat, with our blankets wrapped around our shoulders, shivering till daybreak, for sleep was out of the question with the temperature below zero.

As soon as it grew light we were astir, anxiously scanning the ground before us, and soon we made out dense masses of English infantry on the plain. First came a screen of horsemen, and behind a multitude of infantry, guns and wagons throwing up huge clouds of dust.

We looked in dismay at the advancing host, for there were thirty thousand men approaching, whilst on our meagre front there may have been between three and four thousand Boer horsemen, strung out in a ragged line on the rising ground to right and left of us.

It was plain from the very way in which the men sat their horses that they would not stand, and indeed, on this bare veld and against such heavy odds, the task was manifestly beyond them.

The enemy forces came steadily on until their scouts were close to us. When we fired at these they fell back upon their regiments; the batteries unlimbered and in a few seconds shrapnel was bursting over us.

Our line gave way almost at once. The 'A.C.C.' stayed as long as any, but we recognized the futility of remaining, so we went galloping back with field-gun and pom-pom shells besprinkling us as we rode. We had no casualties, but a number of men from other commandos were killed and wounded before we got clear, and after a hard ride we slowed down at a deserted farmhouse to breathe our winded animals.

The English troops being mainly infantry, their progress was slow, and, although they were quickly at us once more, we were able to retire before them with very little loss for the rest of the day, firing on their scouts when they pressed us too nearly, and moving back in extended order to escape the shell-fire that came in gusts as the guns were brought forward. We were in the saddle until sunset, for we had to exercise ceaseless vigilance to keep the English horse from the wagons that were struggling to get away.

There must have been over a thousand of these, for, in addition to General de la Rey's transport, there were a great many vehicles belonging to the civilian population fleeing before the oncoming invasion.

By dark the English had pushed us right back to the Vet River, a distance of twenty miles or more, and next morning we had scarcely time to prepare a hasty breakfast before we could see the columns again advancing towards us.

General Louis Botha was standing at the drift as we rode through, for he had hurried round by rail from Natal to see for himself what was going on in the Free State.

He and General de la Rey disposed such commandos as were available along the river from the railway bridge to a point about four miles down, with orders to take a stand. The 'A.C.C.' was allotted the extreme right, so we searched out a suitable spot on the river bank beyond the next farthest commando, and, leaving our horses in the bed below, took up our posts. As we expected trouble, we sent the native boy Charley to the rear with our spare kit loaded on my Basuto Pony (which we had brought from Natal as a pack-horse).

The British were by now feeling their way over the plain that ran down to the river, and before long were volleying at us from tall grass in which we could only just see where they lay. Then their guns came forward and started shelling us. Our horses were safe in the river bed behind, but owing to the thorn trees fringing the bank our view was impeded, and we had to crawl to the outside edge of the bush to see the enemy, with the result that we had practically no cover and had casualties almost at once. Several men were killed and wounded close to me, and altogether it was a beastly day.

The shelling was not confined to our portion of the line, but ran up and down, like a piano, as far as the bridge and back again, and at times was as heavy as that on the Tugela. It continued until far into the afternoon and it was only at three o'clock that we saw the infantry preparing to charge.

We had six killed and about fifteen wounded by then. The dead had been laid on the sand in the river bed, and the wounded had been placed on their horses and told to get away as best they could, while the rest of us stayed on in such holes and hollows as we had been able to scrabble in the soil. The shell-fire and the casualties had shaken us, and when the British rose to their feet, and from their rear some three hundred cavalry came riding, sword in hand, we rose to fire a few wavering shots, and then broke for the river behind, tumbling down pell-mell to get our horses. Leaving our dead, we rode up the opposite bank and went racing across the open to the hills a mile to rearward. We were heavily fired on, but reached sanctuary with only two or three men down and a few wounded, including my younger brother Arnt with a scalp-wound from a glancing rifle bullet. The English horsemen that had been the chief cause of our flight came no farther than the river, but the infantry were breaking through at several places, and we could see them well on our side of the stream, the rest of the commandos also retreating wildly.

Before long we were again being shelled, and near sunset the soldiers came on to drive us out of the hills to which we had fled. As we were holding the extreme end of the Boer line, we were soon outflanked. We saw a regiment change direction and before we could stop them they were climbing into the very hills on which we ourselves were at a point about fifteen hundred yards off, from which they began to work their way towards us.

We fronted round to meet them, but the sinking sun was straight in our eyes, making accurate shooting difficult, and, when the soldiers came swarming towards us at short range, another stampede took place. The whole of what remained of the 'A.C.C.' rushed for their horses and made haste to be off. By the time I was in the saddle, the nearest infantrymen were so close that I could see their faces and the brass buttons on their tunics, but they were blown with running and their aim was poor, and although several horses were hit, none of the men were injured. My eldest brother's pony was shot through the body from saddle-flap to saddle-flap, but the plucky little animal carried him a thousand yards before he fell dead. Riderless horses were careering all over the place, and by cornering one of them we succeeded in providing my brother with another mount. Bullets and shells were striking everywhere, so we hurriedly transferred his belongings to the new horse and followed the rout now fast vanishing over the next rise. In the darkness we galloped on to catch up with the press, for all positions along the river had been given up and a wholesale retreat was in progress.

The 'A.C.C.' had over thirty men killed and wounded during the day, and if this was a fair average the total Boer casualties must have been heavy.

We trekked on till after midnight, our only crumb of comfort being our native boy awaiting us beside the road, his voice quavering with emotion at seeing all four of us still alive.

The withdrawal was continued next morning without waiting for the enemy, and by midday we were across the Sand River, thirty miles and more from the scene of yesterday's encounter.

The wagon convoys were far away by now, so we were free of that trouble, and we had moved to the rear so rapidly that it was twenty-four hours before we saw the English on the skyline once more. It was towards evening of the next day that they came - a small advance guard of two hundred horsemen with a gun, riding so fast that before we could stand to arms they were on the south bank of the Sand River, and killed one of the Irishmen preparing to dynamite the bridge. The commandos were some distance back, but the 'A.C.C.' was halted near by, so we ran for our horses and recrossed the river lower down to outflank the intruders. When they saw that they might be cut off, they fired a few shells at us and fell back on their main troops, masses of whom we could now see on the far horizon. We got near enough to use our rifles, bringing down two troopers from their horses. I rode up to have a look at them. They were both Canadians, badly wounded, one of whom told me that many thousands of their people, as well as Australians and other Colonial forces, had volunteered for the war, as if the odds against us were not heavy enough already.

It was getting dark, so we left the wounded men to be fetched in by their own side, and for the next two days we were not disturbed, the English apparently resting their men before resuming the advance. On the morning after this, Commandant Malan sent me with a message for General Botha, whom I found, after a fifteen-mile ride, camped beside the railway line. Having delivered my dispatch, I started back for the Sand River where I had left the 'A.C.C.', only to find them gone. Men in the neighbourhood told me they had ridden away hours before, going west on some unknown errand. It was growing dark and bitterly cold, and as it was useless to try and follow, with no idea of where they had gone, I broke enough timber from the pumping station at the railway bridge to make a bonfire, and spent the night in solitary comfort within, my old roan horse snug beside me.

As soon as it grew light next morning, high dust-clouds rising south of the river showed that the English were coming, so I saddled and hastened to fall back to where a force of six hundred burghers was approaching under the personal command of General Louis Botha. He ordered us to open out, and each man stood before his horse awaiting developments. These were not long in coming. Soon the English scouts had crossed the river, and infantry were coming down to the drifts, while the country behind was black with more troops and transport columns. Batteries came into play, and, as the ground was devoid of cover, we mounted and sullenly retired. Now began anew the long-drawn humiliation of retreat. All day we were driven relentlessly; the British herded us like sheep to the incessant shriek of shells and the whizz of bullets, and by evening we were a demoralized rabble fleeing blindly across the veld.

After sunset the pursuit tailed off, I spent a cold night on a kopje with a few other stragglers, and next morning we rode into the town of Kroonstad. Here we found President Steyn addressing a crowd of burghers from a market-table in the square. He had succeeded my father as President of the Free State in 1896, a burly, heavily bearded man, not brilliant, but possessed of dogged courage.

For the moment his words fell on deaf ears, for so universal was the discouragement that few paid any heed to his appeals. His audience consisted mainly of Transvaal burghers, more concerned with getting back home than with forlorn hopes, so there was little response, but I stopped to listen, and was so carried away by what he said that I rode back the way I had come with a dozen more until we reached the scattered hills a few miles south of the town. From here we could see the English columns advancing towards us, and after some time several hundred other men rode up, coming across the plain from various directions. By midday the troops were within range and began to shell us, but made no attempt to push home an attack. In the afternoon my brother Arnt made his appearance from the rear. He brought me bad news of the 'A.C.C.' He said that after I had left them on the Sand River, they had received orders to go west, to watch the movements of a cavalry force in that direction.

In the neighbourhood of Kopje-Alleen they were ridden down by a regiment of horse. It was a case of every man for himself, and he had escaped by hard riding, but he could not tell whether our remaining two brothers and the native boy had got away.

This was serious news, and when a retreat was called after nightfall we rode back into Kroonstad greatly troubled. The town was in darkness, and we went right on for twenty miles without a halt until we overtook the commandos.

Next day the retreat was continued to the Rhenoster River. In the course of the morning we came on our boy Charley, who had not only escaped but had brought out the Basuto pony as well, thereby saving much of our gear, but he had no word of the other two.

An hour later we saw my eldest brother ambling along in company with the rest of the 'A.C.C.' They had got off better than we thought, having lost only twelve men in the fight. Of my brother Joubert they could tell us nothing; no one remembered having seen him and it was a long time before we heard of him again.

The 'A.C.C.' had now lost, in less than a week's fighting, nearly a third of its strength, with very little to show for it, but at any rate we were still a coherent unit, which was more than could be said for most of the other commandos, as the process of disintegration was gaining so rapidly that the major portion of the burghers riding in the retreat were no longer members of any recognized force, but merely individuals on their way home.

At the north bank of the Rhenoster River, we lay for nearly a week without sign of the British, during which time the Boer Army melted still further until General Botha had a bare handful of men left.

One morning a dozen of the 'A.C.C.', of whom I was one, were ordered to go back in the direction of Kroonstad to reinforce a small body of Scouts under Captain Daniel Theron, who was keeping touch with the enemy.

We recrossed the river, and after a forty-mile ride south over the plains, we found him and his men on a hill over-looking the English camps that had sprung up around Kroonstad. Captain Theron had gained considerable notice before the war for thrashing Mr Moneypenny, the well-known journalist, and had of late added to his reputation by his daring at the time when Cronje was surrounded at Paardeberg. He was a light, wiry man of about twenty-six, dark complexioned and short-tempered, and although I never once saw him really affable, his men swore by him for his courage and gift of leadership.

For two days we watched the camps, and then one morning pillars of dust slowly rising and troops marching on every road showed that once more trouble was afoot. We made immediate preparations to depart, for we were only there as an observation post. Before we started, a companion and I went down to a farmhouse to fill our saddlebags with meal and biltong from a supply stored there, and in returning we rode into a troop of English horse that unexpectedly appeared through the trees. We whipped up and raced away towards where we could see Theron and his men retreating in the distance, but the patrol was hard on our heels, and galloped after us for over a mile, firing about our ears, until at last our men, seeing the danger, came to the rescue. We fell back slowly until dark, and spent the night in view of their camp fires, and next morning, when we reached the north bank of the Rhenoster River, we found it deserted.

A solitary member of the 'A.C.C.', left behind for the purpose, told us that General Botha was summoned to Pretoria and that General de la Rey had taken the remainder of the forces towards the Transvaal border. We were to follow after.

12. THE BRITISH INVADE THE TRANSVAAL

Travelling on through empty abandoned country, we overtook some sort of a rearguard by next evening at Viljoensdrift, and in their company we crossed over that night into the Transvaal at Vereeniging. Here there were only a few Irishmen of the dynamite squad, who told us that the 'A.C.C.' was camped a few miles on, and that some of de la Rey's men under General Lemmer were ten miles down the river, but that for the rest the Boers had vanished.

Captain Theron asked me to remain with him, but I refused as I wished to rejoin my brothers, so I said good-bye next morning, and went in search of the 'A.C.C.' This was the last I saw of him, for he was killed a few miles from here; a man who would have made a name for himself had he lived.

The 'A.C.C.' now decided to join General Lemmer's men, and, after a long ride, we came up with them just in time to see a strong body of English cavalry crossing the Vaal River, cheering loudly at setting foot in the Transvaal again, for it was twenty years since a British soldier had trodden its soil.

They had batteries posted on the Free State side, and, as we had ridden too close up, Lemmer lost three men killed and several wounded, with no corresponding advantage to himself. He thereupon drew off into rougher country where we halted for the night, and next morning, seeing the British troops advancing from the Vaal, we retreated in the direction of Johannesburg, thirty miles away.

By noon we found General de la Rey, with nearly a thousand men, holding some low hills within sight of the mine-stacks. I was surprised that he had managed to keep so many with hills, considering the way in which things were going to pieces, but he had more control over men than any officer who I had thus far seen.

At four o'clock the advance was on us again. Armstrong guns were unlimbered, and we were severely handled. The position we held was a strong one, however, and despite casualties we stood our ground until dark, by which time word came through that we must fall back on the Klip River, a small stream on the outskirts of Johannesburg. We groped our way through the night with hundreds of other men all jostling each other on the narrow road, and, having forded the river, we slept till daybreak. We were now practically backed right up against the city, so close that sightseers and even women came out in cabs and on foot to view the proceedings, and soon after dawn the English came pouring over the ground to the south of the Klip River with horse, foot and guns. As we were watching them, Commandant Gravett, of the Boksburg Commando, came riding by asking for volunteers to accompany him to a low ridge just beyond, from which he said we could make a showing against some English cavalry that had crossed the river and were approaching in our direction. The men of the 'A.C.C.' hung in the wind, for they were sulking over some gibe Gravett had flung at us when we elbowed his people off the road the night before, so only a man named Jack Borrius and I went. We rode rapidly forward, reaching the hills just in time to forestall the English horsemen from getting there first. We brought down three, whereupon the rest galloped back through the river, but soon returned reinforced, and they came at us so determinedly that we loosed only a few shots before running for our lives. We came under brisk fire without any casualties, but my roan horse had a piece clipped from his ear by a rifle bullet before I got back to the 'A.C.C.' in the rear.

My two brothers had been absent since earlier in the morning. For several days the younger one had been ailing, and now he was so ill that Hjalmar and our boy Charley had taken him to Johannesburg, one riding on either side to hold him on his horse. We did not know what was wrong with him, but it subsequently turned out to be typhoid fever from which he barely escaped with his life.

They had not yet returned when I rejoined the 'A.C.C.' and in the meanwhile we were kept busy enough, for the British troops were by now crossing the Klip River in large numbers, deploying on the open ground between us, and before long shelling had commenced. No doubt they knew by now that Johannesburg was theirs for the taking, and they ran no risks with their infantry, confining themselves to most unpleasant gun-fire.

For the first time for many days we, too, had guns in action, and there were several batteries of Creusots blazing away from close by. The gunners suffered terribly, and I counted seven artillerists killed in less than fifteen minutes during one particularly violent burst. We of the 'A.C.C.' were snugly tucked away in a kopje where the shelter was so good that we did not lose a man or a horse, and we passed most of the day idly watching the scene. Shortly before sunset we saw activity away to our right, and there came line upon line of infantry, with guns roaring. General de la Rey had his Lichtenburg men there, but although they are reputed the best fighting men in the Transvaal, they were overborne by weight of numbers and were soon riding back in full retreat. This was the last effort to defend Johannesburg. When the line gave, all was over, and during the night de la Rey drew off to the west to his own country, where the doughty old warrior was to fight many another battle in days to come.

All semblance of order or resistance now disappeared. Wherever one looked, men were departing wholesale, and the universal cry was: '*Huis-toe*, the war is over'. Several of our 'A.C.C.' men deserted at this juncture, but most of them remained, and we fell back that evening to Langlaagte, a suburb of Johannesburg, where we spent the night. My brother Hjalmar and our boy were waiting for me. They had reached Johannesburg railway station, and had succeeded, in spite of the disorder, in getting Arnt on board a goods train for Pretoria. They said that all trains were crammed with fugitives, but that they had left him in the care of a man who promised to deliver him into my father's hands. With this they had to be satisfied, but they returned towards the firing very worried as to the outcome, for by now he was delirious. Next morning (it must have been about the 1st or 2nd of June) we saw the British feeling their way into Johannesburg, so we followed the drift of retreating men going round by the eastern side of the town. As we passed the gold-mines that lay on our route, there was a small column of cavalry drawn up not far off watching us go by, who made no attempt to interfere with us, probably thinking that we were refugees and not worth bothering about.

When we got to the main road leading to Pretoria, we found it crowded, with mounted men, wagons and herds of cattle, and we had to make our way through dreadful confusion. To the right was another British column moving parallel with us, which caused our native Charley to remark, 'Baas, those English people don't know the road to Pretoria, so they are coming along with us to make sure,' and, indeed, I believe that the English could have ridden in amongst us that day without firing a shot, so strong was the conviction that our army was disbanded and the war at an end.

By sunset the 'A.C.C.' worked itself out of the throng and halted at Six-mile Spruit, a rivulet that distance from Pretoria. Commandant Malan intended to wait here until next morning, but my brother and I pushed on as we were anxious to get home and see our father.

We reached Pretoria by ten o'clock, and rode through the deserted streets to our home in the Sunnyside suburb. Here disappointment awaited us, for the place was in darkness and the house was empty. We went to several neighbours to make inquiries. They seemed to think that the enemy was upon them, for it was only after we had tried at several doors that at last a shrinking figure appeared in response to our knocking with rifle-butts, and, seeing who we were, curtly told us that President Kruger and my father had run away, and that Pretoria was to be surrendered to the British in the morning, after which the door was slammed in our faces. We knew the President and my father too well to believe that they had ignominiously run away, and the fact that they had left Pretoria together was proof to us that they had gone to carry on the war, so we returned home, and after stabling and feeding our weary horses, broke open one of the doors and went inside.

We made a roaring fire in the kitchen, at which we cooked a dinner with supplies from the pantry, and then slept in comfortable beds, a change after the freezing nights we had endured of late.

It was nevertheless a dismal homecoming. Our younger brother had been left stranded in a cattle-truck weak and ill, amid the chaos of a general retreat, our other brother was missing, and for all we knew dead, while my father was gone and our home was deserted.

We only heard later that my stepmother and the younger children had been sent to Delagoa Bay and thence by sea up the East Coast of Africa to Holland, where they still are.

Early next morning we set about making plans for the future. First we saddled our horses and rode uptown to find out what was happening. The streets were swarming with leaderless men, knowing even less of the situation than ourselves. Of the 'A.C.C.' there was no trace, and all was utter confusion with looting of shops and supply depots, and a great deal of criticism of our leaders.

After commandeering provisions for our future requirements, we returned home. The British by now were shelling the forts outside the town, and an occasional 'over' fell in our vicinity, but we were accustomed to gun-fire by now, and remained quietly resting until the afternoon.

Towards three o'clock a gaunt figure appeared before us. It was our missing brother Joubert, whom we had given up for lost. He said that his horse had been killed when the 'A.C.C.' were rushed at Kopje-Alleen a fortnight before, but he had succeeded in escaping on foot. After tramping it for many days, he reached Johannesburg in time to board the last outgoing train, which had just brought him to Pretoria. As burghers now came galloping past, shouting that the English were entering by the road above the railway station, I hurried back on horseback to the centre of the town, where I annexed a saddled-horse, from among several standing before a shop that was being looted, and absconded with this remount for my brother. We now prepared to leave, though as a matter of fact the English only occupied Pretoria next day, but, as we did not know that the rumour was premature, we thought it safer to get away in good time.

In the circumstances it seemed best to leave our faithful old native boy behind, as we felt that with the increasing difficulty of securing horses and food we could no longer indulge in the luxury of a servant, and besides, we needed his animal as an additional pack-horse. The poor fellow piteously entreated us to keep him, but we had to harden our hearts, and, having no money to give him, we allowed him to take from the house as many blankets and other articles as he could carry, and so parted from him after an affecting scene. Our arrangements were easily made. We loaded what we needed from pantry and wardrobes on to our pack-horses, and after a last look round at our home we rode away on the main road leading east, along which many other fugitives were already hurrying.

By dark we had got as far as the big distillery eight or nine miles distant, where we spent the night. By morning so many other horsemen had arrived that there must have been nearly fifteen hundred, few of whom were under officers, and none of whom seemed to know what to do next. My brothers and I rode about, looking for the 'A.C.C.', but, although we round no trace of them, it did not worry us overmuch, and we agreed to remain on our own until we fell in with them again or until we had made further plans. In going round we met Mr.

Smuts, the State Attorney, off-saddled under a tree with his brother-in-law, P. Krige, who had been one of Isaac Malherbe's men and had been seriously wounded at Spion Kop. I had not seen him since, for he had only just left hospital to avoid being captured in Pretoria by the British.

As Mr Smuts was a member of the Government, we persuaded him to tell us where my father and the President had gone to, and what the general position was. He said that the President and my father were at Machadodorp, a small village on the Pretoria – Delagoa Bay railway line, at which place they had set up a new capital. So far from making peace, they were determined to carry on the war by means of guerrilla tactics. They hoped to stop the rot that had set in, and Mr. Smuts himself was starting immediately for the Western Transvaal to reorganize that area, while similar steps would be taken elsewhere; and in the Free State, President Steyn and Christian de Wet had undertaken to pull things together. The Commandant-General, Louis Botha, was lying not many miles away, collecting as many burghers as he could to form the nucleus of a fresh army and everyone was to be directed thither. All this was better news than we had heard for a long time, and already we could see, from the animated way in which the men were standing around their fires talking and laughing, that there was a more hopeful feeling in the air.

My eldest brother and I decided that, before joining a commando, we should seek out my father at Machadodorp, partly to find out his views, and partly to hear whether he knew what had become of our younger brother Arnt. My brother Joubert refused to accompany us and rode away to look for General Botha, so that once more we lost sight of him for many days. Machadodorp lay a hundred and seventy miles due east, and Hjalmar and I set out on the long ride without delay. We did the ninety miles to Middelburg in two days, and here we were lucky enough to get a lift by goods train for the rest of the journey, arriving at Machadodorp by the following morning. This village was for the time being the capital of the Transvaal. Long rows of railway coaches constituted the Government Buildings, where such officials as had not preferred surrender made a show of carrying on the public business of the country. In one of these coaches we found my father installed, and his welcome was a warm one, for he had received no news of us since we had left him in April to go south into the Free State. We were greatly relieved to hear that our brother Arnt was at that moment lying in the Russian ambulance at Waterval-onder, in the low country, forty miles down the line. He had arrived delirious some days before, but there was hope of his recovery. My father confirmed what Mr Smuts had told us of the military position, and he said that guerrilla war was better suited to the genius of the Boer people than regular field operations. He spoke of George Washington and Valley Forge, and of other seemingly lost causes that had triumphed in the end, and although we did not altogether share his optimism (for we had the memory of demoralized and flying columns fresh in our minds), yet his faith cheered us tremendously.

When we asked after President Kruger we were told that he too was down at Waterval-onder, for he was an old and feeble man in these days and was unable to stand the bitter cold up here.

Before returning west in search of General Botha, Hjalmar and I took train down the mountain to see our sick brother. We found him with many wounded men in a hospital improvised by that very Russian ambulance corps which General Joubert had refused to accept, but which had nevertheless come to our assistance.

He was conscious when we got there, and the Russian nurses said that he had turned the corner, although still in grave danger.

At Waterval-onder we had our last sight of President Kruger. He was seated at a table in a railway saloon, with a large Bible open before him, a lonely, tired man. We stood gazing at him through the window, but as he was bowed in thought, we made no attempt to speak to him. He left for Portuguese territory not long after, and I never saw him again, for he was taken to Holland on a Dutch man-of-war, and he is still an exile.[2]

We now returned up the Berg to Machadodorp, where we said good-bye to my father, and travelled back to Middelburg by rail to get our horses, which we had left in charge of one of the townspeople.

Here there was a small contingent of German volunteers, about sixty strong, under an Austrian, Baron von Goldeck, whom we had known in Natal. As we had no idea where the 'A.C.C.' had gone, and as one commando was as good as another, we obtained admission to the 'German Corps', as it was somewhat grandiloquently called. Von Goldeck was preparing to ride his men west to scout for General Botha, so we trekked away the next day, going via Balmoral Station, until in three days' time we gained contact with the British patrols on the outskirts of Pretoria.

Lord Roberts was resting his army around the capital, so we spent the next ten days skirmishing over the uneven country to watch his movements. We had several exciting encounters, in the course of which we lost five Germans, but it was an enjoyable time. We lived on what we could forage, and, what with scouting to within sight of Pretoria and raising alarms in the big camps, there was not a dull moment. Then the country got too hot to hold us and we fell back twenty or thirty miles to where General Botha was busy collecting as many men as he could get together. We found him halted near the old battlefield of Bronk-horstspruit, where Colonel Anstruther's force was cut up in the war of 1880. He lay by his saddle on the open veld, and save for a few dispatch-riders and some pack-horses, there was nothing to distinguish his headquarters from any of the other groups of burghers dotted about.

He said we had done well and could now take a holiday, so we rode to a deserted farm some distance off, and remained there quietly for some days.

---

[2] *He died in Switzerland in 1904.*

13. FARTHER AFIELD

It was by now becoming generally known that General Botha was assembling a new army, and the more spirited elements were gradually coming back from their homes and elsewhere in order to rejoin him.

Already he had three thousand men, and more were riding in daily. Things were, therefore, shaping better and there was, at any rate, a visible recovery from the deplorable conditions that had held during the retreat through the Free State.

At this stage, remnants of the Natal commandos began to come through. The forces we had left there had been driven out, much as we had been hustled from tile Free State, and had endured the same humiliations. Thousands of the weaker men had surrendered or gone home, and in many cases entire commandos had melted like snow, whilst those that did remain were mere skeleton formations. The remainder, however, were seasoned fighting men, and nearly two thousand of them joined General Botha here, bringing his total force up to five thousand or more.

One evening I saw a Natal contingent approaching over the hills. When they reached us the men turned out to be the remnant of our old Pretoria Commando, now dwindled to about one hundred and fifty, amongst whom were many old friends of the Ladysmith days. The burgher-right men had deserted in a body, and the commando had lost heavily in killed and wounded since we had left them. Mr Zeederberg, the Field-Cornet, had broken down in health; and one Max Theunissen, a young fellow of twenty-five, was in command.

Old General Maroola, they said, and his brother Swart Lawaai, had been deposed, but they had remained in the field and were serving as privates with some other commando.

I had got on well enough with von Goldeck and the Germans, but I decided to return to the Pretoria men. My brother Hjalmar preferred to stay where he was, so I said good-bye, and rode away with my roan horse and the little Basuto pony to join my former unit. The morning after we moved off, going south over the plains for two days and then bending round so as to make for the railway line between Pretoria and Johannesburg, as Max Theunissen was under orders to destroy the English communications. There were, however, so many English soldiers guarding the track that we never got within five miles of it, and for the next fortnight we wandered about searching for an opportunity that did not come. The English troops clamped about Pretoria occasionally flung a few long-range shells at us, but otherwise there was nothing of importance.

While we were operating in this quarter I had unexpected word of the 'A.C.C.' We were taking cover one morning in a hill from the shell-fire of a column that had appeared, when two burghers galloped up to seek shelter. They belonged to the 'A.C.C.', and when I asked after the others they pointed to a farm far out on the plain, where they said Commandant Malan and the rest were off-saddled, so when they rode away I went along with them, partly to see my old companions, and partly to explain to Commandant Malan about my brothers and myself.

To reach the farm we had to ride across the front of the English column, but they let us go in peace, and I was soon shaking hands with Malan and his men. A little later, the English force moved nearer, and began to drop lyddite shells from a howitzer posted on a distant rise. This caused the worst incident I saw in the war. For a time the shells burst harmlessly on open ground, but as the aim grew truer, Commandant Malan ordered us to take cover, and we distributed ourselves behind the garden wall and behind the wall of a small dam that stood near the dwelling-house.

Beside the dam wall was a huge willow tree, in the rear of which seven men of the 'A.C.C.' took station. Suddenly a shell hit the bole about two feet from the ground and, passing right through the tree, exploded as it emerged on the other side. The result was terrible, for the seven unfortunate men were blown to pieces which strewed the ground for thirty yards beyond. They were so mangled that, when the English gun ceased firing, their remains had to be collected with a shovel, a most sickening spectacle. And a further trial was in store for the 'A.C.C.' After the howitzer had gone, Commandant Malan mounted his horse and with a few men rode up towards the English troops to fire the intervening grass. Half an hour later, as I was returning to the Pretoria commando, I saw by the way in which his men were standing that something was wrong, so I galloped up to find him lying with a rifle bullet in his throat, and he died in a few minutes, and any lingering idea I may have had of rejoining the 'A.C.C.' now vanished, for they seemed under an unlucky star. For another week or to the general military situation remained quiet; British columns came from Pretoria now and then, but they were only on the prowl, and there was no serious fighting.

This spell of calm was invaluable, for it gave the Boer leaders breathing space in which to reorganize their scattered forces, and it gave the men time to recover from the demoralizing effect of the long retreats, with the result that when Lord Roberts resumed operations in the middle of July a far better spirit prevailed.

The British advance started early one morning on a broad front. We of the Pretoria commando took up a position in the nearest kopjes, but before long were so heavily shelled that we withdrew, the other commandos also falling back. The direction in which the English were moving was east along both sides of the

Delagoa Bay railway line. Up to now this way to the Portuguese port had been open and the Transvaal Government had been importing supplies on a large scale, but apparently Lord Roberts intended to close this final loophole and cut us off completely from the outer world.

Accordingly great numbers of troops, apparently more than thirty thousand, moved to right and left of the railway, sweeping us easily before them. They were spread fanwise over a distance of fifteen miles, and as the usual curtain of scouts approached, followed by shell-fire from the guns moving up behind, we pursued the same methods that we had employed in the Free State, fading back from hill to hill and rise to rise, firing when opportunity offered, but not really fighting. In this manner we retreated for four or five days, by which time the English had pushed us along the railway line through the town of Middelburg, and right up to Belfast village forty miles beyond. On the night we reached this place there was such a press on the road that in the dark I lost the Pretoria men. By next morning they were nowhere to be seen, but, as I was getting accustomed to quick changes of commando, I joined a body of Boksburgers who happened to be passing. They were part of a larger force under that same Commandant Gravett with whom I had gone down to the river the day before Johannesburg was taken.

Boksburg is a small mining village on the Reef, and the Boksburg men for some reason or other were known as 'Gravett's Guinea Fowls' (*Gravett se tarantaal-koppe*), a title in which they took great pride. Gravett was of English extraction, a fine big man, greatly liked and trusted by all. He was killed a month or two later, and I was with him when he died. In the company of the 'Guinea Fowls' I trekked from Belfast to Dalmanutha, another forty miles up the line. After being marched about for some days over mountainous country, we were allotted a position on the edge of the escarpment near Machadodorp, where General Botha intended making a stand athwart the Delagoa railway.

Along this crest he was going to fight a last pitched battle before taking to guerrilla war. All through the retreat we knew that sooner or later it was planned to break away from before the advance and scatter in smaller bands, and this knowledge had kept the men in good heart. Although they had been badly harried, there was no tendency to dissolve as had been the case in the Free State, and when they were called upon to make a final stand they were willing enough. The position General Botha had selected was a natural fortress. Between us and the enemy there stretched a level plain that could be swept by rifle-fire, and immediately behind us the ground fell steeply into a valley, giving excellent cover for men and horses. We were practically on the farthest rim of the high veld, for a few miles back the country drops into the malarial lowlands that lie towards the Portuguese border. The British had come to a temporary halt at Belfast, and for a week there was no sign of them. Towards the end of that time, while I was working on the defences, I saw the Pretoria commando come riding up, and with them were my two elder brothers Hjalmar and Joubert. Needless to say we were all three glad to be together again, and I at once took leave of the Boksburgers in order to join them.

The Pretoria men were given a portion of the line close by, and at sunrise on the next day heavy dust-clouds arose in the distance, and before long masses of British infantry appeared on the skyline.

They were calculated to be thirty-six thousand strong (but it is difficult to count infantry on the march), and within an hour their skirmishers were firing, and their batteries were unlimbering almost within rifle-range of us.

By ten a heavy bombardment was in full swing, although no actual advance was attempted, as they evidently intended first to batter down our works.

This lasted until sunset, but our cover was so good that the casualties were nowhere heavy, and the Pretoria commando went scot-free. By dark it had all died down, and we passed a quiet night lying around our fires. Next day the programme was repeated. We were shelled to such an extent that one dared scarcely look over the edge of the breastworks for the whirring of metal and the whizzing of bullets. Several of our men were wounded, and my brother Hjalmar was shot below the eye. My other brother led him down into the valley, for he was partially blinded, and there placed him on his horse and rode with him for the nearest medical assistance.

This second day of the bombardment was a crowded one. Shortly after my brothers had left there was an earthquake, the first I had ever experienced. It came with a loud rumbling, and the ground rocked beneath us like a ship, while stone fell from the works, causing much alarm, for disturbances of this kind are practically unknown in South Africa. We thus suffered a bombardment from above and an earthquake from below at one and the same time, and this remained a topic for wondering discussion months afterwards. When it was over, a lyddite shell from a howitzer dropped almost on top of me. It was like another earthquake. I was stunned for several minutes, and, after that, lay for a while in a semi-conscious state, hardly knowing whether I was dead or alive.

In the afternoon a detachment of infantry came down a defile on our left. We saw them in time to drive them back, killing and wounding about fifteen, but owing to the cross-fire we could not reach the fallen men until some time after dark, when we groped our way to get their rifles and equipment. The night was so cold that we found only three soldiers alive, some wounded, who might otherwise have survived, having died of exposure. We carried the three men back, and laid them by a fire, where one more died before morning.

As soon as it grew light on the third day, the bombardment recommenced more furiously than ever, but, instead of being spread all over our front, it was concentrated on that section held by the Johannesburg Police, a mile to our right. Tremendous gun-fire was poured on them, and from the massing of the infantry columns we knew that a crisis was at hand. The police behaved splendidly. Twice they threw back the attacks, and hung on doggedly under some of the fiercest pounding of the war. While this was going on the rest of us could do little, and for the most part we sat perched on our *schanses* watching the struggle. By sunset the police were all but annihilated, and in the dusk we saw the English infantry break into their positions. Here and there a hunted man went running down the slope behind, but the majority of the defenders were killed. Our line being broken, we had to give way too, and after dark General Botha ordered a withdrawal. We fetched our horses from the valley below, and fell back for two or three miles before halting for the night.

Next morning we made for Machadodorp, long-range shell-fire accompanying us. We found the village deserted, the movable capital having left the day before for Waterval-onder below the *berg*.

Beyond Machadodorp a single road climbs the last range, and from here one can look down upon the low country. As this was the only avenue of retreat, we soon found ourselves travelling among a medley of burghers, guns, wagons, and a great crowd of civilian refugees fleeing with their flocks and herds and chattels. It was pitiful to see this exodus, for the English brought their guns up with great speed and the road was heavily shelled over at times, as the wagons with women and children came under fire, but on the whole their behaviour was good, and in the end the shelling proved more unpleasant than dangerous.

After a while the Transvaal Artillery managed to get a battery of Creusot guns into action, which held up the advance sufficiently long to enable the non-combatants with their wagons, carts, and animals to get out of range, after which we too moved slowly up the mountain. I had a narrow escape when we halted to rest our horses. I was sitting on an ant-heap reading a book, when someone called to me that my roan horse was in trouble. He was plucking grass some distance off and had got his legs entangled in the reins, so I went to free him. While I was away a shell burst on the ant-heap, blowing holes in my book, and tearing up the mound itself.

We spent the night at Helvetia on the mountain, and next morning rode down the pass to Waterval-onder, a drop of two thousand feet in less than three miles. The British appeared above the *berg* an hour or two later, but did not follow us down, so we wended our way at leisure.

At Waterval-onder the railway comes out of a tunnel from the high country, and here, standing beside the line, were my father and my brother Hjalmar. They had come from Machadodorp by train the day before and were halted to let the engine get up steam, after which they were to be hauled farther down with other officials and a number of wounded. Hjalmar had a bloody bandage over his eye like a pirate, but otherwise he made light of his hurt. Our remaining two brothers were missing, but we were so continuously losing and finding each other nowadays that their absence caused us no undue anxiety, as we felt they would turn up sooner or later.

After a while the engine-driver ran up to say that he was going off, so my father and brother had to climb on board, and I continued down the road behind the retreat which was crowding the long valley that runs towards the Godwan River.

By dark I caught up with the Pretoria Commando, and we spent the night pleasantly encamped beside a stream. Since morning we had at one stride descended from the bleak highlands to the warmer climate of the low country, and I for one spent the first comfortable night for many weeks.

Next day the Boer forces retired still farther down the valley to Nooitgedacht, where about two thousand English prisoners were confined in a camp. They were lining the barbed-wire enclosure beside the railway line to watch us go by, and were in high spirits, for they knew that they were to be liberated that day. They exchanged good-natured banter with us as we passed, although one of them, less amiable than the rest, said to me: 'Call this a retreat? I call it a bloody rout!' I must say it looked like it, for by now the English advance was on our heels once more, and the narrow valley road was thronged with horsemen, wagons and cattle, all moving rearward in chaos. With the Boers, however, appearances are often deceptive - what might seem to be a mob of fugitives one day, might well prove to be a formidable fighting force on the next, and the soldier who spoke to me little thought that the men pouring by in disorderly flight were yet to test the endurance and the patience of Great Britain to its utmost.

We now headed down along the banks of the Godwan River for another twenty-five miles, by which time the pursuit had slackened, and for the next three days we lay in peace amid beautiful surroundings of mountain and forest. The English probably thought that General Botha meant to cross over into Portuguese territory for internment, rather than surrender, so they lay on their arms and rested. But General Botha intended far otherwise. One morning my father came up by special train from Nelspruit, where another temporary capital had been established, and he told us that the Commandant-General was going to strike north into the wilds. He would then make for the mountains beyond Lydenburg where the forces were to be reorganised for the carrying on of guerrilla warfare.

My father had really come up to see how my brothers and I were getting on, but I was the only one there. Hjalmar was at an ambulance recovering from his wound, Joubert had not returned since he had ridden back to the fighting at Dalmanutha, and the youngest was wherever the Russian ambulance wagons had gone, so that at the moment we were a pretty scattered family.

My father remained with me for the day, and then steamed back down the valley. Unfortunately the engine that brought him ran over and killed my poor little Basuto pony. Besides having served me faithfully since the first day of the war, he was an intimate link with our old home-life, for he had come with us from the Free State as a foal, and the loss of this loyal companion was a great blow to me. However, there was not much time for repining, as the English resumed their advance early next morning. The commandos fell back at once; some retired down the valley, but others slipped into the mountains. Among the latter was the Pretoria Commando, which climbed up to a place called Devil's Kantoor, where we arrived that night. The Pretoria men had for some days been discussing the question of doubling back to the high veld. They felt drawn towards their own part of the world, and wished to return to where they might get occasional word of their families left behind in Pretoria: so they now held a meeting and decided to break away along bridle-paths through the mountains. I refused to accompany them, as my father and brothers were ahead, so I said good-bye, and soon they were riding off into the dark. I did not see them again, but they succeeded in making their way back to their own district, where such of them as were not killed or captured remained in the field to the end of the war. I myself joined a party of burghers whom I found on the mountain, and in their company I rode all night, until dawn found us far down on the plain that runs by Barberton towards Kaapmuiden. Beyond this we got into rugged country and, travelling slowly, reached Hectorspruit in three days' time.

This was the last railway station before the Portuguese border, and here lay nearly five thousand horsemen awaiting General Botha's orders. We had shaken off the English army by fifty or sixty miles, and I found all three of my brothers there before me. Hjalmar's wound was better and Arnt had so far recovered that he could sit a horse, while Joubert was none the worse for his wanderings during the retreat. My father was missing, but he arrived two days later. He had abandoned his railway coach owing to a stoppage on the line, and had come across the difficult area above Crocodilepoort on horseback, so our family was united again for the first time after several months.

General Botha now got everything ready. Surplus guns were destroyed or thrown into the Crocodile River, and the sick and wounded were sent over the Portuguese border, while such stores as had been accumulated were distributed among the men or else burnt. Then, on a morning early on September (1900) he led the way into the uncharted bush to begin a new phase of the war.

14. NEW CONDITIONS

Our road ran through the Sabi low country teeming with big game of all descriptions. By day great herds of zebra, wildebeest, and sable stood fearlessly gazing at us, and at night lions prowled roaring around our camps. Of hunting we had our fill, and to me this journey through a strange and remote region was full of fascination, for we were passing through country as untouched as that upon which the old pioneers had looked when first they came north in the days of the Great Trek.

After long marches we reached the foot of the mighty range that runs north as far as the eye can see. From here General Botha sent the commandos on, with instructions to follow the base of the escarpment to the Murchison Range, two hundred miles away. He himself, escorted by the remnant of the Johannesburg Police and accompanied by the handful of officials who still remained, climbed up by a hunting-path to make for a lost village called Ohrigstad in the Steelpoort Gorge, our way leading by Gras Kop and Pilgrim's Rest amid mountains and forests and gorges more beautiful than any I know of in South Africa.

Now that President Kruger had left the country, the Transvaal Government consisted of my father and Schalk Burger who was the Vice-President, together with a few other heads of departments, and they naturally followed General Botha up the mountain, as did my brothers and I. We remained at Ohrigstad for a week, but when malaria broke out the Government moved to within a few miles of Lydenburg village on higher ground. General Botha now went off to plan guerrilla operations.

He did this so effectively that in a few months' time he had mobile forces in every quarter of the Transvaal harrying and worrying the British far and near, a reawakening that must have been particularly galling to them, considering how close we had been to a general collapse.

All this, however, was still to come, and in the meanwhile my brothers and I lay in the Government laager, fretting at our enforced idleness. We endured it for two weeks, after which we made up our minds to leave. My youngest brother was still so weak from his illness that he had to remain, but the other three of us made ready. My brother Hjalmar, who had a queer bent of his own, preferred to go off by himself, and although we tried to keep him with us he rode away towards the eastern Transvaal. He was subsequently captured and sent to a prison camp in India, and I did not see him again. My brother Joubert and I decided to go west. We had heard from a passing burgher that General Beyers was collecting a force at the Warm Baths, two hundred miles distant, so we agreed to ride thither. Our preparations were soon made, for they were simple enough. We shot a koodoo in the mountain, and made biltong, and we collected a supply of mealies from a neighbouring field. This was all the commissariat we had, for now that we were cut off from the outer world through losing the Delagoa Bay line, we were on spartan diet, and for the next two years such luxuries as sugar, coffee, tea, bread, and soap were only to be had on rare occasions by capture from the enemy.

We said good-bye to all, and set out.

I did not see my father again for twenty months. He remained in the field until the end of the war with the Government laager, handling his rifle like a private soldier when they came under fire, which was quite often, and doing much to keep up the spirits of the fighting men by his poems and his personal example.

It was a long ride to the Warm Baths. Our way went through bush country, with neither track nor road to guide us, for the region we traversed was untenanted save by native tribes and wild animals. I was on my splendid old roan who had carried me from the start, and my brother rode the horse which we had taken back from our native boy at Pretoria.

On the third day of our journey we had a mournful encounter. We came on Commandant Gravett dying of wounds in the bush. He had been hit by a shell ten days before, and his men had brought him here to prevent his falling into the hands of the British. He knew his end was approaching, but he bore his sufferings without complaint, and spoke of his coming death with resignation. He called us to him a few minutes before the end to tell us of his friendship with my father in former days, and a little while after he lapsed into unconsciousness from which he never recovered. We helped to bury him under a tree, and rode saddened on our way.

For ten days we journeyed, straying far north beyond the Olifants River, misled by natives who told us of a commando in that direction. When we came up with this force, it was only a patrol on their way to Secocoeni's country to inquire into fighting that had broken out between two native tribes. Among the patrol were old General Maroola and his brother Swart Lawaai, now serving in the ranks.

They were dressed as in the Natal days, only shabbier from long exposure on the veld, but they greeted us as if nothing had changed since. At length we turned south, and eventually reached Warm Baths, where we found General Beyers with a thousand men. He had been a lawyer before the war, and was now in command of the North-West under General Botha's new scheme of reorganization. He was a brave man, but I never liked him.

Here we were surprised to find our old 'A.C.C.' commando almost intact. After that unfortunate day, when Commandant Malan and seven men were killed, they had left the high veld and had made straight for these parts. This was why we had never come across them during the retreat to the Portuguese border. They were still about sixty strong, under command of a newcomer, a young officer named Lodi Krause, who invited us to rejoin, which we did at once. We remained in the neighbourhood of the Warm Baths for the better part of a month while General Beyers was raising more men, and the time passed pleasantly enough. We hunted a good deal and several times rode out on patrol to Pienaars River, twenty-five miles towards Pretoria, to watch the doings of a large English camp there. On one of these occasions we had a narrow escape. Six of us were approaching a kopje overlooking the camp, when suddenly a strong body of horsemen tried to cut off our retreat. We turned and made a dash for it, passing so near to some of the troopers that I heard them shouting at us to halt, while their bullets whipped around us as they galloped through the bush. We shook them off, however, without getting a scratch.

Except for these patrols and hunting for the pot, we spent a quiet time. Late in November my younger brother Arnt arrived at the Baths looking fit and well, having ridden hundreds of miles to find us, for he too had found life in the Government laager too slow once he was restored to health. We were very glad to see him, and the three of us built a weatherproof hut and fared well as food was plentiful. Rations were chiefly game and mealie meal, last of which General Beyers had accumulated a large supply from the Waterberg farms. He himself was camped close to us, a dark moody man who lost no opportunity of holding prayer meetings. With him was the Reverend Kriel, a Dutch Reformed parson, equally zealous; so between the two we were continually bidden to religious services, and they even went the length of ordering all the younger men to attend Bible classes. When my brothers and I ignored the order, General Beyers and Mr Kriel rode over in person to expostulate with us, and even threatened to turn us out of the commando, but we stuck to our guns and heard nothing further of it; in fact we rather gained in reputation, for the Boers, although a religious people, are not intolerant in matters of faith.

I did not care for Beyers, but I liked the old *Predikant* for all his narrowness, and afterwards in the Cape Colony I grew to admire him as a steadfast man.

On about the 7th of December (1900) we were told to be in readiness to move south the next day. My brother Joubert now surprised us by saying he was not coming. He said that he was going to be a gunner with a Creusot gun, one of the few still left, and was leaving at once with his new unit. He had always wished to be an artilleryman, and his obstinacy defeated our arguments. He rode away that same afternoon and I have not seen him since, for he was captured and sent to Bermuda, where he still is. General Beyers left a few hundred men and his guns behind to oppose the English columns that were preparing to invade the northern Transvaal, and with the rest, about eight hundred strong, he marched off. His purpose was to make south over the Magaliesbergen to the high veld beyond, in order to carry on guerrilla warfare there.

Our first day's trek brought us to the big native *stad* of a local chief named Koos Mamogali. From here we looked across a valley, twelve miles wide, towards the Magaliesbergen. The mountain range stretches east to west for a hundred miles and more and, in this area, forms the dividing line between the high veld and the bush country from which we were emerging. We crossed the valley that night, and by daybreak reached the foot of a disused pass known as 'the old wagon road'. Here there was evidence that General de la Rey had lately been in the vicinity for we found a burning convoy of fifty or sixty English supply wagons, and one of his men who came riding by told us that they had ambushed the wagons in a stiff fight and had taken many prisoners.

We looked on this as a good omen after the unbroken run of ill luck that had dogged us for so long, for it showed that General Botha's reorganization was beginning to take effect.

After a rest we climbed the pass, reaching the top by four that afternoon. From there, southwards, we had a wide view over the grass-covered plains, and far away on the skyline we could even see the smoke-stacks and goldmines of the Witwatersrand. The sight raised our spirits, and the men crowded the edge of the cliff animatedly discussing the improved outlook, for we were back from the wilds to within hail of Pretoria and Johannesburg.

Then we came down the south side, and by dark were off-saddled among the gardens and orchards below. We had had no sleep the night before and were looking forward to a good night's rest, but this was not to be. As we were preparing our supper, General de la Rey came riding amongst us on his famous little white-faced pony, and word went round that we were to attack an English force camped at the foot of the mountain not far away.

15. A SUCCESSFUL AFFAIR, AND AFTER

I had last seen General de la Rey during our great retreat through the Free State. Since then he had been busy in the western Transvaal raising fresh commandos, and infusing new spirit into the fighting men by his ceaseless activity, and by the great affection they had for this wonderful old man. Only two days before he had fallen upon and captured the British convoy that we had seen on fire beyond the *berg*, and now he had crossed over to this side with four hundred men, to strike another blow.

An English commander, General Clements, was camped round a bend of the mountain about nine miles off, with many troops, wagons, and guns, and when Beyers arrived, General de la Rey was quick to seize the opportunity for combined attack.

A plan of action was soon arranged. De la Rey with his horsemen was to rush the English camp at dawn from the landward side, while we were to return up the pass and make our way along the mountain-top under cover of night, until we could fire down on the enemy from the cliffs.

Having completed his dispositions, de la Rey rode away in the dark to find his own men, and soon the whistles blew for us to saddle our horses. General Beyers led us up the road down which we had come an hour or two before, but when we reached the head of the pass we changed direction ace picking our way eastwards along the boulder-strewn crest of the range. We had to lead our animals, for riding was out of the question over the uneven surface and progress was slow.

Towards morning, tired and sleepy, we were halted for an hour, to enable de la Rey's guides who had accompanied us to reconnoitre. When they returned they reported that General Clements's camp stood at the base of the mountain and was held by about five hundred soldiers. On the cliffs above, close to where we now lay, was a force of equal strength entrenched behind sangars and breastworks in case of overhead attack. These men we were to deal with while de la Rey's men fell upon those below.

General Beyers, whatever his faults, was a bold and resourceful leader, and he made immediate preparations for the assault. Ordering all horses to be left behind, he passed word that we were to advance on foot. We knew no drill, so it was difficult to keep alignment in the semi-darkness, but we got ourselves sorted out into some kind of extended order and moved forward in a long ragged front.

We of the 'A.C.C.' were on the extreme right at the edge of the cliff, with a drop of five or six hundred feet below us. Beyers was with us, and to our left walked the Waterbergers, and beyond them the Zoutpansberg men. Before we had gone far, dawn lit the mountain-tops, and with it came a fierce rifle-fire from the enemy *schanses* some distance ahead.

We had gone without sleep for two days and two nights, so that our spirits were low, and our advance came at once to a halt. Our line fell down behind rocks, and whatever shelter was to be had, leaving General Beyers walking alone, his revolver in one hand and a riding-switch in the other, imploring us to go on, but we hugged our cover against the hail of bullets lashing around us.

From where I lay on the tops of the crags, I could look straight down into the English camp hundreds of feet below. I could almost have dropped a pebble upon the running soldiers and the white-tented streets and the long lines of picketed horses.

As I looked down on the plain, from behind a jutting shoulder of the mountain came winging into view a force of mounted men who galloped hard for the English camp. It was General de la Rey timing his attack to synchronize with our own. They closed in, and for a moment it seemed as if they would overwhelm the British, but then the soldiers rushed to their posts opening heavy fire. The plain became dotted with fallen men and horses, and the attack wavered and broke. The survivors turned towards the shelter of the buttress whence they had come, and in less than ten minutes the assault was over.

The troops facing us on the mountain now made a mistake.

Like ourselves, they were able to look down at the attack, and when they saw our men retire in confusion they set up loud shouts of triumph. Stung by their cries, our whole force, on some sudden impulse, started to its feet and went pouring forward. There was no stopping us now, and we swept on shouting and yelling, men dropping freely as we went.

Almost before we knew it, we were swarming over the walls, shooting and clubbing in hand-to-hand conflict. It was sharp work. I have a confused recollection of fending bayonet thrusts and firing point-blank into men's faces; then of soldiers running to the rear or putting up their hands, and, as we stood panting and excited within the barricades, we could scarcely realize that the fight was won.

Our losses were severe. On the ground across which we had charged lay a trail of dead and wounded, and yet more by the schanses.

In all we had about twenty-five men killed and some seventy wounded, and we shot down nearly a hundred of the English, besides taking as many more prisoners. But it was a heavy price to pay for success, even in this strange affair in which our men who had been cowering disorganized behind the rocks suddenly flung themselves upon a fortified enemy with a furious desire to silence their shouts of triumph[3].

We had now taken the main defences, but scattered rifle shots were coming from a nest of granite boulders to the rear, and General Beyers ordered Krause, Commandant of the 'A.C.C.', to clear the place. Krause took a dozen of us, and we worked our way forward in short rushes. But he grew impatient and told us to close in more quickly. The result was disastrous, for as we rose a salvo rang out which brought down four of our men. Having fired this parting volley, the soldiers, of whom there were only six, went running towards the mouth of the ravine which led down a cleft to their camp below.

I hit one of them through the thigh, and Krause shot another dead, but the rest escaped. We walked back to see the extent of the damage, and it was bad enough. My old school fellow Jan Joubert, son of Piet Joubert the late Commandant-General, had a bad chest wound, and the other three men were dead. Two of them were young brothers named Koekemoer, about eighteen and nineteen years old, who had been with the 'A.C.C.' since the Free State days. I also went to see the soldier whom I had shot. He had a nasty wound, but he was bandaging it himself with the first-aid pad which they all carried, and he said he could manage. He was a typical Cockney, and bore use so little ill will that he brought out a portrait of his wife and children, and told me about them. I made him comfortable, and left him cheerfully smoking a cigarette. Jan Joubert was badly hurt, a portion of his rifle-stock having been blown into his lung, so Krause asked me to take a water-bottle from one of the dead soldiers, and go down into the ravine in search of water. I got a flask and went down the slope to the mouth of the gorge. Unknown to us there was a path to the English camp, along which reinforcements were climbing up to dislodge us. I saw twenty or thirty soldiers already near the top, standing in a group not a stone's-throw from me, while many more were coming on behind in single file.

I fired at once and dropped a man, the remainder disappearing amongst the trees. From here they opened fire on me, and I in turn had to take cover, dodging from rock to rock to get back to Krause. On hearing my news he took a number of men, and we ran down just in time to see the path crowded with soldiers. We lost no time in pouring close-range volleys into their midst. In less than a minute only dead and wounded were left; more than twenty men of the Imperial Yeomanry of London lying in the space of a few yards.

---

[3] *Of this attack The Times story of the War gives the following account: In a bold reckless fashion for which there was no precedent since the attack on Wagon Hill a year earlier, and which was a startling novelty to the troops present, the Boers rushed forward on foot, cheering and shouting as they ran. Indifferent to loss, with great skill and dash . . . they shot down most of the British officers, rolled up the pickets and, in spite of a stout resistance, mastered the position after killing and wounding ninety-seven officers and men.*

This was the final clearing, and we now had the camp below at our mercy, for we were able to fire into it without opposition. Soon we could see the occupants retiring with their guns, and we descended the ravine and entered the camp.

In passing by the intake of the gorge, I found the soldier whom I had killed. I was horrified to see that my bullet had blown half his head away, the explanation being that during one of our patrols near the Warm Baths I had found a few explosive Mauser cartridges at a deserted trading-station, and had taken them for shooting game. I kept them in a separate pocket of my bandolier, but in my excitement had rammed one of them into the magazine of my rifle without noticing it. I was distressed at my mistake, but there is not a great deal of difference between killing a man with an explosive bullet, and smashing him with a lyddite shell, although I would not knowingly have used this type of ammunition. I flung the remainder into the brook that ran by, now red with the blood of dead men lying in the water.

Having sent back for our horses, we hastened down the path into the camp.

On my way down the gorge I found two wounded officers beside the track, one with his thumb shot away and the other with a broken arm. As I came up I heard one of them remark: 'Here comes a typical young Boer for you', and they asked me whether I understood English. I told them 'Yes', and the man with the thumb said: 'Then will you tell me why you fellows are continuing the war, because you are bound to lose?' I replied: 'Oh, well, you see, we're like Mr. Micawber, we are waiting for something to turn up.' They burst out laughing and the one said: 'Didn't I tell you this is a funny country, and now here's your typical young Boer quoting Dickens.'

The camp was filled with supplies of all kinds, and such a smashing of cases, and ransacking of tents and wagons, had not been seen since we looted the Dundee camp long before. While we were at this, General Beyers came riding among us in a rage, and ordered us to follow the enemy, but we thought otherwise. We considered that the object of the attack was to capture supplies, and not soldiers, as soldiers would have to be liberated for want of somewhere to keep them, and besides, if we went off, we might return to find the camp already looted during our absence. So we attended to the matter in hand, more especially as de la Rey's horsemen had recovered from their setback earlier in the morning, and could be seen stringing out across the veld towards where Clements and the balance of his troops were withdrawing down the valley in the direction of Pretoria. We told ourselves that we had done our part in the day's work, and that they could do the rest.

My brother brought my roan and his own two riding-horses down the ravine, and we took two more horses from the English lines, where many stood picketed.

Searching out saddles and wallets to match, we loaded our caravan with spoil in the shape of tea, coffee, salt, sugar, food, clothing, books and other luxuries of which we had long been deprived. Then we followed the other men who, having taken what they wanted, were riding along the foot of the mountain to the spot below the Old Wagon Pass from which we had started the evening before. Thus ended our share in the fight.

The 'A.C.C.' had lost five men killed and five wounded. Among the latter was our Commandant Krause with a bullet in his foot, and my Corporal Jan Nagel, with his right shoulder-blade badly shattered. A French gentleman-adventurer, Georges de Gourville, who belonged to us, was also badly wounded, but the worst was Jan Joubert, who was carried down to the English camp with the other serious cases, and left there until the British could be asked to send them surgical aid, for we had neither drugs nor doctors.

My brother and I had a glorious feast, and then, having gone without rest for forty-eight hours, we slept the clock round.

Next day, such of the dead as had been carried down the mountain by friends or relations were buried in a single large grave that I helped to dig. General de la Rey was present and he addressed us in eloquent words that moved many to tears, for besides being a fighter he had a fine gift of simple speech.

Here we remained for several days, during which time my brother and I enjoyed high living, after the straight diet of meat and maize on which we had subsisted for so long. We were refitted from head to heel, we carried a Lee-Metford rifle apiece, in lieu of our discarded Mausers, and above all we were well found in horseflesh. My gentle loyal old roan was as flourishing as ever, and I had a fine little chestnut pony, which I had chosen in preference to the larger but less reliable chargers in the English camp. I gave the other horses away in order to reduce our stable to manageable proportions; my brother had the two horses which he had brought with him from the north. One was a toll-free chestnut[4] and the other was the strangest horse I have ever known. My father had purchased him in the Lydenburg district from a homegoing burgher, who omitted to tell us that he was possessed of the devil. He indulged in such extraordinary antics that the police at the Government laager had declared him insane, and christened him 'Malpert' (the mad horse). Sometimes he would allow a single man to walk up and catch him without trouble, but at other times we had to turn out the whole Government from the Vice-President downward to form a cordon around him. He would pretend to be quietly grazing, but as soon as he was completely hemmed in, he would look up in assumed surprise and start to back against the ring, kicking and lashing so furiously that we had to give way, when he would go capering off, heels in air, to crop the grass near by. If another cordon were made he would repeat his performance, until he left the men helpless between cursing and laughing. The only persons for whom he had any respect were my brother Arnt and myself. He was afraid of me because once at the Lydenburg Camp, after he had twice kicked his way through I leaped at him from a distance of several feet and flung my arms about his neck. He reared and bucked and tried to bite and roll, but I locked my legs around his, so that he

---

[4] *Among the Boers a chestnut horse with white face and four white stockings is called toll-free, there being a tradition that in the old days horses thus marked went through the toll-gates free of charge.*

could not shake me off, and in the end I bested him. With my brother he was tractable, because he had doctored him for a badly ulcered back, and the 'Malpert' showed his gratitude by obeying him. His reputation had followed him down south, and he was quite an institution among the commandos. Often we would hear a warning cry 'Look out, here comes the 'Malpert',' and the burghers would scatter beyond reach of his heels. Nevertheless, his tricks and pranks were taken good-humouredly, for he had magnificent staying-powers and the men looked upon him with the admiration that born horsemen have for a good animal, and as for Arnt and myself, we had a very soft spot in our hearts for this queer outlaw.

Well mounted as we were, my brother and I felt that we could ride anywhere and be ready for anything, and we looked forward with interest to the next move. General de la Rey, restless as usual, had gone off, leaving us behind with General Beyers. On Dingaans Day, December 16th, he and the Reverend Mr. Kriel held a religious gathering on a neighbouring hill. They invited all to join in piling a cairn of stones like that raised at Paardekraal in 1880, during the first English war. My brother and I thought the proceedings somewhat theatrical and kept away, but so far as I know the beacon is still standing in testimony of vain hopes.

On the following day General French, the English cavalry leader, was reported to be moving up the Hekpoort valley from Pretoria, and General Beyers marched out to meet him.

Near Hekpoort the 'A.C.C.' was ordered to take post in a range of hills skirting the valley, to guard our main body against surprise. We spend an uneasy night on a rocky crest overlooking the broad 'Moot' as it is called, and at daybreak next morning we saw an English force of three or four thousand horsemen approaching. We had strict orders from Beyers to keep out of sight, so Krause led us into a gorge to hide our horses, after which we climbed up and peered over the rocks to view the enemy advance. The valley here lies four or five miles broad, and the British scouts were strung across it from side to side, their nearest horsemen passing so close beneath us that we could easily have shot them down. We could see General Beyers' men riding to occupy a line of hills farther up the valley, and before long they were hotly engaged. We had a fine view of the fight, but our interest in the spectacle was dampened by the fact that by now the British were between ourselves and our parent body, so that if General Beyers fell back we should be left isolated in the rear.

And as the gun-fire increased and the troops began to mass, we saw our men running for their horses and galloping away. This was not unexpected, considering the heavy odds, but nevertheless there went the commando, pursued hotfoot by the English, and here were we stranded far behind.

Krause decided to recover contact by riding round the left flank of the troops, but we fell foul of so many of their patrols, and were so often shelled by pom-poms and field guns, that we were forced to take refuge in the parallel hills. From here we could make out our men about six miles off, moving west from the valley, white puffs of shrapnel breaking over them as they went, and horsemen hard on their heels.

Krause now led us into the broken country north-west of Johannesburg (Skurwe-bergen), where a small force like ours could lie in hiding for a while, and by dark we were well within the region of its tumbled hills.

Although the rainy season was overdue, we had thus far experienced only sunny days, but now the weather broke, and for the next six days it rained without ceasing. We sought out a lonely farmhouse, and here we lay over, waiting for the deluge to lift. The farm was deserted, but sheep were straying near, and dry fuel was stacked in the barns, so we fared moderately well.

Georges de Gourville, the Frenchman, had insisted on accompanying us in spite of his wound, and he nearly died here, my brother and I nursing him through his fever. On the evening of the sixth day the clouds thinned, and we decided to set out that night in quest of General Beyers.

We had no idea where he was, but we counted on finding him sooner or later, so we started off immediately after dark. We rode all night, save for short halts, and towards morning came to a farm where a woman told us that General French was camped close by with his columns. She said that the English had given up the chase after Beyers and were on their way back to Pretoria, but had got weather-bound by the rains and were waiting for dry roads before going on.

On hearing this, Commandant Krause in his impetuous way rode off with only two other men to look around, and that was the last we ever saw of them. He and his companions must have ridden straight into the arms of the English, because soon after they left we heard a few distant shots and then silence. We waited until daylight, after which we decided to go on without him.

As a heavy mist hung over the veld, we made our way carefully, and it was as well that we did so, for when my brother and I with another man turned aside to water our horses at a dam lying off the road, four English troopers came riding out of the fog and let their horses drink about a hundred yards away. We gazed at each other suspiciously in the uncertain light, and then one of the soldiers shouted: 'Look out, those men are Boers', and pulling round they galloped away. We dismounted and fired before the mist swallowed them, bringing two to the ground. Riding up, we found one dead and the other rolling in agony, but both their horses had bolted after the others. While we were trying to help the wounded man the mist lifted somewhat, and a large English camp was outlined close by. We could hear our men splashing over the muddy ground in haste to get away, for they too had caught sight of the camp.

Bugles started calling and we caught glimpses of soldiers scurrying for their horses, so we galloped away, guided by the tracks lying clear across the sodden veld.

After a long ride we caught them up, and, when the sun broke through a little later and the fog dissolved, we could see some five-hundred English horsemen coming towards us, but had no difficulty in outpacing them, for in spite of our long night's journey their heavy troop horses were no match for our hardier and lighter mounts.

Krause having been captured, we were now leaderless, but with the Boers each man is practically his own commander, so the loss did not weigh heavily upon us and, having shaken off our pursuers, we rode along westward at our leisure, until in two days time we came on General Beyers and his men camped around the source of the Mooi River in the district of Potchefstroom.

Beyers appointed Corporal Jan Nagel to be our new Commandant, a popular choice, for, although a rough and illiterate man, he was well liked. He was still suffering from the wound received on the berg, but had remained in the saddle nevertheless.

We passed Christmas Day undisturbed, but next morning an English column came from the direction of Potchefstroom, and as there was no object in fighting except on ground of our own choosing, General Beyers gave them the satisfaction of thinking that we were running away, and at dark we drew off to spend the night near the village of Ventersdorp. From here we moved about at random, seeking for a chance to strike, but no favourable opening presenting itself, we saw the year 1901 in without further incident.

16. FROM WEST TO EAST

We now came into the Lichtenburg district, within a day's ride of Mafeking and the Bechuanaland border. This was General de la Rey's military area, but he was farther south at the time, and we only met an occasional roving patrol of his.

Beyers had a mind to raid Mafeking, but before he could do so a messenger arrived from the east with orders from General Botha to bring all his men to the Ermelo district. This meant transferring our force right across the breadth of the Transvaal, a matter of three hundred miles. Fortunately our horses were in good condition, thanks to the abundant rains and consequent good grazing, so we prepared to start at once. We now began our long march, riding eastward until some days later we reached back to the Magaliesberg Valley once more, close to where we had taken General Clements's camp. Since that event the English had apparently decided to garrison this fertile stretch, for we found a strong force a few miles down, busily constructing a fortified camp as though they intended to hold the valley permanently.

We left the camp alone, but for a few hours we lay on a ridge overlooking the troops who sent some shells at us, one of which killed a Waterberg man within a few yards of me. While we were halted here, I rode across the valley to the farmhouse near General Clements's camp to see my friend Jan Joubert, who had been left there with our other seriously wounded, after the fight. Although not yet out of danger, he was on the mend, and he told me that the British were treating them very well. A surgeon came over nearly every day, and medical orderlies were on duty to tend to their wants. They had brought his old mother from Pretoria to be with him, and officers from the camp down the valley often brought them fruit and other luxuries. I did not stay long for fear of a stray English patrol, and rode back after a hurried greeting. I did not hear what happened to him afterwards, but I believe that he made a complete recovery.

We now resumed our march, making for the railway line between Johannesburg and Pretoria. This had to be carefully approached as the track was patrolled night and day by armoured trains.

The 'A.C.C.' was sent ahead to reconnoitre, and after an absence of twelve hours we reported back that the crossing was practicable. On our return journey to rejoin the main commando at the hill called Swart Kop, we found a suspicious-looking native watching our movements, and arrested him for further inquiry. We interrogated him closely, without getting any evidence that he was a spy, but for safety's sake we kept him by us during the night, intending to release him next morning. Just before daybreak, however, while I was lying asleep by my saddle, I heard shouts, and looking up, saw the prisoner running as fast as he could go towards Swart Kop Hill. Several of our men were already astir, and as he would not stop when called, they dropped the unfortunate savage dead in his tracks, for which I was sorry, but in the circumstances it could not be helped.

That evening we started off on an all-night march for the Johannesburg railway, which we struck soon after sunrise. The 'A.C.C.' were scouting well in advance, so we were the first to cross the metals. As we were riding over, an English trooper came cantering up to see who we were, and he was considerably taken aback when he found out. We relieved him of his horse, rifle, and equipment, and told him to go off, a command which he obeyed with alacrity, and when we saw him last he was marching steadily for Johannesburg.

On the far side of the line stood a small homestead, out of which several more soldiers came tumbling. They all surrendered except one man, who made a bid for liberty by running into an orchard, but we shot him dead before he had going far. At the same moment a trolley came down the line from Kaalfontein Station, and as the crew tried to turn back, we fired on them, killing one and wounding a native. The dead man turned out to be a railway-ganger, as were the other four white men with him. They were on their morning round of inspection, so we let the survivors go after telling them that it was their own fault for not halting when challenged.

Our main commando now coming up, some of the burghers foolishly rode along the track towards the station, with the result that they left three men killed and several wounded in the hands of the garrison there. Our whole force now being across the line, we rode to a large farm over the rise to off-saddle.

This crossing of the railway proved a relatively simple matter, but later on in the war, when the English had completed their blockhouse system, it became increasingly difficult; and from all accounts it required something like a pitched battle to negotiate a passage over the Transvaal and Free State lines, though in the Cape Colony I saw none of this.

While we were resting at the farm, patrols were sent out, and in less than an hour one of these came galloping back to say that a strong force of English was approaching from Johannesburg. Scarcely had they returned, when we heard a succession of loud bangs and the roar of shells tearing overhead.

Our horses were out grazing, so that there was a good deal of confusion before we had the frightened animals collected, but we managed to saddle up and get away without loss, our whole force moving in a north-easterly direction with the English following. We could hardly have fought them on such open ground, armed as they were with field-guns, but in any case our object was to effect a junction with the Commandant-General, so we made no pretence of standing. The troops tried to head us off, and an armoured train from Pretoria made a belated appearance, firing heavy lyddite shells, but with our greater mobility we left the soldiers far behind, and by midday were able to come to rest after our long ride.

Next day we trekked to Olifantsfontein, where the seven 'A.C.C.' men had been killed the year before. At this place I suffered a most serious loss, for a young fellow claimed the pony which I had brought from the English camp after the Magaliesberg fight. He brought me and the horse before General Beyers, to whom he proved that it had belonged to his father, who was among those killed that morning during de la Rey's attack. I could not but admit the justice of his case, and handed over the pony, but this left me with only my old roan, a narrow margin of safety in these days when to be horseless meant almost certain capture.

At Olifantsfontein, General Botha came up with a small escort. He looked thinner than when I had last seen him in the Lydenburg Mountains four months ago, but he was full of energy and confidence. He told us that Lord Roberts had decided to bring the Boers to their knees by a series of drives, in which vast numbers of troops were to sweep across the country like a dragnet. To that end, all through this month of January (1901) they were assembling fifty thousand men along the Johannesburg-Natal railway line, ready to move over the high veld on a front of sixty or seventy miles, with tile intention of clearing the Eastern Transvaal, after which the process was to be repeated elsewhere, until every one was dead or taken.

The Boers were as yet mercifully unaware that this new system was to include the burning of farms, the destruction of crops and herds, and the carrying into concentration camps of their wives and children, but they were soon enough to learn that the British had taken the dread decision of laying waste the two republics, regardless of the suffering of the non-combatant population, and ignorant of the fact that these methods, so far from subduing the Boers would merely serve to stiffen their resistance.

Two days after General Botha had ridden away, the storm broke upon us. As the sun rose, the skyline from west to east was dotted with English horsemen riding in a line that stretched as far as the eye could see, and behind this screen every road was black with columns, guns, and wagons slowly moving forward on the first great drive of the war.

General Beyers, when he grasped the situation, divided his force in two, and rode away with one half to find the left flank of the enemy, while the rest of us were told to do what we could in front of the advance.

Far away, to our left, parties of General Botha's men were visible from rise to rise, scattered specks before the great host.

All that day we fell back, delaying the enemy horsemen by rifle-fire as far as possible, and breaking away when the gun-fire grew too hot. This went on till sunset without heavy losses on our side, despite the many batteries brought into play from every knoll and kopje. Once I saw my brother disappear from sight as a shrapnel shell burst on him, but he rode out laughing, he and his horse uninjured.

During the course of the morning, pillars of smoke began to rise behind the English advance, and to our astonishment we saw that they were burning the farmhouses as they came. Towards noon word spread that, not only were they destroying all before them, but were actually capturing and sending away the women and children.

At first we could hardly credit this, but when one wild-eyed woman after another galloped by, it was borne in on us that a more terrible chapter of the war was opening.

The intention was to undermine the morale of the fighting men, but the effect was exactly the opposite, from what I saw. Instead of weakening, they became only the more resolved to hold out, and this policy instead of shortening the war, prolonged it by a year or more.[5]

Towards dark the chase slowed down. It rained steadily all night, and we spent a miserable time lying in mud and water on the bare hillsides. At daybreak we were all on the move again, but, owing to the rain and the heavy going, the English could only crawl in our wake, and we had little difficulty in keeping our distance. By now, the news had spread that the English were clearing the country, with the result that the entire civil population from the farms was moving.

The plain was alive with wagons, carts, and vehicles of all descriptions, laden with women and children, while great numbers of horses, cattle, and sheep were being hurried onward by native herd boys, homes and ricks going up in flames behind them.

General Botha directed all non-combatants, wagons, and live-stock to make for Swaziland, and he ordered us to give way before the troops, and let them expend their blow in thin air.

Owing to these measures the drive went to pieces during the next few days. The British could not maintain a continuous front over the increased distances, and the troops were left groping about after the elusive Boer forces, which easily evaded the lumbering columns plodding through the mud far in the rear.

The drive caused an immense amount of material damage to farmhouses and crops, and much live-stock was taken, but so far as its effect on the burghers

---

[5] *The Times History of the War says: The policy of burning down farmhouses and destroying crops as a measure of intimidation had nothing to recommend it and no other measure aroused such deep and lasting resentment. The Dutch race is not one that can be easily beguiled by threats, and farm-burning as a policy of intimidation totally failed, as anyone acquainted with the Dutch race and the Dutch history could have forseen. Applying this system against a white race defending their homes with a bravery and resource which has rightly won the admiration of the world was the least happy of Lord Roberts' inspirations and must plainly be set down as a serious error of judgment....*

went it was a complete failure, for it left them more determined than ever to continue fighting.

As soon as the main pressure of the drive had eased, we of the 'A.C.C.' were deputed to patrol the areas around Bethal and Ermelo, and although we did much hard riding on the flanks of various columns that were trekking along, we had no actual fighting, I now suffered the loss of my dear old roan horse. One morning he came staggering and swaying up to me from the grazing-ground, and I saw at once from his caving flanks and glassy eyes that he was stricken with the dreaded horse-sickness, from which scarcely one animal in a hundred recovers. Nosing against me he seemed to appeal for help, but he was beyond hope, and in less than an hour, with a final plunge, he fell dead at my feet. This was a great sorrow, for a close bond had grown up between us in the long months since the war started, during which he had carried me so well.

I had to leave him, for as he fell, English scouts came swarming over the rise. I threw my saddle on a borrowed mount, and galloped away with the rest, and as my brother was absent on patrol with both his horses, I was forced to rely upon a succession of loaned animals, but there was no help for it.

On his return a week later he unselfishly made over the '*Malpert*' to me, and we now spent some time scouting over the plains in small parties to see what the English were doing, for, although the drive had petered out, large columns were still aimlessly wandering over the country, and our orders were to keep count of them. We had several sharp brushes with their outposts, and one evening were caught by a burst of shrapnel which blew a Carolina man to pieces within an arm's-length of me, and wounded his horse so severely that I had to shoot it.

After thoroughly scouring the countryside as far as the Swaziland border, our various 'A.C.C.' patrols reassembled at a place called Klipstapel, said to be the highest and coldest spot in the Transvaal. That same day instructions came from General Botha that the 'A.C.C.' were to be with him by midnight, as he was going to attack an English force camped near Lake Chrissie.

The attack took place, but we were held in reserve. We heard the sound of heavy firing shortly before dawn, and a rumour passed that the camp was taken. This proved only partly correct, for by sunrise came the trampling of many riderless horses, followed later by galloping riders, who told us that, although they had succeeded in overrunning the camp, the English troop horses had stampeded, creating such confusion in the dark, that our men gave way when success was practically in their grasp.

As it grew light, we could see the English camp lying intact below, and, as the troops turned several guns on us, and on such others as were in sight, we went scurrying away for the shelter of a neighbouring valley, where we found General Botha and most of his men. There was dejection in the air, for our loss overnight had been heavy, about forty killed and many wounded, with nothing to show for it.

But General Botha was not discouraged, for he addressed us, saying there were bound to be ups and downs, and he talked the men into a better frame of mind without any trouble.

After this, he split up his commandos. We had to live by foraging for sheep that were roaming about the veld, and by gathering maize from the unharvested fields, so he hived us off into smaller bodies, for easier provisioning.

As the drive had gone to pieces and there was no immediate need for our further services in the Eastern Transvaal, he ordered Beyers to take his men north to the new storm-centre in tile Waterbergen, which the English were now penetrating and from which urgent calls for help had come.

Most of Beyers' men were Waterbergers, so it was only natural to send them up to the threatened parts, but we of the 'A.C.C.' were a mixed community, a sort of Foreign Legion, not hailing from any particular area. As, moreover, we were not over-fond of General Beyers, we decided instead to return west and rejoin General de la Rey, especially as messages had come that there, too, another great drive was in progress.

Beyers accordingly started on his long march without us, and we took our leave of General Botha next day. After some days' riding over the plains we got back to the country between Pretoria and Johannesburg, in order to recross the railway line.

This time the track was better guarded, for we found numerous little camps on either side, and the line was closely patrolled by mounted men.

Jan Nagel, our commandant, sent me with another man after dark to find a convenient crossing. We crawled right up to Irene Station, ten miles from Pretoria, passing within a few yards of the tents there, and a thousand yards down we found a suitable spot in a hollow.

We were at this all night, returning to the 'A.C.C.' at a neighbouring farm by daybreak. Here we rested quietly until dark, and my companion and I then led the commando over the railway line without any trouble. We rode on all night, reaching our former haunts near the Swart Kop by morning.

We were now back in the Skurwe-bergen country near Johannesburg, where we had taken refuge before, and here we rested for seven or eight days, as the British troops rarely visited these broken hills.

This mistake proved our undoing, for the area is notoriously unhealthy for horses during the rainy season, and our animals began to die so rapidly that, by the time we made for higher ground, more than half the 'A.C.C.' were dismounted, but as the 'Malpert' and my brother's toll-free chestnut had escaped the contagion thus far, we were still in the saddle.

Jan Nagel decided that we must reach General de la Rey's commandos in the west, in the hope of getting fresh horses, so we started off, a miserable band, most of the men on foot, carrying their saddles and equipment on their backs, and the rest of us not knowing when we should be doing the same.

17. THE END OF THE "A.C.C." – I
START FOR THE CAPE COLONY

We struggled along for two days, making west, and losing more horses as we went, until we found our way barred by a body of troops stationed on the height known as Ramagothla, from which they had a wide view over the surrounding country.

Hampered as we were with dismounted men, we could not venture into sight across the open, so we turned north to the friendly refuge of the Magaliesbergen that we could see once more on the far horizon.

By stealing down kloofs and valleys, we made the foot of the mountains unobserved, reaching the very spot where the 'Old Wagon Pass' comes down, the same road along which we had travelled from the Waterbergen, two months before.

On this march the '*Malpert*' showed signs of distress, his staring coat and lagging steps telling only too plainly that his course was spent.

A column of English horse was near, so we had to hurry up the pass as it grew dark, and I was obliged to leave him in an orchard below, to give him this slight chance of recovery. Next morning, on looking over the cliffs, I saw him lying dead. He had been game to the end - '*puure paert*' ('all-horse') - as the men called him, and my brother and I climbed down to pay a last visit to his poor emaciated carcass.

On our return Nagel discussed the situation. With more horses dying every day, our prospect of safely crossing the open plains and reaching General de la Rey was a poor one, and he suggested that we should return to the hill country from which we had just come. He said that we could wait there until word was got through to General de la Rey, who would doubtless send sufficient fresh horses to enable us to join him.

About half the men agreed to this, but the others refused. They said de la Rey was short of horses himself, and, with winter approaching once more, they preferred making north over the mountain-range for the warmer climate of the bush-veld. My brother and I decided to go north, too, although for a different reason. I was without horse, and he might be so at any moment, so we decided to find my father, as we counted on him to fit us out again, after which we would return south.

There was very little discussion and no ill feeling, for Nagel was a sensible man, and that same afternoon all was concluded. He, and those who were accompanying him, said good-bye, and filing down the pass again were soon lost to view. With him went de Gourville the Frenchman, the two sons of our late Commandant Malan, Fred Hancock, an old Bloemfontein school-fellow, and many other friends and companions, none of whom I ever saw again.

I think most were hunted down, or shot out, before they could obtain re-mounts, for, as I was to discover, their hopes of getting horses from General de la Rey were practically nil as he had none to give.

The men who had chosen for the north now started over the mountains, some on horseback, the majority on foot, and thus ended the A C.C..

My brother and I were in no hurry, so we remained resting among the boulders that night.

My father was somewhere in the Lydenburg country, and this was three hundred miles away, no easy journey with a single horse between us, but we reckoned that by riding and walking in turn we should find him in the end, and we hoped that as a member of the Government he would be able to recondition us.

Next day we loaded our gear on the chestnut, and descended the north side of the Magaliesbergen into the great valley which we had crossed with Beyers the night that we found the burning convoy.

We reached the bottom in the afternoon, by which time the 'A.C.C.' men who were travelling the same road had long since disappeared, leaving us seemingly alone in the broad rift. Towards evening, however, we came on an ox-wagon, outspanned in a patch of scrub, and owned by a stout-hearted old Boer lady who told us that she was on her way to the bush country. Her husband was fighting with de la Rey, and as the English were harrying and burning in the west she had thrown her belongings on a wagon, and, leaving the farm to look after itself, she had crossed the Magaliesbergen with her children and a native herdboy. She said she was going north at once, and offered us a lift. As this would save us much walking, we helped to fetch and yoke the oxen, and started off overjoyed at this timely relief. Before we had gone many yards, however, I remembered that by some oversight I had forgotten my saddlebags where we had halted that morning on our way down the mountain: a slight matter that altered the whole subsequent course of the war for me.

Saddlebags were scarce and valuable, and moreover mine contained a supply of salt that I had been lucky enough to discover at a deserted farm the week before, so it was agreed that my brother would go on with the wagon, while I returned up the pass on his horse to retrieve the missing articles. We thought that I should easily be able to catch up next day, so, leaving the wagon to jolt along, I trotted the chestnut back along the road towards the mountain.

By the time I reached the spot where I had left my wallets it was dark, so I built a fire and spent the night there. At daybreak when I untied the hobbles of the horse he savaged my arm, a sure sign that he was not himself, for ordinarily he was gentle, but I saddled up none the less and rode him down the mountain and halfway across the floor of the valley, by which time the tell-tale flecks of foam at his nostrils showed that the horse-sickness was on him. Seeing an empty farmhouse not far away, I led him there and kept him in the shade (which is said to be the only chance), but in less than an hour he was dead.

I could see up the northern road for ten miles or more, with no sign of the wagon, and, as the sun was blazing down, I decided to rest in the house until it grew cooler, before walking on in search of my brother.

The farmhouse had apparently been used as a place of call for English supply columns, coming and going between Rustenburg and Pretoria, for there was a litter of empty tins and other debris outside and the floors within were strewn with cigarette-ends, matches, and other marks of recent occupation. In going through the rooms looking for a cool spot, I found an unopened packet of newspapers on the floor, and as I had not seen a paper for over nine months I lost no time in reading them. I learned for the first time that Queen Victoria was dead; that there was a war in China; that Lord Roberts had been superseded by Lord Kitchener; and I read of a great many other events that had been passing in the outside world. What interested me most was an account of a Boer commando that was raiding far down into the Cape Colony, and I resolved at once to go south in search of them.

It was not so clear how I was to set about this, for the Cape lay many hundreds of miles away, and I was alone and on foot. But my mind was made up and, abandoning all thought of overtaking my brother, I threw my saddle across my shoulders, and carrying my rifle in one hand, and my cooking-tin in the other, I started back on a journey that was to take me very far indeed.

As I trudged along the road I had come, clouds of dust rising from the direction of Pretoria warned me that an English column or convoy was approaching, so I took to the bush and spent the night there. Starting long before daylight next morning, I reached the foot of the Magaliesbergen once more, at the Old Wagon Pass, and here I found about fifty Rustenburg men who had come in overnight They were horseless like myself, owing to the ravages of horse-sickness, and, having observed the approach of the English troops, they, too, had made for the shelter of the *berg*.

By climbing a little distance we could follow the movements of the soldiers, whom we made out to be about three thousand strong, with guns and many wagons, all making in our direction. We fled up the heights to a gorge near the top, where we lay secure, but the weather took a turn for the worse and it rained for eight days and nights without stopping, during which time we had no shelter but over-hanging rocks. It was impossible to find dry fuel, so we existed on biltong without a mouthful of anything warm.

We could not descend the mountain, because parties that went down reported that both north and south there was not a dwelling or a barn within reach that was not occupied by weather-bound English troops, who had been driven in from all directions to take cover against the unprecedented downpour. The knowledge that our opponents were comfortably housed merely added to our misery, and every time that the clouds and mist swayed aside we could see smoke cheerfully ascending from every building and shack below.

When the rain ceased, after a dreadful week, we impatiently watched the troops getting under way, and then made haste down the north side of the mountain, to re-occupy some of the farms which they had vacated.

My boots meanwhile had rotted and I had to climb down the sharp slopes on my bare feet, which became so swollen and blistered that I lay for a fortnight in a tobacco shed to which I was carried. The men were kind to me, one old *takhaar* actually walking twenty miles to fetch a piece of leather of which he knew, to make me a pair of rawhide sandals which served me for many a month to come.

These burghers were *Doppers*, a religious sect said to be somewhat like the Quakers. They held strange views on many things, but for all their primitive ways they were brave, unspoilt men.

Among them were some who had been serving with General de la Rey before they lost their horses, and they now began to discuss the possibility of returning to him.

This meant crossing over the Magaliesbergen to the south once more and going thence on foot over the open plains of the high veld, at the mercy of the first mounted enemy patrol that caught sight of us, so that it would not be at all plain sailing.

However, after discussing the pros and cons of the venture, thirteen of us decided to take the risk, in spite of the warnings of those remaining behind.

The prospect of a two-hundred-mile march on foot, burdened with our saddles and other belongings, was not an attractive one, but we began our preparations. While out after game one morning I chanced to pass the derelict English wagon-convoy that had been burnt last year, and looking over the remains I had an inspiration. There was not a single whole wagon, but it seemed to me that by taking an undamaged wheel here and there, and axles and planks from other parts, we might piece together a composite vehicle.

Returning to my companions, I put forward this suggestion, which was so well received that they went off in a body to inspect the skeleton convoy, and in two days' time had built up a strange-looking but quite trustworthy wagon.

The question of transport animals was just as easily solved. In a deep kloof some miles away ran a large herd of cattle, kept hidden there by General de la Rey's orders, as a reserve supply depot for his commandos in the west. We visited the cattle-guards, and got a dozen good trek oxen from them.

My fellow-travellers were born stockmen, who could tell at a glance which animals were trained to the yoke, and after a trial run they could even tell the exact place at which each ox bad previously pulled in the span, so they quickly selected an excellent team, with which we returned to complete our plans by rough-hewing sufficient yokes and curing the necessary straps and riems. In a few days' time all was ready, and loading up our goods we said good-bye to the rest of the Rustenburg men, and with our improvised wagon jolted up the Old Wagon Pass on our journey of discovery.

We climbed over the mountain range in one day, reaching the orchard where poor *'Malpert'* had died, in time to see the English still crowning the rise at Ramagothla. The night was black with heavy rain under cover of which we crawled on to the open plain, hurrying the oxen past the camp until by daylight we were well out of sight in the folds of the hills, cold, drenched, and weary, but pleased with the good progress that we had made. We found ourselves on the scene of recent fighting, for the ground was littered with rotting carcasses of horses and mules, and there were newly made graves.

I heard later that Mr Smuts, the State Attorney, had here besieged a force of Australians, who defended themselves so bravely that they beat off our people with loss.

We now travelled onward for several days through devastated country. The counterpart of the great drive we had witnessed in the east had since rolled over this area, leaving behind it only blackened ruins and trampled fields, so that our course lay through a silent unpeopled waste, across which we navigated our wagon like a lonely ship at sea.

My companions were big heavily bearded men of the old school, who looked on me as something of an alien, for I was town-bred, and they did not always understand my ways, but they were simple kindly souls and we got on well together. The Boers had their full share of laggards, but they had a full share, too, of steadfast yeomen such as these; men whose farms were lying in ruins, whose wives and families were scattered they knew not where, but who, unpaid and unbidden, returned to risk their lives in the fighting that swayed continually backward and forward over the western plains, and I got a truer insight into the fine courage and high qualities of their fighting-men during this journey than at any other time of the war.

On our fourth or fifth day out, a woman came walking towards us with her two small children and a native servant girl. She told us that she had been sheltering for the past ten days in a wooded kloof where her wagon was hidden, but the oxen having strayed into the open had been captured by passing soldiers, so that she was stranded. She said that General de la Rey's wagon-laager was camped at a place called Rietpan, near Tafel Kop, so, ascertaining that she was in no immediate want, we turned south-east, coming in view of the shimmering waters of the pan by noon next day. There was a considerable number of wagons on the shore of the lakes with many horses and cattle out at graze, and we were just congratulating ourselves on having at last found de la Rey when we saw a sudden stir—men began to run for their horses, and oxen were rapidly driven in, and, as we realized that something was amiss, we halted our wagon to await events.

Soon horsemen came riding furiously past, followed after an interval by the wagons and carts, also urged forward in a panic. We managed to stop one rider, who only stayed long enough to say that the English were upon us. We looked in vain for any sign of the enemy, but assuming that they must be near, we turned our tired oxen, and rattled along behind the retreat, which did not slow down until we had covered about six miles. Then horsemen from the rear overtook us with word that the alarm had been a false one.

All concerned had the grace to look ashamed of the stampede, but there was at any rate some excuse for them, as de la Rey had been severely handled early that morning in a surprise attack, in which he had lost over a hundred men. Some of his wounded, galloping up to the wagons, had precipitated a rout among the drivers, cattle-guards, and camp-followers, who formed the bulk of the laager.

In the afternoon General de la Rey himself rode in with his men, and he used withering language.

We now went into laager at Tafel-Kop, where de la Rey's commando and the wagons remained for the next few days. There were about a thousand mounted men and perhaps two hundred wagons. A few of these were used to bring maize from the Magaliesberg foothills, but the majority belonged to non-combatant refugees. De la Rey looked with an unfavourable eye on these and their vehicles, and the men said that the old man prayed to the Almighty night and morning for the enemy to relieve him of this incubus.

I saw a good deal of him at this time, as he held a daily levee beside his cart, where all were free to hear his views.

Attached to his person was a prophet, van Rensburg, a strange character, with long flowing beard and wild fanatical eyes, who dreamed dreams, and pretended to be possessed of occult powers. I personally witnessed one of the lucky hits to which he owed his reputation, for one morning while we were congregated around the General's cart, van Rensburg was expounding his latest vision to a hushed audience. It ran of a black bull and a red bull fighting and goring each other, until at length the red bull sank defeated to its knees, which he interpreted to mean that the British would soon be in like case. As he stood before us, his arms outstretched and his eyes ablaze, he suddenly called out: 'See, who comes?'; and, looking up, we made out a distant horseman spurring towards us front the cast. We waited in silence for the rider. When he came up, travel-stained and weary, he produced a letter from General Botha, hundreds of miles away.

When General de la Rey opened and read it, his face lighted up, and in a voice ringing with emotion he said: 'Men, believe me, the proud enemy is humbled' (*Die trotse vijand se nek is gebuig*). He went on to tell us that the letter contained news that the English had proposed a peace conference. Coming immediately upon the prophecy, it was a dramatic moment and I was impressed, even although I suspected that van Rensburg had stage-managed the scene. Of General de la Rey's sincerity there could be no doubt, for he was not a man to stoop to subterfuge, and I knew that he firmly believed in the seer's predictions.

These tidings created a great deal of stir and excitement during the next few days, and many of the men thought that the war was as good as over.

A peace conference did in fact take place a little later between General Botha and Lord Kitchener, but it proved abortive, and the only immediate result was to establish van Rensburg's reputation more firmly than ever.

I asked General de la Rey for a horse, but he said I should have to wait until parties he had sent into the Free State had returned, and, indeed, I could see for myself, from the number of dismounted men with the laager, that he was unable to assist me, so in the meanwhile my companions and I clung to our wagon and team, taking turns at herding the oxen and foraging for maize. Like everyone else, we had to find ourselves in food, excepting meat, which was supplied from a communal drove.

By this time my clothes had fallen from my body, owing to the rains, and my entire wardrobe consisted of a blanket and a pair of sandals, so that, as it was towards the end of March by now, with winter coming on, I felt the cold pretty severely. General de la Rey had noticed my scanty attire, and one morning he walked over to our wagon with a pair of breeches and a coat, a gift I much appreciated, for he could have been none too well supplied himself, but it was of a piece with his natural kindliness and consideration towards all.

From Tafel Kop, after some days, he rode off with the mounted men, and we poor infantrymen and other camp-followers were ordered to a place ten miles away, where there was better grazing for the trek-oxen. Here we remained, my prospects of reaching the Cape Colony looking pretty uncertain, although I was as determined as ever to get through.

On the 3rd of April, or the day we calculated to be that date, the wagon crew and myself were busy preparing a dinner to celebrate my birthday with an ox-tongue and a few odds and ends that we had managed to collect. Suddenly there came the crash of a field-gun, followed by the roar of a shell exploding close by, and almost immediately some of de la Rey's horsemen came riding out of the heavy mist that lay over all the country. They were riding hard to warn us that the English were coming. In a moment there was a wild rush to fetch the oxen, and fortunately the fog was so thick that none of the other shells fell among us and the entire wagon-laager was able to get under way without being seen.

To the sound of small-arm fire where our horsemen were engaged in the mist, the convoy spread out for better speed, each wagon striking out a course of its own, without regard to the others. The fog held, and heavy rain setting in still further decreased the visibility, so that my companions and I got clean away, although at times the English horsemen splashed past so close to us that we could hear them shouting to each other for their bearings.

The bulk of de la Rey's fighting men were not in the vicinity at all, but only some twenty or thirty of them had been approaching, the wagon-laager, for a few days' rest, when they unexpectedly stumbled on an English force that was stalking the convoy under cover of the mist. But for this we should have been taken by surprise, and I doubt if a single man would have escaped. As it was, the warning we received enabled us to escape wholesale capture, but it was touch and go, for the boom of the guns, the splutter of rides through the fog, and the hallooing and galloping sounded very near. As a matter of fact a number of wagons were taken, although we did not know it at the time. As for our party, we ran beside the team, keeping the oxen at a trot, and as our wagon was light, carrying only our saddles and cooking-tins, we made good progress. The other wagons and carts were almost immediately lost sight of in the mist, but we forged ahead by ourselves, and towards evening reached broken ground to the north, where we were safe enough.

We built a large fire on the banks of a stream and resurrected the remains of my birthday-dinner, which had come along in a leather bag. Afterwards my companions stood in a circle round the blaze, and solemnly sang hymns of thanksgiving for our escape. Then we camped for the night.

Next morning as it grew light, other wagons came crawling over the plain, also making for the safety of the hills, so we yoked our oxen and joined them, heading for a valley in the heart of the rugged tract known as the 'Swart Ruggens', where we found the remnant of our laager assembled.

We could not yet tell how many wagons had fallen into the hands of the enemy. Nearly half were missing, but most of these drifted in during the next day or two, and in the end it was found that less than a dozen had come to grief.

While we were camped in the valley, General de la Rey came up with some of his men to see how the convoy had fared, and, before riding back to the fighting area, he left orders for the wagons to proceed to a spot some thirty miles away, where there were two hundred horses from the Free State, which were to be given out by ballot to the dismounted men of the laager.

Many English columns were moving west at this time in continuance of a drive they were making, but we were able to trek along in comparative safety behind the line of their advance, and in due course reached our destination. Here we found a patrol that had come up from the Free State in charge of the remounts. The animals were mostly unbroken mares, and, as there were over three hundred horseless men, the drawing of lots was followed with keen interest.

I drew a blank, but no less than nine of our original wagon party got a horse apiece. I was cast down at the result, although we were comforted by an assurance that further horses were expected, and those of us who were unsuccessful in the drawings had at least the fun of seeing the winners break in their mounts, a diverting spectacle.

Nearly two hundred horses were bucking and squealing at the same time, their riders biting the dust in all directions, while we sat on the wagon-rails cheering them on. It was wonderful how quickly the men mastered their unruly steeds, so that by the third day practically every animal was broken to the saddle, and the newly mounted force could ride off to the war.

With them went the nine men from our wagon, leaving the rest of us to wonder disconsolately when we should sit astride a saddle again, and leaving me to wonder as well whether, at this rate, I should ever see the Cape.

The wagon-laager was now instructed to return to the Swart Ruggen Hills from which we had come, so we lumbered slowly back, halting after some days at the head of a beautiful stream that gushed from the rocks. Here we went into permanent camp, and the place soon became a sort of base depot for de la Rey's fighting commandos. The sick and wounded were brought here, and there was a steady influx of horseless men drifting in from the plains, and of men who had left the firing-line for a rest.

Our numbers varied from two hundred to over four hundred at times, and so securely were we hidden that not once did the British troops come near us, although their columns were ranging far and near over the adjoining open country. Two days after our arrival at the new camp I tried to smash a log for fuel by bringing down a heavy stone on top of it. The stone came back at me like a shot from a catapult, breaking my right tibia halfway between knee and ankle, and for three weeks I lay in great pain and discomfort with splinters of bone working their way out from a suppurating wound.

Luckily there were some Germans here, marooned like the rest of us for want of horses, and one of them had a working knowledge of surgery. Thanks to him and to a healthy constitution, I was at length able to hobble about, so I was doubly fortunate in having his assistance, and in being left in peace by the British while I was incapacitated. By now all but one of our original wagon complement had received horses and ridden away, and all the Germans except two were gone, and it began to look as if I was to become a professional camp-follower, for winter was upon us, and the arrival of more horses from the Free State was very unlikely.

A chance turn, however, brought me relief. One morning, soon after I was able to limp around, a small party of Germans rode into camp under command of a little hunch-backed Field-Cornet named Mayer. At this time there was still in the field a German contingent about thirty strong, with Mayer at its head. In a sense they were the direct descendants of Baron von Goldeck's force, with whom I had served the year before; for although most of the Baron's men had melted away during the retreat to the Portuguese border, some of them had remained, and had collected themselves into a self-contained little commando forming part of General de la Rey's army.

Mayer had heard that there were a few of his compatriots stranded at the wagon-laager, so he had brought some spare horses to remount them. This stood me in good stead, for there were only two horseless Germans left in camp, the others having drawn animals in the lottery and ridden off, and Mayer agreed to let me have a little grey mare on condition that I joined him. The wound in my leg was still far from healed, but as I could not afford to miss the chance I made over my half-share in our wagon and team to the only remaining member of our original and company; and with my leg in a splint accompanied the Germans when they set out on their return to de la Rey's forces.

It was a harsh journey. My leg throbbed and ached at every stride, and the winter had set in with great severity. I had not felt the cold so much in the seclusion of the valley where we had been camped up to now, but out in the open it was a different matter. By day clouds of dust and biting winds drove across the bleak plains, and at night we could hear the crackle of ice forming on the pools, as we lay shivering beneath our threadbare blankets. From now lay onward, indeed, until the end of the cold season, five long months ahead, we endured great hardship and suffering, for never, even in the memory of the oldest man, had there been so prolonged a spell of bitter weather all over South Africa.

For three days we rode on without meeting anyone. Another great drive was in progress with de la Rey's men hanging on to its flanks, the country behind being left wasted and ruined. At length we came on some of his commandos in the ridges near the village of Hartebeestpoort, where they lay in attendance on a large concentration of English troops, said to number twelve thousand. Here we found the balance of Mayer's Germans, with whom we took post in the line that had been established in a half-moon before the enemy columns. For the moment the troops were resting, so we lay watching their camps, guns and convoys, waiting for them to make the first move.

They sent shells over us at times, but were obviously holding their hand until they were ready, an event to which we looked forward with considerable misgiving, as there were only about six hundred burghers present, the last of de la Rey's men being elsewhere engaged.

But the General himself was with us and, happening to ride past one afternoon while my leg was being dressed by one of the Germans, he sent me off to a kind of field hospital that he had established some miles back. I found it in a ruined farmhouse, with a young Hollander doctor doing what he could for the sick and wounded under his care. It was a cheerless place, with only dried grass to lie on, and in the absence of medicines or bandages there was little enough comfort for the patients. They were mostly lighter cases, as the serious casualties were left for the British ambulances to pick up. Amid all the cruelty of farm-burning and the hunting down of the civilian population, there was one redeeming feature, in that the English soldiers, both officers and men, were unfailingly humane. This was so well known that there was never any hesitation in abandoning a wounded man to the mercy of the troops, in the sure knowledge that he would be taken away and carefully nursed, a certainty which went far to soften the asperities of the war.

A few days after I joined the hospital we heard the sound of heavy gunfire about nine in the morning, and realized that the expected attack had come. I had kept my horse by me all the time, so I saddled and rode back to where I had left the Germans in the firing-line, while the doctor loaded his charges on a mule-wagon and made off to safer quarters. When I reached our men I saw the English attacking away to our left. Under cover of a severe bombardment their cavalry rode cheering towards a spot in our position a mile away, and broke through almost at once.

We of the German contingent were merely spectators, but we were close enough to see the men at the threatened point run for their horses and take to flight. Here and there a man went down, but our casualties were not heavy, as there had been scarcely any resistance in face of the shell-fire to which we could not reply, and when the burghers on either side of the breach saw what was happening, they too fetched their horses and beat a retreat. Naturally the Germans and I went as fast as the rest, to join the stream that flowed to the rear. We fell back until two in the afternoon, when the English gave up the chase and we were able to come to a halt in a bush-covered hollow, where General de la Rey addressed us in his half-humorous half-serious manner, and soon he had the men laughing and making light of their misfortunes.

We rested our horses here until dark, and then rode west for several hours, as there was word of further columns converging upon us.

There had been a magnificent double-tailed meteor in the sky of late, the two streamers of which looked like the letter 'V', and van Rensburg, the General's Prophet, had been giving out that this stood for '*Vrede*' (peace), but on this night as we rode along, I heard a boyish voice from the darkness ahead call out: 'Mijnheer van Rensburg, that letter V up there does not mean Vrede, it means Vlug (retreat).' There was wry laughter in the ranks at this sally, which the discomfited oracle bore in meek silence, although it did not diminish his output of prophecies, which continued right up to the peace.

We spent a cold night beside a pan, and at daybreak could make out a large body of English troops in the distance, but we could not tell whether they were our pursuers of yesterday or a fresh column. In any case they were too far away to cause us any immediate anxiety, so we shot some oxen (a number from the larger communal herd having accompanied us) and began to prepare breakfast.

After this General de la Rey divided us into two parties. With half the men he rode south, and before sunset we heard the boom of guns thirty miles away, where the indomitable old man was once more attacking an enemy column.

He left Commandant Jan Kemp in command of the rest of us, with orders to carry out a raid into the territory of Bechuanaland, with a view to capturing a supply train on the Rhodesian railway line. Accordingly, for the next two days, we rode on through barren country, until we reached a point on the Harts River, from which we were to make a night march to our objective.

Mayer asked leave to scout in advance with his men, a request that was granted, so we started two hours ahead of our main body, riding through the Cunana Native reserve until, at four in the morning, we crossed the British border. The railway ran only a mile or so beyond, and we soon reached the metals. We started tearing up the track, with poles from a neighbouring fence for our only tools. Presently Mayer handed me a pair of pliers, and told me to climb up one of the telegraph standards and cut the wires, no easy task with my sore leg. As I was swarming up, there came a sudden volley from a culvert about fifty yards away. I slid down and in a moment we were on our horses, and away, for now that we were discovered there was no hope of surprising a train.

We rode back to a hill half a mile in the rear, to wait for daylight. When we got there we found a little native village nestling behind it, and went there to get information as to the number of soldiers guarding the line below. It was growing light as we rode through the gateway of the thorn enclosure surrounding the *stad*, and when we entered, two khaki-clad white men rushed out of a hut, rifle in hand, followed by a native also armed. Mayer was off his horse at once, firing almost before he touched the ground. He hit the native through the chest, and the other two men put up their hands. This single shot caused a panic in the village. The natives grabbed their karosses, mats, babies, and whatever else they could lay hands on, and fled down the slope in the direction of the railway line to seek protection from the British troops, the women setting up a long-drawn wail as they ran.

Mayer ordered me to head off the fugitives, so I galloped round to get in front of them. Unfortunately three or four of the Germans had lagged behind on the way up from the railway line, and, when they saw the rush of natives coming at them in the uncertain light, they opened fire, thinking themselves attacked. Before I could stop the shooting, they killed four and wounded several others, nearly getting me too.

We did what we could for the wounded and had them carried back to the huts, greatly upset at what had happened, for there were two women amongst the dead.

The white men captured in the kraal turned out to be renegades (National Scouts) from Potchefstroom. They were handed over later on to General de la Rey, who had them both executed, I believe.

It had by now grown fully light, and we could see Kemp's men approaching through the bush. They were riding in small parties, making for the railway line, so we sent off a man to warn them that the English were there, but before the messenger got halfway, shells came screeching through the air from a hill beside the line. So far from expecting to be shelled, we had believed this part of the railway to be unguarded, but we could now make out quite a considerable number of tents among the trees and, as the gun kept dropping shells near us, Kemp ordered a withdrawal, and we trekked back into the Transvaal after a profitless venture.

We rode thirty miles that day, reaching Leeuwpan by nightfall, where we found General de la Rey awaiting us. He said there were several English columns halted in a semicircle ahead, and he instructed Kemp to get out of their way that night. Having told us what to do, he rode away with his handful of retainers, and I did not see the doughty old warrior again, for from that night our roads lay far apart.

18. THE NEXT STAGE

As soon as it was dark enough, Kemp led us off in the direction of the English camps, between which he intended passing. We were skilfully guided, for we slipped through a gap between two camps, passing so close that we could hear the murmur of voices, and could see the forms of soldiers outlined against their fires. No alarm was raised until we were through, when there was some shouting and firing which did no damage. Once ,we had put the camps behind us the men were ordered to march on foot to spare their horses, for we had been on the move for over thirty hours, with no rest worth mentioning.

As I still had a limp, I gradually fell behind; and to make matters worse, my poor little mare was delivered of a still-born foal. With this travail coming upon her she had borne the long treks so unfalteringly, that I had not even known that there was anything wrong with her, but now her strength was gone. After a while she staggered to her feet, and as I could not risk remaining in too close proximity to the English camps, whose fires were still visible in the distance, I led her slowly forward. By this time the rest of our men had long since vanished in the darkness, and I had to plod on alone for an hour or two, dragging my horse behind me, until she could go no farther, when I decided to halt till morning. It was bitterly cold - so cold that earlier in the evening I had heard the men say that it was the coldest night they had ever known. As I could find no fuel for a fire, I wrapped my blanket round my shoulders and sat with chattering teeth until sunrise. When it grew light I found myself on a cheerless expanse, with a view that extended for many miles, but there was no sign of the commando.

By a distant thorn tree, however, I found four of my German friends, huddled together against the cold. They said that they had missed me during the night, and, knowing that I was crippled, they had generously remained behind to wait for me.

After collecting what fuel we could in such barren country, we built a small fire to fry some meat, and then set out on the spoor of the commando, making slow progress, for my companions' horses were not in very much better condition than my own. By nine or ten o'clock in the morning, ominous pillars of dust rising in the rear warned us that the English columns of last night were turning in our direction.

The troops were not as yet in sight; but considering the state of our animals, we stood a poor chance of keeping ahead of them once their scouts topped the skyline, so we hurried on as best we could. Just as we were beginning to see an occasional horseman far behind us, we providentially came on the Harts River. It was more of an earth-crack across the plain than a river. No trees stood on its edge, and fifty yards off the banks were invisible, but it was our salvation, for hardly were we and our horses out of sight in the dry bed below, when the troops came swarming towards the river. All went well, however. The English, when they reached the bank, set to digging gradients for their guns and wagons, and, although it was hours before they got their transport through, during which time we anxiously peered over the top in fear of discovery, we had the satisfaction before dark, of seeing the tail of their convoy vanish over the horizon.

This was good as far as it went, but the question was bow to catch up again with our own people, though the fact of being temporarily cut off was not of vital importance having regard to the fluid nature of guerrilla warfare, and we were not greatly troubled on that score, our worst anxiety being the weak state of our horses.

For the next three or four days we toiled on behind the enemy, who in turn were following our men. We kept some distance to the rear, only moving when the dust-clouds ahead of us showed that the English were advancing too, and in this manner we crawled along on foot, leading our horses by the reins.

One evening a burgher rode up, the first we had seen since the night we dropped behind. He told us that General de la Rey had dispersed his commandos into smaller bands, owing to the pressure from converging British columns. These bands, he said, were by now scattered all over the Western Transvaal, waiting for the end of the drive.

After taking a look at our animals, he said he thought we stood a poor chance of finding Mayer and the other Germans, then he rode off on business of his own, leaving my companions and myself to digest the information received. They were for attempting to work north to the milder climate of the bush-veld, in order to escape the infernal cold of these open plains. They said, as far as Mayer was concerned, we could always find him again once the winter was over, and in any case it mattered little if we didn't.

Seeing that they attached no particular moral value to the necessity of rejoining our unit, I now sprang on them my long-cherished scheme of making for the Cape Colony. They stared at me in surprise when I first broached the subject, but after I had explained my views, and had pictured the Cape to them as a land of beer for the taking at every wayside inn, they became eager converts, and we agreed to start without delay.

The four Germans were a mixture. The eldest, Herman Haase, was a man of about forty-five, in looks the typical sausage-eater of the English comic papers, but, as I found out, a kindly, good-natured gentleman, a Johannesburg merchant, who had been in the field from the beginning. He was the last man one would have suspected of a liking for war, as his talk was all of his wife and family, and the joys of home life.

Next came W. Cluver, a clever, cynical Berlin student, who told me many interesting things of life in the old world; then there was Pollatchek, also a Berlin student, who had come out to fight for the Boers, as on a crusade. He told me that his initial ardour had long since evaporated, but he liked the life of adventure and so had remained, a pleasant, cheerful fellow whom I grew to like very much.

Lastly, there was a farmhand named Wiese, a clumsy, slow-witted rustic, but brave enough. With these four men my lot was now cast. Wiese and Cluver did not get very far, but with Haase and Pollatchek I was long associated, although they turned back in the end.

Our preparations for going to the Cape were quickly made. We slaughtered a stray sheep, and cut the meat into strips for drying in the wind (as we had no salt), and we ground a quantity of maize into meal in a small coffee-mill that Haase carried on his saddle-tree, and next morning we started.

On the evening of our first day out, we had an exciting interlude. Another of de la Rey's men who, like ourselves, had been left stranded in the rear of the British drive rode up to see who we were. He said he had been lurking around here for some days, seeking an opportunity to regain the commandos. While stripping mealie cobs in a field that afternoon, he had seen a native ride from a *stad* close by to meet an English patrol. The native had conferred with the officer in command for some minutes, after which the patrol went off. As the native was obviously a spy in British pay, the newcomer suggested that we should try to capture him after dark. Accordingly, about nine o'clock that night, we started on foot for the kraal, going quietly so as not to frighten our quarry. When we reached the village, however, we found the headman and all his followers on the *qui vive*. They denied all knowledge of the spy, so our guide cut matters short by seizing the Induna by the throat, threatening to shoot him. On being thus roughly handled, he wrested himself free and shouted loudly, 'Help, help, the Boers are killing me!' In a moment we were surrounded by thirty or forty braves, most of them brandishing assegais and knobkerries in our faces.

They began leaping and dancing about us, uttering fierce yells and menaces, while some tore thatch from the huts, lit it at a fire, and held it aloft instead of torches. From beyond the circle of angry savages came the cries of the women, urging them to kill the white men, and things began to look unpleasant. We could have opened fire, but the space inside the stockade was cramped and they were far superior in numbers. Moreover, all through the war the Boers had observed an unwritten law that it was a white man's quarrel, and that the native tribes were to be left alone. For these reasons we did not fire, but closed up, and slowly backed out through the gateway by which we had entered. Once free of the enclosure we had no trouble in safely reaching our camping-place, much annoyed at the poor figure we had cut. To add to our humiliation, at dawn next morning we saw a native boldly riding from the *stad* and when we sent a few shots after him, he waved a defiant arm and disappeared over the rise.

Having thoroughly bungled the affair, de la Rey's man took his leave of us, and we continued on our way.

For several days we were unable to travel in a direct line, for we found the countryside alive with British troops moving in all directions, and we calculated that we saw twenty-five thousand of them before we got clear. It was plain from the way in which they swept forward on an enormous front that they were conducting another of their drives, but as we did not see a single burgher, or the vestige of a commando during all this time, they must have had little to show for their activity. Clearly General de la Rey was resorting to his usual tactics of avoiding these huge concentrations of troops by scattering his men until the blow was spent.

My knowledge of veld-craft brought our party safely through to the Vaal River, for my early experience was of value, and we threaded and twisted successfully between the enemy columns, never having occasion to fire a shot. Once we were held up for half a day while a body of English troops camped within hail of where we lay hidden in a patch of thorn. Another time Cluver and I tried to ambush two officers, but he showed himself too soon and they got away. In the course of these operations we had to jettison Heinrich Wiese. His horse gave in and he himself had blistered feet, so we abandoned him near an English column, where he was sure to be picked up and cared for. My leg was on the mend, but we suffered a great deal from the cold at nights. Otherwise we almost grew to enjoy the excitement of dodging the enemy forces and patrols, and the Germans said that it was the best time they had had in the war.

At length, on the fifth or sixth day, we breasted the long rise at Leeuwdoorn, from which the country slopes down to the Vaal River, and we saw the wide plains of the Free Slate stretching beyond. We slept a night in an unburnt farmhouse on the Transvaal side, and next morning, as we were riding off, we saw a body of English approaching, so we climbed a kopje to see what their plans were.

The soldiers made for the farm we had just vacated, and soon smoke and flames were issuing from door and windows. As we looked on, two old fellows rode up from the direction of the Vaal River, and joined us on the hill. They reminded me of my former commander, General Maroola, and his brother, for they both wore rusty bell-toppers, and the tails of their ancient claw-hammer coats flapped in the breeze as they came. With a curt greeting they dismounted and sat down on the rocks, silently watching the work of destruction below. for a long time neither of them spoke, and it was only when the roof fell in amid a shower of sparks, that the elder of the two sighed and turning to the other said: 'Brother John, there go those teak-wood beams I brought from Pretoria after the Jameson Raid.' This was his sole comment on the loss of his home, then the couple remounted their horses to ride back to the river.

As we were also going there, we fetched our animals and overtook them, learning on the way that they were making for a women's laager halted beside the water.

We found that the laager consisted of about thirty wagons, with perhaps three or four times that number of women and children, all under the care of our two worthies. Now that the British were capturing the civil population it had become the practice for the women on the farms, when hostile forces approached, to load what they could on their wagons, and join hands with others similarly situated, in order to form a joint laager. Once the immediate danger was past they returned to what was left of their homes, to subsist as best they could, rather than be taken for internment to the British concentration camps. We rested at the laager for a few hours, while one of the old church-wardens rode out to see what the English were doing. He came galloping back to say that about fifteen hundred English horsemen were on the river bank eight miles higher up. In view of this it was decided that the laager must cross through to the Free State shore, and immediately all was in a bustle. There was a ford of sorts close by, over which we helped the women to get the wagons, but it was pitiful to see them standing waist deep in the icy water, tugging at the wheels, and urging on the oxen in their anxiety to put the river between themselves and the column. After working hard for nearly two hours, we had the whole laager safely over. We then waded back to the Transvaal bank to fetch our horses, and on our return found the wagons under way, making across the unlimited open country of the Free State that stretches southward for hundreds of miles.

The Germans and I remained resting under the trees to dry our clothes, and slept the night a few miles farther on.

In the morning the Englishmen came moving down the river, and by nine o clock they were fording the stream into the Free State, so we made off, and for the next three days rode leisurely along, following the south bank of the river, and warning the women on the farms, as we passed, that the troops were behind.

I took this route as I had decided to make for the neighbourhood of Hoopstad, a village and district that I knew well, for my brothers and I had camped and hunted here as boys.

I counted on finding the herds of semi-wild horses that used to frequent the river, that we might remount ourselves, for there was small chance of the horses we rode being able to last out the bitter winter that was upon us. We found the homesteads along the river bank intact, but as the bulk of the male population of these parts had been captured with old General Cronje at Paardeberg more than a year ago, the farms were for the most part tenanted by women and children. They told us that an occasional British column had marched through during the past six or eight months, but thus far the policy of farm-burning and the removal of the civilian population had not been put into operation here.

This happy condition was now coming to an end, for pillars of smoke were rising far behind us, and at night the sky was reddened with the glare of burning homesteads, to tell the unfortunate inhabitants that their long immunity was over.

The women took the matter bravely, although there were tears and weeping at times, but each family, as soon as they realized the danger, fetched the oxen, inspanned their wagon, and trekked away south across the plains, out of harm's way.

At length we came to Hoopstad town. The place was deserted, the English garrison, for some unexplained reason, having set fire to their stores and marched away two days before. That same afternoon a solitary German trader rode in from the south-east, where he was serving with a small Boer commando. He proved a useful ally, as he showed us a quantity of maize concealed in an underground receptacle, on which we fed our horses for some days, enabling the wretched animals to pick up condition a little.

Our new acquaintance said he must now return to his commando, and he suggested that we should accompany him. He said that the horses running on the veld were so shy that, unless we got assistance, we should never succeed in catching any of them, as all fences were down throughout the district. We agreed to go with him and, travelling over endless rolling plains, within a few days reached the force to which he was attached. This consisted of twenty men under an officer of the now defunct O.F.S. Artillery. They made us welcome, but shook their heads when we mentioned horses, and indeed we found next day that we might as well have tried to catch antelopes. There were lots of horses roaming about, but when the men spread out, the mustangs went racing away, manes and tails in the wind, and, in spite of our endeavours, we failed to capture a single one of them. It appeared that the British troops had been firing on them with machine-guns and rifles, ever since they discovered that General de la Rey was getting remounts from here, which accounted for their bedevilment. In any case they were too fleet for us, and, as there were no wires to stop them, we gave up the business for fear of foundering the horses we had.

We spent a week with our friends. They were a ragged crew carrying a queer assortment of weapons, and what little ammunition they had they reserved for shooting game, which abounded, and they seemed quite happy so long as they could keep out of the hands of the British.

They gave us unfavourable news of the grazing to the south, so I determined to make for the mountain country farther east, where, I was told, the grass would be better, and where we might procure fresh horses, as de la Rey himself had latterly been sending thither in search of remounts.

So, when we had shot enough springbok and blesbok for biltong, the three Germans and I set out once more. On the night after we started, a bitter cold wind drove across the plains. We were halted beside a water-hole without shelter for man or beast, with the result that, towards morning, my little grey mare broke loose, maddened by the pelting earth and pebbles. She fled down the storm and I never saw her again.

One of our late friends had given Pollatchek a horse, which he made over to me, so the loss of my own, serious as it was, did not prevent my going on. Having ridden out the blizzard without further damage, we pushed on going roughly east by south. We passed Kopje-Alleen, where my brothers had been ridden down with the 'A.C.C.' last year.

It is a curious isolated hill visible for sixty miles around. As a boy I had sat on its summit watching the game-covered plains below, and now, as then, great herds of antelope and troops of wildebeest were grazing at its foot.

I climbed to the top, partly for old times' sake and partly to see whether the land was clear, but there was really no need for anxiety, as we were in empty country.

The farmhouses stood abandoned, the fields lay unploughed, and we saw neither human beings nor domestic animals, even the natives having fled.

We rode through this unpeopled waste until, some days later, we fell in with a party of Freestaters near the Sand River railway bridge There were nine of them under a Field-Cornet named Botha. They had been trying to derail a train, but the English were building block-houses along here and their attempt had failed, so Botha and his men were returning to their own haunts in the mountain ranges to the east. As we were bound for that region ourselves, we joined them. At eleven o'clock that night we set out to cross the railway line (the main line coming up from Bloemfontein to Johannesburg). The cold was intense and the darkness so thick that those in front had constantly to shout and whistle to give those behind their bearings. After we had been going for some hours we found that Cluver was missing. We called and whistled and fired shots, but got no reply, so Pollatchek and I rode back to look for him. We retraced our steps for more than a mile, and then, as the directing shouts of the others were growing fainter, we reluctantly rejoined our companions. The trouble was that Cluver was subject to epileptic fits. Three or four times since being with us he had fallen into convulsions, and we supposed one of these attacks had come upon him while he was lagging behind. The night was so freezing that to lie unconscious on the ground meant certain death, but Field-Cornet Botha said it was essential to cross the block-house line before it drew light, and, as we were still a long way from the point at which he intended to slip over, he insisted upon our pushing on, so we continued our journey, somewhat heartlessly I admit, but we could not afford to lose the chance of getting through under the guidance of men who knew the lie of the block-houses.

Towards four in the morning we reached a hollow between two fortified posts, and crossed the line without any trouble. We never heard of Cluver again, and I have no doubt that he was dead by morning, for he was not strong enough to have survived that winter night in the open.

By sunrise we were well into the foothills beyond the railway, and now for two days we rode east into increasingly mountainous country, until we reached a lonely farm lying high up amid the crags near Wonder Kop. At this place Botha and his men had their lair. From here they made periodic raids down to the plains, and they must have given a good account of themselves, judging by what they told us, and by their horses, weapons, and equipment, all of which were of British origin. Small private bands like this were common enough in the Free State nowadays, remnants of larger forces that had dwindled away under the misfortunes of war.

Botha told me that he had at one time commanded over three hundred men. Many of them had been killed or captured, others had surrendered, and others again had left him to join larger commandos in the north. He clung to his title of Field-Cornet, and as two of his men called themselves Corporals, the rank and file of his army consisted of but six men. We had reached a very snug haven. The owners of the fame were gone, but there was plenty of good clean straw in the barns to lie on, and in a cave in the cliff over-hanging the homestead was a store of wheat, a welcome change from our eternal diet of maize, while in the valleys below half-savage pigs were to be had for the shooting.

Moreover, there was a huge copper cistern, and, as water and fuel were plentiful, we could prepare a hot bath as often as we liked, a rare luxury in this freezing weather.

For ten days the two Germans and I revelled in the unaccustomed joy of good food, cleanliness, and comfortable sleeping quarters, but then I became restless once more. I succeeded in converting Field-Cornet Botha and his followers to my scheme of raiding into the Cape Colony. They were at first disinclined to move so far from their beloved mountains, but eventually I swung them round, and about the end of June (we were vague as to dates and time) we started down the mountains and headed due west, intending to recross the railway line to the plains beyond, and then make a wide detour round Bloemfontein to strike the Orange River somewhere near Ladysmith. On the morning after our departure from the farm, as we were descending the pass near Breslersflat, a young fellow named Jacobus Bosman came riding up. When we told him that we were going to the Cape he said he would come too. As he was one of the Cape rebels who had joined the Boers during their temporary occupation of Colesberg in the beginning of the war, I advised him to stay where he was, for if he were captured on British territory, it would go hard with him. He said he would take the risk, so we enlisted him, but my warning was justified, for he was taken and hanged, as will be seen later on.

After three days of steady progress we were back on the open plains, within sight of the Bloemfontein-Johannesburg railway line, and we scouted round for a suitable crossing. This was becoming more and more difficult to find, now that the English were perfecting their block-house system.

As I spent the rest of the war roving the Cape Colony, I did not experience the full effect of this network, but I have heard that it caused the Free State and Transvaal Commandos great trouble, and in the end contributed largely to the break-up of the Boer resistance.

There were working parties of soldiers dotted along the railway track, engaged in putting up these block-houses, but we had no difficulty in galloping across the metals, despite a fairly heavy rifle-fire, and, having safely negotiated the line, we rode on, passing not far north of Brandfort village. Towards dark we came on a field of maize into which we turned our weary horses, and here we spent the night.

Next morning, just before sunrise, we beard the crack of distant rifle-shots, and shortly after two burghers rode by. They pulled up to say that an English column was coming our way, and they advised us to go along with them - they were making for a women's laager not far away, to warn them of the enemy's approach - so we caught our horses and rode off. One of these men, Piet Marais, was an old acquaintance whom I had known as a compositor in a newspaper office at Bloemfontein. He had since inherited money and had bought a farm near by, which he and his companion had been about to visit when they came on the advance-guard of the British force.

As the sun rose we were able to see the column crawling along the road some miles behind. We judged them to be fifteen hundred horsemen, with a string of wagons, and several guns. The women's laager consisted of some fifty wagons and carts, with over two hundred women and children, the collective non-combatant population of the district.

On hearing our news, they began to pack up; the poultry were run to earth, children and household effects were rapidly stowed, and in a very short time the laager was moving off. Women trotted alongside the teams with whips and quirts, while the children peered out anxiously from beneath the hoods at the dust-clouds in the distance, which betokened the approaching enemy. Fortunately the going was easy on these undulating plains, and the wagons made good headway in the direction of the Vet River, lying ten miles north.

By now other men were riding up in twos and threes from various points, until we were about forty strong, and we began to practise our old tactics of galloping across the front of the English advance to fire a few shots, and then falling back to repeat the process farther on, as soon as the shell-fire grew too hot.

This served its purpose sufficiently well to give the laager time to get away, and after a few hours we had no fears for their safety.

Towards three in the afternoon the English halted. We could see them turning out their animals to graze, so we rode up to a kopje near by, where we lay resting under the trees while our horses ready-saddled cropped the grass close by. Before long we heard a clatter, and jumping to our feet, saw a troop of mounted soldiers coming at a gallop.

Our look-out lad not troubled to keep awake, and the horsemen were within six hundred yards of us before we heard them. As they had two pom-poms with them, we loosed only a single volley, and then ran for our horses.

Rifle bullets were soon spitting about our ears and shells were bursting farther on, but as we were riding wide no one was hit, although once, when we were bunched together at a gap in a fence, a shell pitched right among us and killed a led-horse, whose blood was spattered in my face.

We spread out once more, and sprinted for the shelter of the Vet River banks, two or three miles beyond, and here we gave our winded animals time to recover. The British made no further attempt to advance that day, realizing perhaps that we had the heels of them. After satisfying ourselves of their intentions, we crossed over the north bank by a bridle-path, to build fires and cook a meal, for we had eaten nothing that day, and after dark we trekked down-stream for a few miles, to be in safety. Burghers, who had ridden away earlier to see how the women's laager was getting on, returned to say that all the wagons had escaped, so we spent an easy night under the thorn trees beside the water.

At sunrise yesterday's English approached as far as the river, where they came to rest. Our little party from the mountains thought that we had come far enough out of our course, so we decided to double back behind the column in order to resume our journey southwards. We took our leave of the Freestaters after hearing from them of an insure mountable barrier that we should meet at the Modder River, where, they said, the English had a line of fortified posts that would stop our progress to the south.

Recrossing the Vet River, we rode back along the way we had come the day before, and the soldiers halted along the stream did not even send a shell at us when we skirted round their camp.

We were getting short of ammunition, so during the next two days we followed the road by which the English force had travelled, to pick up Lee-Metford cartridges. The English soldiers were notoriously careless with their ammunition. If a round or two dropped from their bandoliers they would never trouble to dismount, as they knew they could get more, and at their halting-places one could almost always find cartridges lying spilt in the grass. So much was this the case that latterly it had become a regular practice to trail the columns, sometimes for a week on end, to glean these crumbs from the rich man's table, and I doubt if the British ever realized to what an extent the Boers were dependent upon this source of replenishment.

We followed the road back until we came once more in sight of Brandfort village, by which time we had picked up nearly a hundred rounds. Satisfied with this we now turned west, and then south-west, towards the Modder River.

19. FARTHER SOUTH

We rode on steadily for three days, making a bend so as to strike the river midway between Bloemfontein and Kimberley. Nothing of interest happened, save for a brush with an English patrol that suddenly bore down on us one morning out of the mist.

The light was so uncertain that both sides drew off, after firing a few shots, for neither party could make out how strong the other was.

We passed the *dorp* of Bultfontein on our way and looked in for what we could find, but the place was gutted. For the rest we rode over interminable plains devoid of human beings. We did not see a single homestead that was not in ruins, and at some places lay hundreds of sheep clubbed to death or bayoneted by the English troops, in pursuance of their scheme of denuding the country of live-stock to starve out the Boers.

In spite of this there was generally an odd sheep or two straying about, and there were plenty of springbok besides, so we did not lack meat. Nevertheless we were leading a pretty hard life. Bread and salt, soap, tobacco and books were things of the past. We had almost forgotten the taste of tea, coffee, sugar and vegetables. If a man was not lucky enough to possess a tinder-box, he had to expend a valuable rifle-cartridge every time he wished to light a fire. It was midwinter, with ice on every pool, and we went in tattered clothing and slept under threadbare blankets at night.

We crossed the Modder River at midnight above Abrahamskraal, and day-break found us facing the line of military posts we had been told of, that the English had established all the way from Bloemfontein to the Diamond Mine at Koffiefontein, a distance of sixty miles. This cordon was formed to guard thousands of sheep and cattle taken from the farms. Each post consisted of ten or twelve tents, at intervals of perhaps two thousand yards, and as our horses were in too poor a condition to make a dash for it, we turned westward, seeking a convenient spot at which to slink by without attracting attention. We could see patrols of cattle-guards riding about, but they probably took us for their own men, and for a while we went in peace.

Then a heliograph started winking from a kopje, and before long there was activity; soldiers running for their horses, and others galloping in from the plain. Seeing this, we boldly headed between two of the camps for a chain of hills beyond, firing from the saddle and getting well peppered in return, but we gained the cover of the hills before a real pursuit could be organized. A considerable number of horsemen came towards us, and when we opened long range fire they contented themselves with spattering some volleys against the rocks about us, and then returned to their business of minding the herds. We were now safely across the much-talked-of Modder River barrier, and, continuing our journey, reached the mineral spring near Lotshoek by next day, where we fell in with a small commando of fifty or sixty men under a Field-Cornet named Blignault.

We were now in the Fauresmith district, not more than fifty miles from the Orange River, beyond which lay the Cape Colony, but I was yet to discover that it was farther off than it seemed.

When we told Blignault or our plan of invasion from here, he strongly advised us against the attempt. He said that if we crossed the Orange River here, we should find ourselves in open and arid country, where our horses would surely starve, and where we would be ridden down by the first British force that saw us. On the other hand, if we went east towards the headwaters of the Orange River, a hundred and fifty miles away, and then turned south into the Cape, we should find mountains and good grazing for our horses, and there so small a band as ours would stand some chance of survival. Blignault and his men had much to say of the hardships they had endured when they accompanied General de Wet into the Colony some months previously.

Fifteen hundred men had crossed the river, but they were so beset by enemy columns that they had to return to the Free State with the loss of many men and horses. In fact everyone we met in these parts spoke against further raids into British territory.

We were reminded, too, of the disaster that overtook General Hertzog's venture to the south, and of the fate of almost every other party that had crossed the Orange River. It seemed that, like the cave in the fable, many tracks led over the river, but few came back.

This was not encouraging, and Field-Cornet Botha and the rest of my companions were so impressed that they began to waver, but Jacobus Bosman and I talked them into a better frame of mind, and finally persuaded them that, by accepting the advice we had received and going east, we could get into the Cape Colony and hold our own once we were there.

Next day we said good-bye to Blignault's commando and rode away east, coming within sight of Edenburg village the following afternoon. This place lies about forty miles south of Bloemfontein on the main railway, and, as we found the line strongly block-housed and saw a big English camp on the outskirts of the village, we lay over for the night, to spy out the land next day.

The night after that we saddled at dark and rode towards the railway track, hoping to get over unobserved at a spot which we had investigated during the day. Just before we started, a sturdy little Shetland pony came wandering up from the English camp, and I took him along with me, which was just as well, as it turned out. After an hour's ride we reached the railway line at what we took to be the point which we had selected, but the night was so dark that we had gone astray, and we ran into a block-house instead. We were met with the usual 'Halt! Who comes there?' Followed by rifle-shots, so we bore away to look for a more suitable crossing, and some five hundred yards farther down we made another attempt.

As is the case with most railways in South Africa, a fence ran on either side of the line, composed of thick strands of wire which had to be cut before the horses could be led through. The only implement we possessed was a large file, and with this a young fellow named Verster and I tried to saw the wires, while the others waited a hundred yards back. The file grating across the taut wires made a tremendous noise, and before we had cut even one strand, we were again challenged and fired at by a sentry, who sounded not twenty yards away. We hurriedly mounted to rejoin our companions, but our horses began to plunge and flounder over obstructions staked along the ground. In approaching the railway we had somehow or other missed these entanglements, but now we were in the thick of them, and the tins always attached to them were clanging and jangling, and increasing the terror of our animals. To this din was added a blaze of musketry from a block-house standing only a few yards away, which in the darkness we had mistaken for a mound of rocks.

Rifle-fire at point-blank range is unpleasant at the best of times, but when one is on a maddened horse staggering amid wire loops it is infinitely more so, and had there been even a glimmer of light to guide the soldiers we should both have been shot. It was so dark, however, that they were firing at the sounds, and not at us, and Verster managed to wrench his horse free, but mine was shot and I was nearly pinned underneath him. I undid the buckles of the girth, and dragged my saddle from under the prostrate animal and, stumbling over the rest of the obstructions, we got clear away to where the others stood whistling and shouting to us and anxiously watching, not daring to shoot for fear of killing us. I had left the Shetland pony with them when I went forward to the fence, so I now put my saddle on him, and we galloped off, leaving the soldiers firing blindly into the night. We made a half-moon, until we again reached the railway line, intending to have another try, but as soon as I began to use the file, we heard the sound of men running along the track towards us, so we lost no time in decamping, and abandoned all thought of crossing that night. We spent a cold night behind a kopje, and, when it grew light, we were nearer the English camp at Edenburg than we imagined. We had barely time to get our horses saddled before a hundred or more troopers came racing at us, but, riding fast, we got safely into the hills at Boomplaats, my Shetland pony going surprisingly well.

As the English horsemen turned back after a while, we halted by the little cemetery where those English soldiers lie buried who were killed at the battle here between Sir Harry Smith and the Boers, in 1848. This graveyard was of some personal interest to me, because it had almost caused my father the loss of his position as President of the Free State when I was a boy. The British Government many years before had erected headstones over the fallen soldiers inscribed with the words: 'Killed in action against the Rebel Boers'. Many of these stones, in course of time, fell to pieces, so my father ordered replicas with the original inscription faithfully copied. This gave rise to much ill feeling, for there were indignant patriots who considered the epithet 'Rebel' an insult to the Boers, and my father very nearly lost the next presidential election in consequence. I have another reason for remembering the Boomplaats cemetery, for while we were resting here, Field-Cornet Botha came to me and said that he and the other men had for some days been reconsidering the matter of continuing to the Cape Colony, and he now asked me to give up the plan. Apparently last night's affair and the chase of that morning had put the finishing touch to their indecision, and, with the exception of Bosman and myself, they all declared their intention of returning to the Winburg Mountains.

We two said that we had not ridden thus far to turn back now, and we told them that we were going to the Cape, even if we had to go alone. We argued and entreated for hours, but in the end Botha and his men, with my two German friends Haase and Pollatchek, saddled their horses and rode off, leaving us behind.

Bosman and I spent the night beside the graveyard, feeling too depressed to light a fire, and next morning we found our horses strayed out of sight. It took us the better part of five hours to trail their spoor, and when at last we got back to where we had left our saddles and other belongings, there was nothing there. This was a serious blow, for saddles were indispensable, and blankets and cooking-tins even more so. We could see from the hoof-marks that there were two mounted thieves, and although we could not say whether they were Boer or British, we decided to follow; them. After careful going, on our bare-backed horses, for ten miles or more, we saw two men seated beside a fire below a kopje, and, stalking them on foot came close enough to cover them with our rifles before they could stir. They proved to be two Boer boys from a neighbouring outpost, and they had all our missing gear beside them. They said that they thought the things belonged to English scouts, a palpable lie, and we told them plainly what we thought of them, but we did learn from them of a commando under General Hertzog lying in the hills beyond the Riet River forty or fifty miles away, and we decided to go there.

For two days we rode on, passing through the deserted mining town of Jagersfontein, and reaching the next village, Fauresmith, by sunset. This place had also been abandoned by its original inhabitants, but we found it occupied by men who were little better than bandits.

As we went up the main street a number of unkempt individuals rushed at us, rifle in hand, and ordered us to halt. They crowded round threateningly, with shouts of 'Maak dood die verdomde spioene' ('Kill the cursed spies'), although they must have known that we were nothing of the sort, and only wanted a pretext to rob us. We sat on our horses, uncertain what to do with such ugly customers, and it looked as if we were in for serious trouble, for already greedy hands were clutching at our wallets, and trying to pull us from our saddles. Just then two gaunt, famished-looking women rushed from a neighbouring house, and shrilly ordered them off. They had so much influence over the rabble, that they stood aside growlingly and allowed us to accompany our forbidding guardian angels to their home. They were the daughters of a once-wealthy farmer, ruined and killed during the war, and they had taken refuge in an empty house in the village, where they were living in poverty. They told us that the people who had molested us were riff-raff ejected from the fighting commandos, existing on what they could rob and loot. We now heard that General Hertzog's commando had moved west, so we took our leave next morning, and rode for two days in search of them, until we were right on the Griqualand border, where we met a solitary burgher, from whom we learned that we were a long way out of our course and that the commando was back on the Riet River. We turned northeast, and by dark of the following evening we crossed the river by the wagonbridge which, strange to say, was still intact. On the far bank was a cattle-post in charge of an old man and his two sons. They were looking after the meat supply of General Hertzog's men, lying, we were glad to hear, only ten miles upstream. As it was late, we spent the night with our hosts, an unsavoury trio, who did not belie their looks, for we found next morning that our saddlebags had been rifled. So I stood them in a line while Bosman went through their pockets and recovered our knives, tinder-boxes, and other property, after I had grazed the eldest ruffian's arm with a bullet to teach him better manners.

We then rode on, not particularly impressed by the specimens of Fauresmith men whom we had met thus far, for we had been the victims of three attempted robberies in less than a week. These men, however, were only off-scourings, and our subsequent association with the real fighting-men of the district was much happier.

By midday we came on General Hertzog's force, camped on the banks of the river at a place called Bethal. I knew General Hertzog from the old days, a thin high-cheeked man with angry eyes, though his speech was pleasant and I saw that his men held him ill great respect. He had been a Judge of the Supreme Court at Bloemfontein before the war, but was now in command of the southwestern districts of the Free State. He had with him about three hundred men, the largest commando that I saw on my passage through, and he had other smaller bodies scattered about.

We remained with the commando for ten days, hoping to gain recruits for the Cape, but not a man would come. They said once was enough, and every time we broached the subject we were met with emphatic refusals, and with tales of the privations and losses which they had sustained during the previous expeditions, so it began to look as if Bosman and I would have to go by ourselves after all. During the time spent with the commando we earned our keep by taking part in a sharp little affair in the hills above the Riet River wagon-bridge.

An English column, a thousand strong, crossed to our side of the river one night, on their way to Kimberley, and we held them up for two days, until at length they fell back over the bridge and returned by the way they had come.

General Hertzog lost only two killed and a few wounded, although the English rifle-fire was very heavy at times, and they had guns as well. On the afternoon of the second day, while two of us were riding down to a dam to water our horses, an English trooper came galloping towards us from round a kopje. He was plucky enough, for when he realized his mistake he fired from the saddle, from so close that before he could do so again I was alongside with my rifle in his ribs. He said that he had been scouting and had lost his way, and as my companion was barefooted, we relieved him of his boots, as well as his horse, and we left him gingerly picking his way over the sharp surface towards his own side, a thing I did not envy him, for he had to make a semicircle of several miles to get around our flank, before he could rejoin his companions.

When we found next morning that the English had withdrawn overnight, General Hertzog ordered us to return to our former halting-ground higher up the river, and here Bosman and I had good luck, for, off-saddled close by, was a small party of newcomers, ten in number, amongst whom I recognized several old acquaintances from the Transvaal, and to our great joy they told us that they were on their way into the Cape Colony. This was good news indeed, and we told them of our own plans at once.

As from now onward I was to be intimately associated with this little band, and as so many of them died tragically, I shall give their names:

The leader was Jack Borrius, a short thick-set man of twenty-eight, from Potchefstroom, whom I had met while serving with Captain Theron's scouts and in the 'A.C.C.' Next came Benjamin Coetzee, from Pretoria, whose reckless bravery had earned him a reputation as long ago as the Natal days, when I had known him as a member of the Pretoria commando. Then Nicolas Swart and Cornelius Vermaas, both sons of wealthy Transvaal farmers. Vermaas had been wounded and captured by the British six months before, but he had jumped from the train in the mountains near Capetown while being taken for shipment to Ceylon, and after many trials he had got back on foot to the Transvaal.

Next were Percy Wyndall and Edgar Duncker, two English-speaking boys from Johannesburg, and Frits Balogh, a young Austrian from Pretoria.

Then Jan van Zijl, illiterate but witty, and Piet de Ruyt, a Hollander, and lastly young Rittenberg, also from Potchefstroom.

They were all Transvaalers and, with the exception of Borrius, not one was yet twenty years old; and like myself, they had all been taken with the idea of free-lancing it into the Cape Colony.

By way of ironic comment on their tattered clothing and ragged appearance they called themselves the 'Rijk Section' (or 'Dandy Fifth', as Duncker translated it). Of this small band four were to meet their death by execution, and six were wounded or captured, a result that fully justified the many warnings which we had received against entering the Colony.

While we were discussing whether to try the Orange River in this vicinity or to take the advice we had received, and go east towards the headwaters, there arrived another party of horsemen, who decided us for the latter course.

These were Commandant George Brand and a score of followers from the south-eastern districts, come to confer with General Hertzog on military affairs.

He was a son of Sir John Brand, who had preceded my father as President of the Free State. He told me that as soon as he had finished with General Hertzog, he was returning east across the railway line to the area between the Caledon River and Basutoland, and when he heard or our intention to enter the Cape Colony he advised us to accompany him as far as the Caledon River, where the passage would be safer than here.

As we had already received similar advice, and as he assured us that we could get as many horses as we liked in the mountains, we agreed to travel with him.

The very next day, saying good-bye to Hertzog and his men, we set out and made such good progress that by the following afternoon we were back in the same hill over-looking Edenburg village from which we had started with our previous companions on our unsuccessful attempt to cross the railway line.

Now things went better, for we were with men who knew the exact position of every block-house and every sentry along the track, and by midnight we were over without a single casualty, although there was a good deal of firing from block-houses on either side of us as we went through.

The railway is regarded as the dividing line between the Western and Eastern Free State. To the west lie the great plains, while to the east the country grows more and more mountainous as one approaches the Basutoland border.

I knew this region quite well, having hunted here as a boy, so after sunrise we took our leave of Brand and his men, whose course lay in another direction, and we rode on for the next few days in the direction of the upper reaches of the Caledon River. Only once did we see an English column, to which we passed so close that we heard the bugles sound the alarm and saw the soldiers running for their horses; but after the exchange of a few shots, we went on our way.

Most of the livestock lay clubbed to death around the burnt farmhouses, and there was no sign of the civilian population, for those who had escaped capture were hiding in caves and gorges.

We did not see many fighting-men either, for they were dispersed in small guerrilla bands among the mountains.

Troops of wild horses were fairly common between Sikonyella's Peak and the Elandsberg, so we searched our a local outpost, and with their help were able to corral sufficient horses to give each of the 'Rijk Section' two fresh mounts, my own share being two spirited mares, a brown and a roan. The horses were entirely untrained, but in a few days we had them broken to bit and rein and our prospects were vastly improved, for the animals we had been riding thus far were in wretched condition. To these we gave their freedom, knowing that when they had picked up flesh they could be recaptured and used by others, and it was pleasant to see them trotting up the mountain-side to a well-earned rest, my little Shetland pony kicking up his heels and whinnying joyously at their head.

It was near the end of August (1901) by now, and the rainy season might be upon us at any moment, when a single freshet might render the Orange River impassable, so, as we were come to within fifteen miles of it, we made ready for our final effort.

Upon the very morning, however, on which we hoped to cross, a large body of horsemen appeared over the shoulder of a distant hill. By their formation and manner of riding we knew them to be Boers, but as there was no commando of that size round here, we waited for them with considerable interest. After an hour the column came abreast of us and we were astonished to see that at its head rode Mr. Smuts, the Transvaal State Attorney, now a General, who, after hearty greetings, told us that he was on his way to the Cape Colony with three hundred men.

This was another stroke of luck! Falling in with the 'Rijk Section' had been the first, but to meet with a whole commando making for the river was the greatest fortune of all, far greater than we realized at the time, for our subsequent experiences went to show that a small force like ours would not have lasted a week in the troublesome country beyond.

It was the finest commando with which I ever served. The rank and file were mostly keen young farmers from the Western Transvaal, the pick of de la Rey's fighting men, and in command of them was perhaps the one man in South Africa who could have led us through the perilous days to come.

General Smuts halted his men and ordered them to off-saddle. This gave me time to go among them, and I had another pleasant surprise, for I came on my Hollander uncle, Jan Mulder, whom I had not seen since that time in Natal, nearly two years before. I also found the General's brother-in-law, Krige, one of the few survivors of Isaac Malherbe's corporalship, who had been so badly wounded.

I learned from them of the great hardships and dangers which they had encountered on their way through the Free State. The English had wind of their intention to invade the Cape Colony and strenuous efforts were made to head them off. Large forces were hurried up from all sides, giving them no rest either night or day, and it was only by hard riding and hard fighting that they had escaped, with the loss of many men and horses.

From what I could gather, General Smuts proposed a flying raid into the central districts of the Cape, to test a large-scale invasion later on, in order to relieve the increasing pressure in the north.

Whether this was really his object I do not know, for he was an uncommunicative man, but at any rate here he was, and we were only too eager to go with him, whatever his plans might be. When we went to tell him that the 'Rijk Section' proposed joining his force he said he was very pleased, and he appointed us to be his scouts, a distinction which we accepted gladly, but for which we paid dearly an the long run.

20. WE GO INTO THE CAPE COLONY AND MEET WITH A WARM RECEPTION

"The adventures of this handful of resolute men led by General Smuts forms one of the most interesting episodes in the whole course of the guerrilla war."—The Times History, v, 302.

The place of our meeting with General Smuts and his commando was in sight of the little village of Sastron, about fifteen miles from the Orange River, and his intention was to march nearer that day, and cross during the night. By noon a start was made, and towards five in the evening we could see a dark line in front of us marking the gorge, at the bottom of which runs the river between high mountain walls.

Unfortunately this was not all that we saw. Our side of the canyon was held for miles in each direction by a cordon of British troops, stationed there to bar our way. Whenever a footpath led down the cliffs, there stood a tented camp, and the intervening ground was patrolled by strong bodies of mounted men who clearly knew of our coming.

On seeing this, General Smuts led us back into a range of hills, where we waited until next day, whilst men were sent in search of some neighbouring outpost to act as guides. At dusk a young officer named Louis Wessels arrived with fifty men, a hard-bitten crew, with whom he had been operating for over a year.

He reported enemy columns closing in on us from the rear, and said that unless we were able to effect a crossing that night, we should be trapped. He said, moreover, that the river was everywhere difficult, owing to the depth of the gorge and the perpendicular cliffs, but he had brought with him a veteran of the Basuto wars who knew of a path which might be practicable.

General Smuts decided to start at once, and in the falling dark our force rode out, accompanied by Wessels and his men, who agreed to enter the Colony with us we travelled on, hour after hour in the dark, over rough ground, and then, towards three in the morning, we caught a glint of white far below, where the Orange River boiled and eddied in its narrow channel. It was yet night when we commenced the final descent, but after toiling down the precipitous path to which our guide had brought us, and along which assuredly no other mounted troops had ever passed, we reached the edge of the water. In single file we began to cross the river, a strong and turbulent mountain torrent, not broad, but so swift that our horses could scarcely maintain their footing, and as dawn lit the cliffs above, the hindmost man was through, and I stood in the Cape Colony at last.

After a short halt we took a path that led to the top of the cliffs opposite, by a deep cleft, up which we tugged our leg-weary animals, until, far above, we emerged on a wide grass-covered tableland, pleasantly dotted with native villages and herds of cattle at pasture.

We were now actually on British territory, but the country here lies in an angle between the Free State, Basutoland, and Cape boundaries, and the region seemed exclusively occupied by Basutos, for there were no European habitations in sight.

As soon as we gained the top, we scattered into small parties, riding from one native village to another, in quest of tobacco and fodder for our horses. While we were thus ranging, a body of mounted Basutos, about three hundred strong, came moving swiftly towards us. Some were armed with rifles, others carried battle-axes, assegais and knob-kieries, which they brandished in the air as they approached. We did not know what to make of this, but we thought that they could not be contemplating an unprovoked attack on a white force equal to their own. General Smuts, therefore, contented himself with sending word for the various foraging parties to close in, and the commando continued on its way without paying much attention to the horsemen, who at a shouted word from their leader came to a halt on a knoll close by, where they sat their horses in silence, watching the Boers pass.

At this stage, my uncle and I, with five others whose names I did not know, lagged behind to feed our horses from the grain-baskets to be found in every native village, and as we were not frightened by the Basuto parade, which we put down to curiosity, we allowed the commando to get a considerable way ahead of us. At length, seeing that we were being left too far behind, we mounted and followed our men, the last of whom were just vanishing over the edge of the tableland by a road leading to the plain below.

By the time we could look down, the bulk of the commando was already at the bottom. They were riding along a road flanked on the left by a ledge of overhanging natural rock, part of the footwall of the tableland which they had just quitted, and on the right by a Mission Church and a long rubble fence, separating the road from fields and gardens. A force moving down this enclosed alleyway could be easily ambushed, and we were alarmed to see that the Basutos had left their horses above, and were scrambling down the final shelf of rock overhanging the road, crawling forward to the edge, to look straight down on our men riding unconsciously below. We expected to see them open fire on the crowded ranks at any moment. Indecision, however, came over the natives; they began nudging one another as if each wanted someone else to start shooting, and by the time that they had made up their minds the opportunity was gone, for the commando was already debouching from the confined space of the road into the open plain. My fellow-stragglers and I were worse off, for although the Basutos had hesitated to attack the larger force, their intentions were clearly hostile, and we wondered how they would deal with our little band left isolated in the rear.

After hurried consultation we decided to follow on, and attempt to catch up with the commando, so we began to descend the slope. We reached the bottom unmolested, but as we passed the church beside the road we caught sight of many dark faces pressed against the window-panes, and white eyeballs peering at us from within. Then came a deafening crash, as a volley was fired at us point-blank from the building, sending showers of splintered glass about our heads. Fortunately the native is a notoriously bad marksman, for he generally closes his eyes when he pulls the trigger, so not one of us was hit, although the range was under ten yards. When the Basutos lying on the rocky shelf overhanging the road heard the volley, they took courage and also opened fire. The five men with us did the only reasonable thing under the circumstances. They dug their spurs in and rode off as fast as they could, but my uncle with his usual impetuosity loosed his pack animal, swung his horse in behind a massive boulder that had calved from the ledge above, and jumped to the ground. I had to follow suit, relinquishing my own led-horse, and riding in behind the rock, a huge cube that leaned against the parent crag in such a manner as to give us cover against the Basutos overhead as well as from those firing through the shattered windows of the church across the way. We opened fire in turn at the church, but we saw at once that our position was untenable. Immediately above, the natives were excitedly shouting as they fired at our retreating companions, and at such of the rearmost commando men as were still within range.

Already we could hear the voices of several of them craning over to get at us from above. With some of the enemy standing on the roof, as it were, and others shooting from the church not fifteen yards off, we realized that to remain here could have only one ending, and we prepared to mount once more, although our chances of escape seemed desperate.

Looking down the road, we could now see only two of our men, riding for their lives across the fields, for they had succeeded in leaping the dividing wall. The other three men were nowhere to be seen, but two dead horses lay in the road, and a third was galloping riderless in the distance. This looked bad, but no other course was open to us, so we leapt into the saddle and rode out from the sanctuary of the fallen rock. The moment we did so, the natives in the church saw us, and redoubled their fire, while those on the bank above raised blood-curdling yells and also fired.

As we sped past, more natives rose from behind the fence lining the road. Fortunately these last were armed only with assegais and knobkerries, which came whirring about our ears. In this pandemonium we took every moment to be our last, but we ran the gauntlet safely for perhaps sixty yards, when the road fell suddenly into a deep spruit which neither of us had noticed in our excitement. It meant salvation although at first it looked as if it only meant more danger, for, riding down, we saw some fifteen or twenty natives squatted in a circle, intent upon something that lay on the ground between them. Before they could do more than spring to their feet and strike blindly at us, we were through. Instead of riding up the opposite bank of the spruit, where we should come under fire again, we galloped along the bed under cover of the high banks, until we were able to emerge out of range.

Of the five men who had been with us, the two whom we had seen making across country got clean away, but the other three were either killed on the road, and then dragged into the spruit, or else they were destroyed on reaching there, for we learned long after that their bodies were found on the causeway, dreadfully mutilated by the natives for medicine, in accordance with their barbarous custom. I have little doubt that when my uncle and I rode down amongst them, they were busy at their grisly task of dissection, which we ourselves so narrowly missed.

We were out of danger now, but the prospect was not reassuring. True, we had got off without a scratch, but our pack animals were gone with most of our gear, and looking over our saddle-horses. We were dismayed to find that they were both badly wounded. My brown mare had been hit by a jagged missile that had smashed her lower jaw, and my uncle's horse had a bullet through the crupper and another through the hind leg. I put my poor animal out of her misery at once, but my uncle thought that his might recover (which it did). I shouldered any saddle, and, leading the injured horse, we advanced on foot, dolefully speculating upon our future, for we had only a wounded horse and a handful of cartridges between us in this inhospitable country.

Far away we could see the commando posted on a ridge, to cover the retreat of those who were still in danger, for some of the men had been within range when the firing started on us at the church, and there were several wounded painfully making their way across the plain.

When at last we reached the commando and had time to look around, my uncle and I had a pleasant surprise, for there stood our two led-horses safe and sound, with our blankets and cooking-tins intact. They must have fled straight on when we loosed them on the road, and they had overtaken the commando while we were fighting below the shelf. Now they were contentedly ranged in line with the rest of the horses behind the hill, as if nothing out of the common had happened, so at any rate we still had a riding-horse apiece.

While we were halted here, we saw that another party of ten or twelve men was in difficulties. They, too, had got separated from our main body, while foraging on the table-land earlier in the morning, but no one had missed them until now when we heard the sound of distant firing and saw them riding into view two miles away, hotly pursued by numbers of mounted Basutos.. They were in grave danger, for between them and ourselves ran a deep ravine, towards which they were being shepherded, and as the ravine seemed impassable, it looked for a time as if we should have to stand by helpless and see them killed.

In order to do what we could, the whole commando mounted and rode to the edge of the chasm, and here, fortunately, we found a piece of high ground from which we over-looked the scene on the other side, and were able to drop our bullets among the advancing natives with such good effect that they reined in. This gave the cornered men time to search the cliff for a way down, which they succeeded in finding under cover of our fire, and ultimately they rejoined us without casualties.

This final episode reduced my ammunition to four rounds, and indeed many of the rest were no better off, for the long chase to which they had been subjected during their dash through the Free State had depleted their bandoliers to such an extent that the question was becoming a very serious one for a column such as ours, starting to invade hostile territory.

After this we halted for an hour to give the wounded men a rest, and to enable those whose horses had been killed to get remounted. There were seven men hit, and, as we had no lint, bandages, or medical supplies, there was little that we could do for them.

After a while the injured men were placed in their saddles, and we trekked away, with several bands of natives hovering in our rear, as if they contemplated a further attack, but in the end they retired. After a wearisome ride we got beyond the area of the Native Reserve, and towards afternoon we came across the first European farmhouse, where we left our wounded to be fetched in by the British.

We rested our exhausted animals till dusk, and then, saying good-bye to the wounded men in the house, we rode on for five or six miles before camping.

For months past we had experienced an unbroken spell of fine weather, bitterly cold at night, but cloudless sunshine by day. Now, however, there was a change, and it came on to rain heavily, so that we spent the long hours of darkness dismally lying in mud and water. This weather, coming on top of the crowded events of the last twenty-four hours, gave us our first taste of what was awaiting us in the Cape Colony, and thus early we began to appreciate the fact that our road was likely to be a thorny one.

Next morning the sky cleared somewhat, although a penetrating drizzle continued for most of the day, through which we rode shivering, our thin clothing being but little protection. My own wardrobe was typical; a ragged coat and worn trousers full of holes, with no shirt or underwear of any kind. On my naked feet were dilapidated rawhide sandals, patched and repatched during eight months of wear, and I had only one frayed blanket to sleep under at night. Few of the men were better off, and we looked with apprehension on the change of weather, for it meant that the rainy season was upon us, with its attendant hardships, the full extent of which we were yet to learn.

Our course during this day took us through more settled parts, and for the first time we looked at farms and homesteads untouched by the hand of war. There were men peacefully working in the fields, and women and children standing unafraid before their doors as we passed, a very different picture from that to which we were accustomed in the devastated republics.

The people were almost exclusively of Dutch origin so they gave us unselfish hospitality. In the matter of clothing they were hardly able to assist us, on account of the military embargo which prevented them from buying more than certain quantities, but gifts of coffee, sugar, salt and tobacco were ungrudgingly made, and the first slice of bread and butter and the first sip of coffee I had tasted for a year almost made the long journey worth while.

In spite of the bad weather, our first day among a friendly population was a pleasant experience, which put the men in good spirits, and I dare say we posed a little before the womenfolk, laughing and whistling as we rode along.

Our course, later in the afternoon, took us up a mountain-pass, and when we reached the top towards evening, we could see in the distance the comfortable hamlet of Lady Grey nestling to the left, while in a glen below was the old familiar sight of a British column, crawling down the valley. This gave us no anxiety, for, being without wheeled transport of any kind, we turned across the heath and easily left the soldiers far behind.

That night it rained again, and a cold wind drove against us from the south. Our commando presented a strange appearance as we wound along; we had no raincoats, so we used our blankets as cloaks against the downpour, and the long line of draped horsemen looked like a tribe of Red Indians on the warpath.

Long after dark we came to a halt, spending a wretched wet night, and at dawn, cold and miserable, we trekked over bleak country, the biting wind in our faces, until at four in the afternoon we came to rest near a place ominously called Moordenaar's Poort (The Murderer's Way). The rain how ceased, and a passing herdboy having told us that English troops were camped a few miles off, General Smuts decided to go and see them for himself. He took with him two young Freestaters who had joined him on the way down, and another man named Neethling from Pretoria an old friend of mine. With these he left, saying that he would be back by dark. At sunset he had not returned, and for hours we anxiously waited for him until, shortly before midnight, he walked in among us on foot and alone. He had been ambushed by a British patrol, who had killed all three of his escort and all the horses, he alone escaping down a nullah. Had he been killed I believe that our expedition into the Cape would have come to a speedy end, for there was no one else who could have kept us together. The commando was divided into two portions commanded by Jacobus van Deventer (later Sir Jacobus van Deventer in the Great War) and Ben Bouwer respectively, both good fighting-men but neither of them possessing the personality or the influence over men that General Smuts had, to save us from going to pieces during the difficult period upon which we were now entering.

We spent the night where we lay, and there was more trouble before daylight, for a porcupine came grunting through our lines, with the result that the horses stampeded in a body. They thundered off in the dark, crashing through fences and undergrowth in blind terror, and at sunrise there was not an animal to be seen.

With an English force in the vicinity this was a serious predicament, for they would make short work of us if we were dismounted, so all hands turned out to hunt for the horses. Luckily a few of the men had hobbled their mounts, which prevented them from going as far as the rest, and as these were run to earth in a hollow not far away, they were used to track the others, and after three or four uneasy hours, expecting to see the English appear at any moment, we brought back all the missing horses safe and sound.

We now travelled on for the next three days across windy barrens, heading south-west. The weather grew more and more tempestuous as we went, and we suffered severely from the cold, and from the intermittent rains that accompanied us. Both horses and men began to show signs of distress. The animals looked thin and gaunt, and the man sat on their saddles pinched, shivering, and despondent, for South Africans are peculiarly susceptible to the depressing effects of bad weather. They can stand cold and other hardships as well as anyone, but continued lack of sunshine soon makes them miserable, and for the time being we were a dispirited band, wishing we had never come.

By day we were wet and cold, and the nights were evil dreams. Dry fuel was almost unprocurable, and after a weary day we had to spend the hours of darkness cowering together to snatch a little sleep on some muddy mountainside, or in an equally sodden valley.

Soon we were losing horses freely, and not a trek was made without some wretched animals being left behind with tuckered flanks and drooping heads, waiting for the end.

We had three days of this, but our real troubles were only beginning.

Towards sunset one evening we came in sight of the village of Jamestown, and saw a strong English column to our right, so General Smuts moved us on. It grew pitch-dark, and a driving rain smote straight in our faces. The night was so black that it was impossible to see even the man immediately before one, and the cold so bitter that we became stiff and numbed, and it was only with difficulty that we could drag our horses along, for we were ordered to go on foot to husband their strength.

When I was crossing a spruit, my sandals stuck in the heavy pot-clay and came to pieces when I tried to withdraw them, and it was only by cutting corners from my blanket and wrapping one about each foot that I was able to go on at all. Our guide, a young man from a local farm, had lost his bearings, so we had to grope our way through icy rain for five hours, until we could continue no longer, and stood huddled together ankle-deep in mud and water, praying for sunrise.

When it grew light, over thirty horses lay dead from exposure, besides others abandoned overnight, and our spirits, low before, were at zero now.

The rain continued pitilessly until midday, when the sky cleared and the blessed sun shone upon us once more. We moved forward, and not far away saw a large farmhouse and outbuildings containing plenty of fuel. Soon we were warming our numbed bodies, and cooking our first hot meal for days.

The housewife at the farm gave me a pair of old-fashioned elastic-sided boots, and I unearthed an empty grain-bag in which I cut a hole for my head, and one at each corner for my arms, thus providing myself with a serviceable greatcoat. My appearance caused much laughter, but I noticed that during the next few days, whenever we passed a barn, grain-bags were in great demand, and soon many of the men were wearing them.

As the people here told us that there was an English force in the neighbourhood, we moved on later in the afternoon, first saying good-bye to Louis Wessels, the young Free State officer and his men, who turned back from here as they had only come thus far to see our force well launched into the Colony. I believe that they reached their own country again in safety.

We continued for an hour, and then halted in a valley. Whilst we were idly resting in the grass two field-guns banged at us from a hill, and shells came tearing overhead. More followed and, taken by surprise, we leaped into the saddle and made for the cover of a line of hills to the rear.

The artillery was poor, and neither man nor horse was hit.

Once in safety, we put our animals out of harm's way, and climbed up to see what the English meant to do. We could now see a column of horse coming down towards us, around a spur that had previously hidden them from view.

There were about six hundred of them, and they had with them two fifteen-pounder Armstrong guns, and several pom-poms which unlimbered and opened fire, while their horsemen cautiously approached us. After a time they quickened pace as though to attack, but coming under our fire, they took cover behind some farmhouses and kraals.

In spite of the shelling, and a lively exchange of rifle-fire, there were apparently no casualties on either side, and the affair terminated after dark. I did not fire a shot on account of the state of my cartridge belts, and the others fired no more than was necessary to stave off the enemy, because, as I said before, the ammunition question was an exceedingly serious one.

When the light went out we withdrew to a farm close by, hoping for a real rest this time as we had not enjoyed a full night's sleep since we crossed the Orange River, more than a week before.

We did not get that night's rest, for at three o'clock next morning we were ordered up in the dark, and started in a cold drizzle of rain on a record march. Our men were weakened by long privations, our ammunition had dwindled to vanishing-point, and our horses were in the last stages of exhaustion, yet during the next six days, beset on all sides, we marched and fought, and in the end successfully got through.

21. HORSES AND MEN

When the sun rose and the rain ceased, we found ourselves crossing a high shoulder of land with a wide expanse of mountains to the south of us, and there, in every valley and on every road, stood the white tents of English camps, to bar our progress.

General Smuts surveyed the blocking forces for a while, and then led us due east across the front of the enemy posts. Our road took us through rough country and he ordered every man to go on foot to spare the horses. The English made no attempt to come after us, their orders apparently being to hold the roads and exits, so we trekked all day, seeking to turn their extreme right flank. Throughout the expedition into the Cape we had no difficulty in getting local sympathizers to act as guides, and on this occasion a young farm-hand volunteered to lead us. He picked his way so unerringly that towards nightfall we had not only succeeded in finding the end of the British line, but had even got round behind them, and could see the town of Dordrecht in the distance. We must have covered nearly thirty miles since getting out that morning, but as we were not yet out of danger of being headed back, we continued after dark, and, hungry and weary but in good cheer, we trudged all through the night, with only an occasional halt, mostly along steep mountain paths, wet and slippery from the rains. When daybreak came our young guide had done his work with such skill that we were well beyond the cordon, and there now lay before us the long mountain chain of the Stormbergen, stretching east to west as far as the eye could see. He told us that we could cross almost anywhere, so he was allowed to return home, and we made for a large farm lying at the foot of the range, where we turned our horses into the fields, and set about preparing a meal, once again hoping to spend the rest of the forenoon in sleep, for we had been on the move for twenty-four hours. But we had scarcely slaughtered a few sheep and broken our fast, when the well-known cry of 'Opsaal! Opsaal!' sent us scurrying to fetch our unfortunate animals; for coming down the slopes was a long column of English horse making our way. Near by ran a pass up the mountain, and as it seemed clear of troops, we made for it, and in an hour stood on the top of the Stormbergen, with the enemy force slewed round and following us. The summit was a grassy tableland about three miles wide, sloping gently to where the southern face of the mountain fell abruptly down to the plains below.

There was no sign of troops up here, but as those in the rear were coming after us, General Smuts disposed his men to hold them back while we of the 'Rijk Section' were ordered to ride forward to the far edge of the plateau, to see whether the way in that direction was clear. We set out in couples, making for different points from which to look down on the Karoo. My companion was Henry Rittenberg, and when we reached the rim of the plateau we saw the narrow ribbon of a railway track winding across the plain at our feet, with train after train steaming up to a small village station and disgorging large numbers of soldiers.

The British, having failed to stop us at their first barrier, were now hurrying troops round by rail to establish a second, and already several mounted columns had detrained, and were beginning to climb up the mountain.

One body was so far advanced that their scouts were appearing on the table-land itself, so Rittenberg and I rode nearer to examine their strength. We had not gone half a mile when some two dozen troopers rode at us from behind a roll in the ground, firing from the saddle as they came. We whipped round and galloped away, but had not the balance of the 'Rijk Section' come to our aid we should have been shot or captured, for there was no cover in which to make a stand, and our horses were in no fit state to compete with the well-fed English chargers.

We now returned to General Smuts, to report what we had seen, and he looked grave enough, for, with the original column of that morning closing in behind and all those fresh troops coming up in front, we were almost invested.

A strong north wind, which had sprung up earlier in the day, had steadily increased to a violent gale, and most of the men were crouching with their backs to the storm to escape the flying grit that stung like buckshot.

General Smuts, with Commandants van Deventer and Bouwer, was, however, on the look-out, standing well forward near the head of the pass up which the commando had come. While we were explaining the situation, about three hundred soldiers appeared on foot, having left their horses below. They did not seem to be expecting us here, or, for, when our men sprang up at a shout from van Deventer, they turned and ran back.

They were out of sight almost at once, and when we reached the edge we saw them scrambling down, but the wind in our faces made accurate shooting impossible, and I do not think any were hit. The soldiers only fired a few shots in reply, and a young man standing near me, named de la Rey, a nephew of General de la Rey, threw up his arms and dropped dead with a bullet through his brain. We left him where he fell, for we had no spade or other implement, nor had we time to bury him, for looking back we could now see more and more English horsemen emerging on the tableland, until we were practically encircled, although they were not yet strong enough to prevent us from moving freely inside the wide ring that they had formed about us.

Nevertheless we could not break out, for soon there were machine-guns at every point of vantage, so commanding the terrain that a burst-through during daylight would have cost us more men than we could afford, and our only course was to try to stave off the pressure until after dark. To that end, with the gale roaring about our ears, General Smuts led us hither and thither all the afternoon, now pushing back one portion of the enemy line, and then another, avoiding the machine-gun fire by using dead ground, and generally preventing them from hustling us too closely. With our tired horses and men the strain was great. Ammunition was at such a low ebb that some had not a round left, and when, towards evening, many more troops had come up our case seemed hopeless.

We and our horses had marched for forty hours on end, and we were all but finished for lack of sleep and rest, while the noose around us had slowly tightened, until by dusk we were at bay around a small farmhouse and kraal, lying somewhat in a hollow, where for the moment we had comparative shelter, but where our speedy capture seemed certain.

When the English troops saw us preparing to make a stand they stayed their advance, in the belief, no doubt, that having cornered us, they could afford to wait for our surrender in the morning.

General Smuts stood before the homestead in whispered consultation with his two lieutenants, while the rest of us leaned on our rifles, too weary to care very much what happened. Then out of the house came a hunchbacked cripple, who said that he would lead us through the English troops to the edge of the tableland, by a way which was unlikely to be watched, for it ran through boggy soil. His offer was eagerly accepted and orders were given to mount at once. six or seven men had been wounded during the day, two of them so badly that they had to be left behind, but the others chose to accompany us, and in a few minutes we were silently filing off into the darkness, the cripple crouching insecurely on a horse at our head. He took us along a squelching path, that twisted for a mile or two so close to the investing troops that we could hear voices and the champing of bits, but at the end of an anxious hour he had brought us undiscovered to the escarpment. From here the mountain-side fell sharply away into black depths below, how steeply we could not tell, but our guide warned us that it was very steep indeed. Dropping from his horse, he plodded off into the night on his crutches, carrying with him our heartfelt thanks, for he had risked his life and goods on our behalf.

We now began to descend what was probably the nearest approach to the vertical attempted by any mounted force during the war. I doubt whether we could have accomplished it by day, but horses are more tractable and surer-footed in the dark, so we pulled them over the edge and went slithering down. At times whole batches of men and horses came glissading past, knocking against all in their course, but luckily the surface was free of rock, and covered with a thick matting of grass which served to break the impact, and after a terrible scramble we got down without serious damage. For the time being we had shaken free of the enemy once more. Our most insistent need now was sleep, but this was still denied us.

Somewhere on the plain before us ran the railway line on which we had looked down that morning, and many miles beyond that lay still another track, both of which had to be crossed before sunrise, if we did not wish to have the troop-trains hurrying up more men. So General Smuts implacably ordered us on, and, leading our horses, we tramped obediently but wearily forward, little dreaming that another twenty hours of unbroken marching lay before us, and several days of even greater trials to come.

It was about ten o'clock by now, and the storm that had been raging throughout the day was subsiding, though the aftermath still blew cold, a blessing perhaps, for it served to keep us awake, and it made us step out to keep warm. After an hour we reached the first railway, a branch line from the Indwe Coal Mines. As we approached we saw the lights of a train, but General Smuts would not allow us to pile boulders on the metals nor to fire as the engine thundered by, for fear of killing civilians, so we stood aside, catching a glimpse of officers and others seated in the dining-car, smoking and taking wine, all unaware of the men looking at them from the darkness. General French, the English cavalry leader, told us long after that he was on board that train with his staff, hurrying round by rail to control operations on the berg where he imagined us still to be, so unknowingly we missed a great opportunity.

After crossing the rails, we went on mile after mile, dazed for want of rest. Whenever there was delay at a fence or a ditch, whole rows of men would fall asleep on their hands and knees before their horses like Mohammedans at prayer, and it was necessary to go round shaking them to their feet to prevent them being left behind. Save for occasional halts we continued thus all night, for it was imperative to cross the remaining railway. As we had no guide we travelled by the stars, and the sun was rising before we struck it at a small siding about five miles east of Sterkstroom village, where, from the activity at the station, it was obvious that our escape from the mountain was known. Several trains were unloading troops, and there was no time to be lost. So mounting, we galloped as fast as we could across the rails for fear an armoured train might cut us off.

Commandant van Deventer and a few of us remained behind to search the railway buildings for anything that might come in useful, and while we were busy at this a long goods-train came clanking up, and we brought it to a standstill by switching the points. It was an empty coal train in charge of a driver, stoker, and brakesman, whose faces were a picture when they saw what we were doing. As the train consisted of nothing but incombustible steel trucks, we let them proceed, after extracting a mail-bag from the guard's van. The letters were all private ones, seemingly written under censorship, for not one of them made any reference to the war, but the newspapers were less reticent, and in one of them was unflattering mention of ourselves, for it said that General Smuts had invaded the Cape Colony 'with the riff-raff of the Boer Armies', which caused much merriment when later on I was able to read it to the men.

There was another surprising feature in the mail-bag in the shape of a Proclamation by Lord Kitchener, wherein every burgher under arms after the 15th of September was sentenced to perpetual banishment from South Africa. This was news to us, and seeing that it was the 13th of that month by now, we were left with a bare two days in which to comply. This announcement was received with equal derision, when made known to the commando, and from what I have heard since, it had equally little effect up north in the Republics where the 'paper bomb', as it was called, got treated with the scorn it deserved.[6] After speeding the goods-train on its way, we overtook the commando at the Klaas Smits River, where we halted for about an hour, to give our poor horses a chance to pluck a few mouthfuls of grass, and to prepare a hasty meal for ourselves. Longer than that we were not given, for a column of troops with guns came up, and kept us on the move all day, slowly retiring from hill to hill, half dead with fatigue, but keeping them at arm's length until sunset, when they turned back and left us free to camp at last at a large farm, where we lay like dead men until morning after sixty hours of continuous marching.

This full night's rest was a great relief, but the strain was by no means over, and the worst was yet to come.

Towards nine o'clock next day, an English column appeared from the direction of Sterkstroom, so we saddled up and rode away, skirting the base of some hills running south. The column contented itself with following us slowly, apparently having been sent to keep us under observation, and they dogged our steps until sunset, when it came on to rain and we saw them go into camp. We halted in a patch of thorn trees and, as it poured heavily till dawn, we had another of those wet and miserable nights which had been so frequent since our entry into the Colony.

Daylight saw the troops once more coming after us, and, owing to the shortage of ammunition and the condition of our horses, we had no option but to give way. The going was heavy, and at times the swollen spruits and dongas held us up, but we were in no great danger of being overhauled, for the column had wagons and guns, which impeded them so much that we had miles to spare.

In the afternoon the English camped again, and we halted for the rest of the day at a small farmhouse standing out on the plain. The rain had ceased since morning, but it was cold and threatening; black clouds hung low in the sky, and there was every promise of more dirty weather to come.

We could see smoke curling from the English camp four miles behind, where whole streets of comfortable tents had sprung up, at which we gazed wistfully, for there were warmth and rest, whilst we stood shivering in the biting wind,

---

[6] *The Times History says of this Proclamation, Vol. V, 321: Lord Kitchener made his first and last attempt to end the war by a minatory proclamation. It began by giving in a solemn legal preamble an account of the military situation, which must have seemed strangely unconvincing to the Boers, and which, it must be confessed, was replete with unconscious humour. The fourth paragraph in particular where the Boers were informed that they were incapable of carrying on regular warfare was a strange tissue of perverted logic.... The operative art of the Proclamation demanded the surrender of all Boers before September 15th under pain of stringent penalties. The results were not encouraging: Botha, Steyn and de Wet sent defiant replies, and among the burghers at large there was a sullen silence.*

wondering how it was all to end. The English numbered about a thousand, and it was useless to attempt an attack in our present condition, for we were wet, cold, and in low spirits, and our ammunition was almost finished. So, when darkness fell, General Smuts gave orders for us to saddle up, intending to make for a larger farm where there was said to be ample shelter.

As we started, hard rain came down once more, and the darkness was so intense that we could not see a yard ahead. We had not gone three hundred paces before we heard horsemen splashing through the mud in front, and ran into the tail of an English patrol or column, we could not tell which, evidently making for the same farm.

Neither side was prepared to risk a fight in the rain and dark. The troopers galloped away, and we sheered off, too, but with this difference, that they were able to continue on to the shelter of the farm, whilst we were adrift on the open veld.

The night that followed was the most terrible of all. Our guide lost his way; we went floundering ankle-deep in mud and water, our poor weakened horses stumbling and slipping at every turn; the rain beat down on us, and the cold was awful. Towards midnight it began to sleet. The grain-bag which I wore froze solid on my body, like a coat of mail, and I believe that if we had not kept moving every one of us would have died. We had known two years of war, but we came nearer to despair that night than I care to remember. Hour after hour we groped our way, with men groaning who had never before uttered a word of complaint, as the cold searched their ill-protected bodies. We lost fourteen men that night, and I do not know whether they survived, but we never again had word of them.

We also lost a large number of horses, and I remember stumbling at intervals over their carcasses. We went on till daybreak, dragging ourselves along, and then, providentially, came on a deserted homestead and staggered into shelter, standing huddled together in rooms, stables, and barns until dawn, still shivering, but gradually recovering from the dreadful ordeal. When it grew light, some fifty or sixty horses lay dead outside. My little roan mare was still alive, but both my uncle's horses died here, and he, with thirty or forty more, was now a foot-soldier. [7]

This night's 'Big Rain', as we named it, left such a mark on all of us that later we used to call ourselves 'The "Big Rain" Men' (*Die Groot Reent Kerels*) to distinguish us from those who had not experienced it, and for my part I passed through no greater test during the war.

The day was cold and wild, but the rain stopped. We broke up the floors and windows, tables and chairs, and everything else that would burn, and made great fires to dry our clothes and blankets, and to warm our chilled limbs. Towards noon, General Smuts ordered us on to another large farm, eight or nine miles away, which had, a native told him, plenty of fodder for the horses.

---

[7] *As practically every man had crossed the Orange River with two horses, the number of dismounted men did not necessarily correspond to the number of horses that were lost.*

No attempt was made to send back for the missing men, because we were too exhausted, and they had to be abandoned.

We plodded over the waterlogged country, a quarter of our number on foot, and the rest soon likely to be, for there was not a fit horse in the commando.

We found this farm also deserted, but there was protection for all, and a good store of oat-sheaves, as well as sheep for slaughter, so that, although the rain came down again, we at last spent a comfortable night.

Although we had managed to avoid the different cordons thrown in our way and had eluded the columns sent in pursuit, we were not yet out of danger, for local natives now told us that southward every road, valley, and outlet was blocked by English troops. This meant that they were once more trying to head us back out of the Cape; but, with so many enemies in our rear, our only alternative was to go forward. Next morning, we set out on what was to be an eventful day (September 17th, 1901).

Our road ran south down a long valley. The sky was clear, and the sun warm and bright for the first time for weeks, so that the men were cheerful again, although there was little other cause for optimism.

As a fighting force we were on our last legs. In front walked those who still had horses, dragging scarecrows behind them; then came a trail of footmen in twos and threes, their saddles slung across their shoulders, and in the rear rode the wounded in charge of their friends.

However, the sun was shining after the wet and cold and we went hopefully along. After a few miles General Smuts ordered the 'Rijk Section' to scout ahead of the commando, so those of us who still had horses mounted and rode forward as fast as our weakened animals could carry us. When we got to where the valley widened into more open country, a Dutch farmer rushed from a cottage beside the road and, in a voice hoarse with excitement, told us that English cavalry were waiting for us lower down. He said that they had mountain- and machine-guns, and he estimated their strength at two hundred men, with over three hundred horses and mules, all of which proved substantially correct.

Edgar Duncker was sent back to report, and before long he returned with General Smuts, accompanied by Commandant van Deventer and a dozen men. General Smuts immediately decided to attack, and I heard him say that if we did not get those horses and a supply of ammunition we were done for. He ordered van Deventer forward with the men who were with him and the 'Rijk Section', to locate the British force, while he himself waited here to bring up the rest of the commando. We set off at once, and in a few minutes reached the banks of a small river which we crossed. As we were going through the fringe of thorn trees on the other side, we rode straight into fifteen or twenty troopers cantering towards us. Most of our men were still among the trees, but four or five of us were in advance, and when we leaped to the ground the soldiers were not more than ten yards away. Opening fire, we brought down several, and the rest turned and galloped back along the road. I fired my last two cartridges here, and my first thought was to run to a dead soldier and seize his rifle and bandolier, abandoning my own rusty weapon, then I rushed for my mare and joined in the chase.

The troop-horses were in much better condition than ours, but the soldiers were delayed by a gate, so we got close again, dropping two or three more from the saddle.

At the gate van Deventer himself and half a dozen men turned aside to a kopje for observation, but the rest of us, about twelve in number, followed the retiring patrol to a low stony ridge farther down the road.

They got there several lengths ahead of us and, abandoning their horses, took to the rocks. It was too late for us to retire back across the open plain behind, so we galloped on.

Before we reached their outcrop the soldiers opened fire almost point-blank, and worse still, a mountain-gun unexpectedly fired on us from a point to our left, not thirty yards off, and a machine-gun rattled into action close by.

So near was the mountain-gun that smoke from the discharge billowed over us although the shells went wide. It was astonishing that any of us escaped, but, owing no doubt to our sudden appearance behind the flying patrol, the firing was wild, and only three men and some horses went down before we reached the rocks in which the soldiers were. Here we, in turn, loosed our horses and ran up, to find ourselves within a few feet of our original quarry and a number of others, who had been posted here before.

Now that we could look over to the far side, we were surprised to see a large English camp less than a stone's throw away, buzzing like a disturbed ant-heap. Officers were shouting orders, and men tumbling out of their tents, some running towards us; others going to the right and left to take their stations.

This placed us in a remarkably tight corner, as we were so far ahead of our main body that they could not help us, for the English, having recovered from their first surprise, were sweeping the plain with gun and rifle-fire. The result was that our little party was stranded on the very edge of an armed encampment, and practically mixed with the English soldiers. Fortunately General Smuts had hurried the commando on, and in a few minutes they opened fire from a hill in the rear, thus preventing us from being overwhelmed, for our opponents were forced to take cover and could not surround us.

Those before us were in rough alignment along the bank of the ledge, so we were able to form a similar front, with a space of two or three yards separating us, while along the perimeter of the camp lay the rest of the troops in a half-moon. A young Transvaaler named Muller and I lay at the end where the rocks ran dead, and from here we could see the mountain-gun close by, busy shelling our commando. The gunners could not fire on us as they would have to hit their own men, and in any case they did not seem to realize that we were so near, for they were unconcernedly loading and firing at our men on the hill six hundred yards back. Standing behind the gun was a tall man handing shells to the three at the breech. I fired at him, and he spun round and sank in a sitting position against the wheel, where I found him dead when the fight was over. The other three ran for the camp at their backs. I fired at one, and he pitched forward dead, while Muller brought down a third, but the last man got away among the tents. Having disposed of the gun-crew in a matter of seconds we turned to the other work on hand. The place we were fighting in was an outcrop of loose rocks, jutting up like a reef, nowhere much higher than a man, although the rear slope fell somewhat more steeply into the English camp. In this narrow space, where we were facing each other almost at handshake, a grim duel began. As the soldiers raised their heads to fire we brought them down, for they were no match for us in short-range work of this kind, and we killed twelve or thirteen and wounded several more, at a distance of a few yards. We did not suffer a single casualty, except for the three men hit as we rode in. Of these, one was Edgar Duncker with a bullet through his foot, and another, a Jew named Cohen, with a smashed ankle. These two had been able to crawl forward to the firing-line and were taking part in the attack, but the third man, Raubenheimer (a brother of Vera, Countess of Cathcart), lay out in the open with his thigh broken, and his dead horse pinning him down.

Before he could reach his men, I hit a sergeant who came running up from the camp, a big heavily built man. He doubled up like a knife, and rolled about, shot in the stomach; then he died.

Nicolas Swart by my side shot two other soldiers in quick succession, as they tried to join those in the rocks. There was a young lieutenant a few feet from me. I found out afterwards that his name was Sheridan, and they said he was a cousin of Winston Churchill. Twice he rose to fire at me and missed, at his second attempt I grazed his temple, and he dropped out of sight, but only dazed, for in a moment he was up again, swaying unsteadily on his feet, with his face streaming with blood, but still trying to level his rifle at me. While I was hesitating what to do, Jack Borrius shot him through the brain. Another soldier fired several hasty rounds at me, and I put a bullet into his heel, which was protruding from behind the rock near which he was lying. The sudden shock made him leap up, and again Jack Borrius, who was wonderfully quick, shot him dead as he rose.

In this manner the fight went on, until a mile beyond the camp we saw a small force of English troops approaching from the south. There were not many of them, but for all we knew they were the advance-guard of a relief force and, should sufficient reinforcements arrive to drive off our commando, those of us here in the rocks would be marooned, so we decided to clear the rocks by charging. After a whispered consultation from man to man, Jack Borrius gave the signal, and, rising together, we leaped in among the surviving soldiers. There were only ten or fifteen left, and so far as I can remember not a shot was fired on either side. Our sudden onslaught took them unprepared, and they surrendered at once. Without troubling about our prisoners we ran down shouting and cheering into the camp, before the rest of the defenders knew what had happened. When they saw us among the tents in their rear, something like a stampede set in. Soldiers went running in all directions, some making away into the thorn trees, others coming towards us and throwing down their arms. One man rushed to the horselines, and mounting barebacked, flourished a revolver and tried to ride off. I shouted to him to halt, but as he gave no heed I shot him dead. When the commando saw us enter the camp, they came galloping across, and the fight was over.

I took part in a final episode, for William Conradi and I, walking through a patch of trees to disarm some soldiers, came on a stone cattle-kraal, in which a dozen men were holding out. When we looked into the kraal, they were leaning on their rifles on the far wall and firing at some of our commando men moving in the distance. We called out 'Hands up! Hands up!' but they turned instead and blazed a volley into our faces. Only our eyes were showing or we should both have been shot.

Conradi killed one man and wounded another with a single bullet, and I wounded one, but even now they did not surrender, for, rushing across the kraal, they ranged themselves against the near wall, which alone separated us, and one of them thrust his rifle so near my face that his shot scorched my cheek and neck with cordite, fragments of which had to be picked out for days afterwards with the point of a knife. When I seized the muzzle he gave an oath and jerked it back so forcibly that the sharp foresight gashed the ball of my thumb and the palm of my hand, and I had to let go.

The situation was fast becoming dangerous, when, to our relief, we heard the sound of voices through the trees, and a number of our men came running up to see what the firing was about. The soldiers now threw their rifles over the wall, but even this was not the end, for, as I hastened round to the entrance of the kraal to receive the prisoners, I collided with a soldier who came crouching along to get us in the flank. He did not know that the fight was over, and if I had not rammed him when I did, in another moment he would have been round the corner, shooting us down while we were engaged with the men inside. He said I was a 'surprise packet', offered me a cigarette, and came with me to join his captured companions in the kraal with his hand amicably on my shoulder. The whole incident had not lasted five minutes, but it had been sharp enough, and Conradi and I reckoned ourselves well out of it as we hastened back to the camp to take part in the looting. The commando was up and there was a great ransacking of tents and wagons. The small relieving force that had given us cause for alarm turned out to be only a patrol, and it had the doubtful satisfaction of watching us from afar as we turned the camp inside out.

When we had done we were like giants refreshed. We had ridden into action that morning at our last gasp, and we emerged refitted from head to heel. We all had fresh horses, fresh rifles, clothing, saddlery, boots and more ammunition than we could carry away, as well as supplies for every man.

Moreover, we had renewed confidence in our leader and in ourselves, a factor of considerable importance to a body of men in a hostile country.

In the fight we lost only one man, who was killed when we rushed the camp, and six wounded, whereas the enemy had thirty killed, many wounded, and many taken prisoners.

I did not count the number of soldiers opposed to us, but there must have been about two hundred. They belonged to the 17th Lancers, one or the crack regiments of the British Army. Among their wounded was their Commander,

Captain Sandeman, and Lord Vivian, whom I found among the rocks where we first rushed them. He it was who told me the fate of the three men killed and mutilated by the Basutos, the day that we crossed the Orange River. He pointed out his little bivouac tent, and said that it would be worth my while to have a look at it. I was not slow to take the hint, with the result that having started that morning with a grain-bag for my chief garment, a foundered horse, an old rifle, and two cartridges I now appeared in a handsome cavalry tunic, riding-breeches, etc., with a sporting Lee-Metford, full bandoliers and a superb mount, a little grey Arab, which his coloured groom said had been the property of Lieutenant Sheridan.

I also selected a strong riding-mule in preference to another horse, for my experience during the past fortnight had taught me that a good mule for long marches and a light nimble pony for use in action were the ideal combination.

After I had completed my equipment, commissariat, and ammunition supply, I walked around the camp.

We considered that the taking of it was chiefly the handiwork of our original storming party, for while we could not have done it without the protection and covering fire of the commando, yet by riding in on the heels of the English troopers and taking post on the very edge of the camp, we had served as the spearhead that made success possible. I also saw the dead gunners and other men whom I had shot, and I looked on them with mixed feelings, for although I have never hated the English, a fight is a fight, and though I was sorry for the men, I was proud of my share in the day's work.

Lastly, I went to see what had become of my roan mare. She was still patiently standing where I had left her at the ledge. On each side of her lay a dead horse, but she had escaped unharmed. The gallant little beast was, however, so exhausted that when I tried to lead her away she could scarcely put one foot before the other, so I unsaddled her, throwing the saddle aside, for it was old and worn with much use since I had taken it from General Clements's camp ten months before. Removing the bridle and halter, I turned her loose in the hope that some neighbouring farmer would look after her, for she too had shown the mettle of her Free State pasture, and the marvellous endurance of the South African horse.

General Smuts now ordered us to set the tents and wagons on fire, and to destroy the mountain- and machine-guns, as well as such surplus ammunition and other supplies as could not be removed. Then, leaving the prisoners, mule-drivers and native servants to shift for themselves, we rode off in triumph.

22. MOSS-TROOPING

Next morning we rode out of the mountain country into the open plains of the Karoo. In the face of great odds we had broken across the successive barriers placed in our way, and although we had still many troubles to meet, the English had failed to turn us back. We now slowly marauded southwards. At the village of Maraisburg, a large number of troops was waiting for us, but General Smuts skilfully led the commando through at night without firing a shot, and we continued unmolested.

During this time the 'Rijk Section" came into its own. Our share in the attack on the 17th Lancers had enhanced our reputation, and in this open country our services as scouts were in greater demand, so we ranged far ahead, hospitably entertained by the Dutch-speaking population, and philosophically tolerated by the English farmers with whom we came in contact.

In our fine khaki tunics, and on our well-found horses, our appearance had undergone such a transformation that when asked at the English farmhouses who we were, our stock witticism was to say that we were 'English-killing Dragoons'. We thoroughly enjoyed it after all the hardships of the past.

The weather had improved, the long winter was over, and cloudless sunny days put still further heart into us. Then we had another stroke of luck, for we were joined by Field-Cornet Botha with twenty-five men, the remnant of a band of free-lances that had been roaming the midlands, until their numbers had so dwindled that they had been forced into hiding among the mountains. Hearing of our passage they had hastened to find us, and practically replaced our wastage since coming into the Cape.

But we had to abandon Raubenheimer, whose thigh had been smashed during the last fight, and a day or two later we had to leave Cohen behind, as his wound became gangrenous.

Besides being a brave man, Cohen must have been a bit of a wag, for I subsequently read in an English newspaper that when he was captured and asked by a British officer why he, a Jew and a Uitlander, was fighting for the Boers, he replied that he was fighting for the Franchise.

The next loss was heavier for me. My friend Jacobus Bosman, who had so loyally stood by me when the others turned back in the Free State, was taken ill with some malignant fever. He gamely tried to keep up but we had to leave him delirious at a farm. I went off with a heavy heart, for I knew that he was doubly in danger. If the disease spared him, the English would be waiting with a charge of high treason, and my fears were only too well founded, for about three weeks later I read that he had been sentenced to be hanged as a rebel at Graaf Reinet.

He was the first of our 'Rijk Section' men to meet a humiliating death by execution, but not the last, for three more were destined to stand before a firing party, and also other members of the commandos.

Two days after we had left Bosman behind, we reached the foot of a high mountain range, the name of which I have forgotten. There was a road running into a narrow defile called Lily Kloof into which the 'Rijk Section' was sent scouting. We rode up the gorge for some distance, until we saw an English foraging party going off, each man with sheaves of oats tied to his saddle. Ben Coetzee killed one of them, a local farmer named Brown, who had joined the troops, and the rest of the patrol raced off. A woman ran out of a cottage to warn us that there were English strongly posted at a narrow point farther up, so we turned back to report to General Smuts. Some miles west lies an equally deep ravine, through which we now tried to find a way, but here again we were warned that the route was held. General Smuts said that he as not going to squander men in forcing his way, when there were other means of crossing, so we retraced our steps, and that night, led by a local guide, we picked our way over the range by a bridle-path. It was a long march with no chance of sleep, but dawn found us on the far slopes, in the English-speaking district of Bedford. From here there was a glorious view, across deep mountain valleys and green uplands of one of the loveliest and most fertile parts of South Africa. We had left all serious pursuit so far behind that for the next few days we rode leisurely on our way, while the men scattered about, visiting farmhouses and enjoying themselves.

The inhabitants took our coming in good part, and there was never any sign of ill feeling, although they hoped that we should get rounded up, and told us so.

We saw an occasional Defence Force patrol, which, however, gave us no anxiety, for they were local levies merely keeping their eye on us, and there was no trouble until one afternoon when a column of horse showed on a hill and opened long-range fire in our direction. Not wishing to be involved in fighting other than of our own making, we turned up a defile that wound into a mass of rugged mountains before us. These were the Great Winterbergen, and we halted at sunset amid gorgeous forest-covered steeps, where we built huge log-fires, and spent a comfortable night, greatly taken with the fine country we had reached.

Next day our path ran through even more beautiful scenery. Around us was primeval forest, and through an occasional tunnel in the trees we glimpsed green fields and white homesteads in the valleys far below.

The following morning, while halted in a picturesque glade, a woodsman in a log cabin told us of a tavern and trading-station at the foot of a pass leading down close by. The men were all for going to see what was to be had, and towards sunset we reached the bottom, where stood a substantial wayside inn flanked by well-stocked warehouses.

So little were we expected in this remote part, that no effort had been made to remove the goods to the protection of the nearest military post, which was generally done when we were approaching, and the owner suffered from our visit, for we were masters by now in the gentle art of commandeering. I would not have mentioned this excursion had it not cost us the life of another member of the 'Rijk Section'.

There was plenty of beer and spirits at the inn, and although few of the men had tasted liquor for a year or more, there was no drunkenness, but Piet de Ruyt, our Hollander companion, took too much, and when the commando moved away at dusk, he was left asleep unnoticed.

Weeks later we learned that he had been discovered in a room, and as, like most of us, he was dressed in a British uniform. The poor fellow was executed, in all probability before his fuddled brain had time to take in what was happening.

Neither then, nor for weeks later, did we know that the death penalty attached to the wearing of khaki, and although after a while rumours reached us through the country people that our men were being executed, these stories left us doubting and perplexed. We could not believe that the English were resorting to the shooting of prisoners, and it was only after many had been executed that we learned of Kitchener's proclamation ordering the death of all Boers caught in khaki. As far as I know no steps were ever taken by the military to acquaint us with its contents.

From the foot of the Winterbergen we rode on for some hours in the dark, by a footpath winding across a bush-covered plain, and we camped in all open space for the night. At daybreak we made out the little village of Adelaide in the distance, but, as it seemed to be strongly garrisoned, we left it alone, and continued all that day slowly making south through broken country.

Here again the inhabitants were chiefly English-speaking farmers, who submitted with good grace to our depredations, for we slaughtered what sheep we required, and helped ourselves freely from their larders and orchards. Towards evening a column came following us from Adelaide, halting when we halted, and moving when we moved, and when after dark we went into camp, their fires were soon winking at us five or six miles away. During the afternoon an armed Colonial had ridden up from a farm with a story that he wished to fight the English. He rode a spirited horse and spoke fluent Dutch, and as he seemed genuine he took us in, but now, while we were off-saddling by a pool, he suddenly pulled his horse round and galloped away. He was gone before anyone could give chase, and, as he was obviously a spy sent to learn our intentions, we re-saddled and rode on for an hour or two before resting for the night.

Next day we bore away in a somewhat more westerly direction, reaching the Great Fish River by sunset. We crossed at a ford, and a mile or two beyond, at Commadaga Station, we passed over the railway line that comes up from Port Elizabeth through the midlands. As there were no block-houses we had no difficulty in getting to the other side after dark, and then, as our horses were tired, General Smuts ordered us to camp at a farmhouse five or six hundred yards beyond. We had scarcely turned our animals out to graze, when an armoured train came puffing up, the beams of its powerful searchlight sweeping the veld, but, as we lay in a fold of the ground, the crew could not see us although they must have suspected our presence, for they sent a number of shells howling into the night, only one of which came within measurable distance of us. It burst harmlessly near by, but we thought that we had been discovered, and ran to find our horses, with the result that there was a good deal of bumping and confusion in the dark before we realized that the English were shooting at random. Then we had a good laugh at ourselves, and spreading our blankets slept in peace till daybreak.

From here we headed south-west, riding at our ease through the district of Somerset, until by sunset we made the foot of the Zuurbergen, the last great escarpment before the country drops away to the sea.

We were by now within fifty miles of Algoa Bay. I do not know what General Smuts's intentions were at any stage of our expedition, for he was a silent man, but I think that at this particular juncture he was contemplating a sudden raid on Port Elizabeth, for next morning, when we saw what looked like over three thousand troops coming after us, he kept us quietly resting at the foot of the mountain, instead of slipping away east or west as he could easily have done. These troops had been brought by rail, and had detrained at Commadaga Station, where we had crossed two nights before, and from their converging front it looked as if they hoped to bring us to bay against the slopes of the range.

We watched them slowly approaching for most of the day, until their scouts were almost within rifle-range, and then General Smuts led the way straight up the steep slope behind us. We spent the night on the crest of the first of the great parallel hogbacks that constitute the Zuurbergen.

From the point where we reached the top, we looked on a world of more mountains, line upon line of high ranges, each separated from the next by deep wooded gorges, and the prospect of being driven into these fastnesses was not inviting. However, with troops closing in on us from the rear, there was no help for it, so we built fires and camped.

On the way up Jack Borrius and I had met a native herd-boy, who informed us that there was a big troop of horses in a neighbouring kloof. On all our journey through the Cape we had not found a single riding-horse on any of the farms, as the English had cleared the country to prevent us from getting remounts, and the boy said over five hundred horses had been collected by the military within the last few days, on hearing of our approach. Accordingly Jack and I left the commando before daybreak and followed the ridge for some miles, until we found a practicable descent down which to lead our horses into the kloof which the native had pointed out. At the bottom we came on a deserted homestead, with the ground trampled by many hoof marks, but a Red Native, who appeared out of the forest, told us that a patrol had come the day before, and driven all the animals away to the coast. We therefore gave up the idea of finding them and, turning our mounts into a paddock, stretched ourselves under a shady tree and fell asleep.

Some hours later we were waked by a couple of men who had ridden out in search of food. They roused us and told us to listen. Bumping to our feet, we heard the sound of distant rifle-fire coming from the quarter where we had left the commando that morning. It was clear that they were fighting, and before long we caught sight of our men on the slope of the next range, crawling like ants up a steep side. They were miles off, but we could see that all was not well with them, for they were strung out in a disorderly line and the firing was coming from an enemy force some where out of view.

We caught our horses and led them up the range which the commando was climbing, and on getting above we could see our men hurrying towards us along the top. It took more than an hour for them to come up with us, and then we learned that while they were encamped a number of English had unexpectedly opened fire on them.

After an interchange of shots the commando had fallen back deeper into the mountain, with only one man wounded and a few horses killed. The wounded man was badly injured about the face, but had come on. We were now on the second range. From here we saw many English horsemen riding about on the first crest. When they came opposite us, with only the deep kloof, through which we had passed, lying between, and then opened fire upon us with several machine-guns and a field-piece. I do not know how they had succeeded in dragging those up the mountain, but there they were barring the way should we try to break back, while behind us lay mile upon mile of tumbled forest-clad mountains and gorges.

The immediate danger from the troops was not pressing as we had good cover for ourselves and our horses, but now a fresh-complication set in.

Up to now we had found so little difficulty in commandeering supplies from the farms we passed, that no one ever thought about the next day, with the result that when we unexpectedly found ourselves in a wild region without habitations, the men had little or no food with them, and were already beginning to feel hungry. Scattered about stood a strange growth known as 'Hottentot's bread' (*Encephelartos Altensteinii*), a wild fruit not unlike a large pineapple. It is edible only at certain seasons of the year, but coming from the north, we did not know this, and as one of the men sampled it and found it to his liking, many unfortunately followed suit.

I had not eaten any, and returning to the firing-line, after going to tie up some horses that had broken loose, I was astonished to find more than half our men groaning and retching on the ground in agony, some apparently at their last gasp. General Smuts was worse than the rest, so, with half our number out of action, we were also leaderless, for he was lying comatose.

The horsemen of the strong enemy force before us were even now descending the opposite slope to attack us, while behind were mountain wastes stretching as far as we could see. We had no food, and could not move without abandoning the sick, so our position was critical.

For the moment our most urgent concern was the soldiers advancing towards us. They had by now reached the bottom of the kloof, and some of them, leaving their horses behind, were already swarming up, firing as they came.

Commandant van Deventer was too ill to take charge, but Ben Bouwer, though bad, was able to order every man who could still handle a rifle to extend along the top. It was nearing sunset, and the light was uncertain, so I do not think we did much damage with our shooting, but it served to turn our assailants, for they went back to their horses, and then climbed up the other side, until their camp fires began to shine in the dark, which meant that they were settling down for the night.

Those of us who had been lining the forward crest now had time to look around, and what we saw was not comforting. The sick men were worse than ever. General Smuts was very bad indeed, and van Deventer, his second in command, not much better. From the groans and cries on all sides it was clear that the sufferers could not travel, and there was nothing to do but to wait, although it was urgently necessary to get away before daylight would enable the English to surround us. I shall not soon forget that night. It was dark, and a chill wind blew from seaward. We dared not light a fire, and those of us who were not ill from the poisoned fruit were starving. We knew that if the men did not recover in time to avoid the pursuing column, our expedition into the Cape would come to a speedy end next morning, and we sat beside the sick men not knowing when we might be fallen upon. However, as the darkness slowly passed, one man after another recovered sufficiently to stagger to his feet and towards dawn there were not more than twenty unable to stand. General Smuts was still prostrate, but able to take in the position, and he gave orders that the men who could not help themselves were to be tied to their saddles, and that the commando was to march deeper into the mountains. He himself had to be held on his horse, and we started off in the dim light, following a game-track that led down into the next gorge. At the bottom we halted to rest the sick men, and then crawled up the far slope, which was almost as steep as the place we negotiated on the night of our retreat from the Stormbergen.

Bringing up the sick men was a difficult task, made more difficult by the fact that the English troops had actually dragged their gun to the top of the second range where we had spent the night, and opened fire on us as we were climbing. The distance was so great that only a few shells fell among us, their chief effect being to spur the men to greater activity and rouse the invalids, some of whom asked to be lifted to the ground, for they did not relish the idea of being trussed up in the circumstances.

As one of the last to gain the top, as I had led my horse and mule very slowly, a few yards at a time, to save their legs. But when I got above and chanced to look back, I was surprised to see that General Smuts was still lying below, with three or four men attending him, while down the path above them came a number or English scouts trailing the spoor which the commando had made. At the rate at which the scouts were descending they would soon come on General Smuts and his men, and I realized that there was no time to be lost. I tied my two animals to the nearest tree, and rushed and slid to the bottom unharmed by the bullets of the scouts. When the men with General Smuts heard the firing overhead they lifted him to his horse, and were already starting, a couple on each side to hold him, by the time I got down.

We did not follow the commando, as we should have presented too easy a mark, but kept away to the right where there was a gully up which we could make our way unseen. When we reached the top I fetched my two animals, and we followed on to find the commando waiting for us in a glade.

We were now in the very heart of the mountains, so far from any farms that buffalo were seen, and their tracks and mud-wallows were frequent. Not one of the sick men had died and most of them were better, perhaps because of the shaking and movement. General Smuts and a few other cases were, however, still in danger, and it was decided to spend the day here, as our scouts reported that the enemy had turned back, and it was thought necessary to give the sick a long rest before continuing. The trouble now was to get food. Parties were sent out in search of native kraals, for smoke had been seen rising from a distant part of the forest, and here, after struggling for hours through dense under-growth, we found a few poverty-stricken huts whose inhabitants had fled. They belonged to a destitute tribe of Red Natives, but we unearthed a supply of millet, enough to give the commando some sort of a meal.

In the afternoon we moved deeper into the mountains, and, breasting a high grass-covered shoulder, caught a distant view, thirty-five miles away, of white sand-dunes, and of a grey haze, which was the Indian Ocean. We were elated, for we knew that we had now penetrated farther south than any other commando during the war, and that we were the first to come within sight of the coast.

After dark, camped on a height, we could see the lights of Port Elizabeth shining far off, and this strengthened our belief that General Smuts, in spite of his illness, still intended to go there. Next morning we went down into a beautiful valley filled with yellow-wood trees, centuries old, and here we camped for the rest of the day, still subsisting on boiled millet.

One of our men recognized this part, having hunted buffalo and elephant here long before, and he said that he remembered a path running south, by which we could get out of the mountains into the valley of the Sunday River, where we might take the small village of Bayville.

On hearing this, a small party, mostly 'Rijk Section', was made up to raid the place. Unluckily both my animals had strayed into the forest, and I had to follow on long after the others had gone. I tracked them until I got clear of the mountains into the wide valley, down whose centre the Sunday River runs to the sea. But the floor of the valley was dense scrub, ten or twelve feet high, in which I got completely bushed, so I had to work my way back with difficulty, reaching the commando at dark, tired and disgusted.

Jack Borrius and his buccaneers had not yet returned, but that night we marched on, as we had exhausted our grain supply.

We led our horses in the dark between high ranges, along a well-beaten path that twisted down a valley, until towards daybreak we reached the Sunday River, at a point still closed in by the mountains, but where, in a clearing, lay a well-stocked farm.

General Smuts remained pale and weak, but he sent for me and thanked me for having come down to warn him two days before.

Some time after sunrise Cornelius Vermaas, Henry Rittenberg and I were ordered to scout up the course of the river, and we set out on what proved to be my companions' last ride. After following the stream and making inquiries from occasional natives, we learned that there were some white men off-saddled close by, and going thither came on Jack Borrius and his detachment, halted under the trees. Jack himself was suffering from terrible wounds. They had entered Bayville unopposed, but on their way back they fell foul of an English patrol, and, in the ensuing encounter, a bullet had entirely blown away his left eye, leaving nothing but a cavity filled with dried blood. In addition his right hand was smashed to pulp, but he had refused to be left behind, and we found him lying in great pain, but determined to remain with the commando. While we were busy with him, General Smuts rode up. He told Ben Coetzee to take over command of the 'Rijk Section', and ordered him to reconnoitre down a lateral valley, to see whether it would bring us out of the mountains, as he intended to enter the lower Sunday River Valley.

Ben Coetzee took with him Rittenberg and myself together with Vermaas and one of van Deventer's men, named van Onselen, who volunteered to come. We five went ahead carefully picking our way, and discovered late in the afternoon that the valley we were in ran to a dead end, against what we took to be the final range of the Zuurbergen.

Coetzee kept van Onselen with him, and told the three of us from the 'Rijk Section' to climb the height ahead, and see what lay on the far side. As we began to lead our horses up the slope, we heard a shout, and van Onselen overtook us, with a message to say that I was to return, as Coetzee thought my horse looked poorly, and that van Onselen was to go in my stead. The fact that my grey pony had a staring coat saved my life, for the three men, on reaching the top, walked straight into the arms of an English force lying in ambush there, and, as they were dressed in khaki uniforms, were executed out of hand. They lie buried where they fell, their graves being the most southerly of any of our republican dead.

We only knew of their actual fate long afterwards. For the moment all we heard was a burst of firing, and looking up we saw large numbers of soldiers on the skyline, so we rode back along the valley full of anxiety.

At dusk we met the commando coming in our direction, and when we told General Smuts that our progress was barred, he halted us for the night.

At daybreak next morning, while we were saddling our horses, the troops opened fire from above our heads. No one was hit, but we were forced to retire back into the deeper part of the mountains, instead of getting out into the open country to the south. During the retreat we lost three more men. They were looking for their horses when the firing began and, as no one noticed their absence, they were left behind. According to an English newspaper which we saw afterwards, one of them was hanged as a rebel British subject, the sixth man of our force to be executed, not counting the three that had been murdered by the Basutos.

As I have said before, we had not heard of Lord Kitchener's proclamation against the wearing of British uniforms, and I went about wearing Lord Vivian's khaki tunic, with regimental badge and buttons, and the 17th Lancers' skull and cross-bones in my hat, not a little proud of my well-earned trophies, and never dreaming that I was under sentence of death. We made a long trek through the kloofs of this wild region until, after midday, we found a disused pass, made, I was told, by Sir Harry Smith in the fifties during the native wars.

This pass ran up a dark ravine, flanked with dense timber, and heavily over-grown with brushwood, but otherwise in good preservation. Its chief drawback was that it led northwards over the mountains back to the plains of the Karoo, from which we had come, whereas our endeavour had been to break seawards; but with the English column of that morning pressing steadily in our rear, we had to go wherever there was an opening. We started to ascend the pass, not knowing if another force was waiting for us above. If so we should have been trapped, but luckily this particular loophole had not been closed, and we found the top clear. Edgar Duncker and I, who were scouting in advance, saw a human skeleton beside the road, a relic or some past tragedy, and we placed the grin-ning skull on a log as a warning to our pursuers.

Not far from the top was a space of level ground with the ruins of an old building, and the remains of walled gardens and orchards, and as we could see the English troops halted in a glade far below, General Smuts stopped too, for he and others were still very ill. The sick and wounded, with poor Jack Borrius, withdrew to a distance, while the rest of us turned our horses out to graze and lolled about at our ease, admiring the grand forest scenery and enjoying the luxury of our beautiful surroundings.

Then some half-savage cattle came out of the woods and we shot several, and had the added satisfaction of eating our fill around big fires. Afterwards, most of the men stretched themselves under the trees, at peace in this pleasant place.

But towards five in the afternoon we began to bestir ourselves. Ben Coetzee, Nicolas Swart and I sat basking in the sunshine on a wall not far from where the pass came out. Suddenly, while we were talking, we saw the foremost ranks of a body of horsemen appear at the head of the gorge, not a hundred yards away. Shouting an alarm, we seized our rifles and ran down, followed by the men who had been lying close by. The English must have been under the impression that we had gone straight on over the berg, for they were riding in a compact body of thirty or more with no advance-guards, and evidently our presence here was as great a surprise to them as their sudden appearance was to us, but we were the first to recover ourselves, and started to fire as we ran.

The English could not deploy on the narrow road, so they pulled round, and made back as fast as they could, for the ground above and below was so steep that they had to keep to the causeway, down which they poured in disorder.

They seemed to be boring and pushing each other frantically under our fire, horses and men toppling over the edge of the road, and crashing into the timber beneath. The road became obstructed with dead and wounded horses, for we were firing into the brown, and we could hear angry shouts, as those behind tried to pass. Only a few men reached the bottom, where I caught a glimpse of them lashing their horses, as they rode through a clearing below. The rest abandoned their animals, and took cover in the forest, directing at us so hot a fire that we dared not climb down to get at the ammunition of the dead and wounded, nor at the holsters or wallets of the fallen horses. The main English column, that had been halted at the foot of the pass, now moved nearer, and when their fire was added we withdrew to the top to avoid casualties, and escaped without any.

After dark we went down the far side of the mountains, still following Sir Harry Smith's road, and daylight found us back in the Somerset district. We had now left the mountains on the same side on which we had entered them five days before, and, although we had failed to break out to the south, we were all heartily pleased to be clear at last of this appropriately named range.

As soon as it was light we halted at a farm for a few hours, and here General Smuts called us together. He said that we had reached a turning-point in the expedition, and he told us that from now onward he was going to make for the Atlantic seaboard, and the old-established districts of the South-Western Cape. After thanking the men for the way in which they had borne themselves, he told us that he was dividing our force, partly to mislead the English columns, and partly for easier provisioning, as the inhabitants of the districts through which we had passed had complained that so large a force as ours was too severe a tax upon them. Accordingly he proposed to send Commandant van Deventer off with approximately half the commando, while he himself would take command of the rest. Both units were to advance independently of each other, and ultimately reunite in the far west.

He still looked pale and ill, but his spirit was undaunted and at midday he ordered those of us who were remaining with him to saddle our horses, and we rode away amid cheers and farewells front van Deventer's men, who were to start later. We went on until sundown, then halted for the night in a thorn-covered hollow. Next morning we struck across a wide plain, with alternating patches of bush and open country, over which we continued till noon, when we came to rest in a wide tree-covered bottom.

Percy Wyndall and Frits Balogh, of the 'Rijk Section', were sent to a neighbouring rise on outpost duty, and from where we lay we could see them beneath a tree evidently enjoying a quiet chat, their horses cropping the grass behind. Before long a dozen English troopers rode out of the thicket in the rear and surrounded them before our eyes.

The distance between us was perhaps half a mile, and when we realized what had happened, we of the 'Rijk Section' (now reduced to six) rushed for our horses and, followed by a few others who happened to have their horses at hand, galloped up the slope. The soldiers were so intent upon their prisoners that they did not see us until we were close by, when they loosed a ragged volley, and leaping into their saddles, abandoned the two captives, and made off.

Shouting to the rescued men to follow, we rode straight after the patrol, and got to within thirty or forty yards of them, bringing three to the ground. Two more, whose horses were hit, surrendered, but the rest scattered in the bush.

A friend of mine, Jack Baxter, one of Bouwer's men was riding next to me, and he and I singled out one of the flying soldiers. We got near enough to order him to halt, but he rode on, not heeding our shouts. We fired at him but missed, for shooting from the saddle is trick-work and he might have escaped had he not been brought up by a wire fence across his path. He jumped to the ground, and leaving his horse, climbed through the fence and disappeared into a patch of scrub. Almost at once his bullets were singing about our ears. Fortunately for us his marksmanship was poorer than his courage, and Baxter and I had time to dash our horses out of sight into a thicket. We dismounted, and, tying our animals, started to stalk him down. Crawling through the fence, we wormed our way from tree to tree, until we located him. As we could take no risks with such a resourceful opponent, we emptied our magazines at the spot where we had seen movement. Silence followed, and after a few more shots to make sure, we went up to find him lying face down, riddled with bullets, but still clutching his rifle. We smashed his weapon, and shared the contents of his ammunition-belts, after which we returned to fetch our horses and his, and rode back, feeling almost regretful at the way in which we had hunted down so brave a man.

The rest of our storming party were collected around the soldiers who had been killed. The prisoners and wounded were there, too, and after depriving the living and the dead of their boots (an unpleasant but necessary task, for there was continual shortage of footwear amongst our men), we rode back to rejoin the commando.

In the course of our return journey Ben Coetzee and Edgar Duncker branched away on their own, and soon after, hearing several shots, we galloped in their direction. When we came up we found them sitting their horses in considerable agitation, while on the ground lay an officer and a trooper, both dead. It appeared that shortly after leaving us, as they rounded a piece of thorn bush, they ran into a small English patrol. So unexpected was the encounter that they were alongside before they could think, and Duncker, on the spur of the moment, called out, 'Don't fire, we are the 17th Lancers!' The officer in charge, a Captain Watson, said, 'I don't believe you; all Smuts's men are dressed in khaki. Put up your hands.' Then Coetzee and Duncker, both of whom carried Webley revolvers fired simultaneously, killing Captain Watson and one of his men, and seriously wounding another, who, however, got away with the rest.

This was a very unlucky incident, for the wearing of British uniforms had without doubt been the proximate cause of the death of these two men, and although we knew nothing as yet of Lord Kitchener's proclamation, General Smuts pulled a long face when he was told of the business. Indeed, long afterwards, when we met Lord Kitchener himself, he cited this very case in defence of the execution of so many of our men for wearing khaki.

Well the harm was done, and I can only say that none of us ever wore captured uniforms with the deliberate intention of decoying the enemy, but only out
of sheer necessity.

We met no more soldiers that day, and towards afternoon the commando
moved to a camping-place ten miles farther on. Next morning, while scouting
ahead, I met a British ambulance-wagon with a doctor and several stretcher-
bearers, on their way to fetch in the wounded of the day before. The Medical
Officer already knew the manner of Captain Watson's death, for he spoke
heatedly of murder, and abuse of military uniforms, although he made no
mention of the proclamation, perhaps thinking that we knew about it. After this
we went steadily west for some days without anything happening of importance,
except that one evening we came in sight of a tiny hamlet called Hobsonville,
where there was a small garrison of a dozen men, with whom the 'Rijk Section'
and two or three more had a sharp brush, one of Bouwer's men being shot
through the thigh. To avoid further damage we galloped in among the houses, in
time to see the defenders rush for their horses, and make good their escape, as
they had seen the commando coming on behind.

There were two well-stocked shops, and a quantity of military stores, so we
did quite well out of the place, and spent the night feasting on tinned food and
other luxuries.

In this manner we journeyed slowly on, until at length we reached the Port
Elizabeth - Graaf-Reinet railway line which we crossed at night, an armoured
train sending a few shells to speed us on our way. Next day we saw the town of
Aberdeen, lying seven or eight miles distant, and as there was a large camp on
the outskirts, we did not need the local farmers to tell us that there was trouble
ahead.

We put the strength of the troops at about fifteen hundred, so we rode up to
a large farm, to keep them under observation. They were not yet ready, but by
the activity in their lines, we knew that they would soon be after us, especially as
their patrols kept hanging about in the offing most of the day.

That afternoon we moved on, bearing slightly north for the Camdebo Mountains, ten or fifteen miles away. We reached the foot next day, by which time a
long English column was marching on our tracks, while various smaller bodies
were skirting round the base of the range, in an encircling movement. General
Smuts did not wish to get involved in a fight against heavy odds, so we started
up the mountain by a gorge, and at sunset reached a high saddle, over which we
passed.

Unfortunately the fine weather which we had enjoyed of late now changed. It
turned bitterly cold, and a biting rain set in, and when darkness overtook us we
had to halt on the rear slope for fear of falling over precipices. The icy water came
down in torrents all night and there was no hope of a fire, so we sat before our
horses until dawn, cold and drenched. Commandant Bouwer and two others
were so benumbed, that when it grew light we had to carry them down in
blankets to a valley, where we at last succeeded in getting fires alight, while

General Smuts, Jack Borrius, and the rest of the sick and wounded must have endured agony that night.

It was still raining when we marched over a bleak up-land, apparently uninhabited. To the north lay a world of barren-looking peaks and heights draped in heavy clouds, a sight that made our hearts sink, for, with an English column in our rear, it seemed as if we were in for another spell of cold and hungry mountaineering.

By midday the rain had stopped, and the sun showed through, and after plodding for hours over sodden turf, we came upon a farm with fuel to dry our clothes, and a flock of sheep for supplies.

A picket had been led behind at the neck which we had crossed the night before, and these men rode in after a time to say that the English column was nearing the top.

General Smuts sent the 'Rijk Section' and other patrols to look for a way down the south face of the mountain, for he liked the idea of being forced higher up as little as we did.

We rode to what seemed a likely kloof, but when we got to the edge and peered down, an enemy force lay waiting for us below. The other parties brought similar reports. All the exits from the tableland were guarded and our position unpleasantly resembled that on the Stormbergen. However, things shaped better this time, for here again the owner of the farm where we had halted (and whose sheep we had freely slaughtered) volunteered to lead as to a bridle-path, and after five or six miles brought us out on another high saddle, over which a faint goat-track led to the bottom. As soon as it was dark, we took our horses along the easy gradient, and got down in an hour or two without trouble. In order to shake off the columns more effectively, and to get clear of the terrible cactus-belt that girdles the foot of the mountains, we trekked on till daybreak.

This cactus (prickly pear) was brought from Central America about fifty years ago, and found the Karoo such congenial soil that there are now vast tracts rendered valueless by it. Our way now ran through a veritable forest of this vile growth, standing twenty feet high in places.

Soon after sunrise we reached the Kareega River, which rises in the mountains which we had just left, and runs due south across the plains.

We camped for the day on its wooded banks, seeing no sign of the English. In the course of the morning the 'Rijk Section', with the exception of my uncle and myself (and Jack Borrius), rode off to forage. I could not go, because General Smuts ordered me to ride through the river to a rise beyond, to watch the country towards Aberdeen. Before leaving I asked my uncle to look after my riding-mule during my absence, and that was the last I ever saw of either of them. It was well that I went off on my Arab pony, for his fleet legs were to be my salvation that day. I kept watch on the hill for many hours without seeing anything of note, but when General Smuts sent a messenger up in the afternoon to say that I was to remain until half an hour before sunset, I sent back a warning that I could not tell what might be going on at the river, as the heavily timbered banks made it impossible to see along its course.

When I judged from the height of the sun that my time was over, I rode down to the river, on my way back to where the commando was camped on the opposite side. Near the ford in a clearing stood a farmhouse, and, being thirsty after my long spell in the hot sun, I touched there to ask for a cup of coffee. The old lady inside was eager to grant my wish, but, as the kettle was not boiling, she asked me to sit down while she piled more wood on the fire. I knew that the commando was moving at sunset, so I decided not to wait, and, bidding her good-bye, rode off.

I had not gone thirty yards when I heard the trample of many horses, and, glancing over my shoulder, saw a swarm of English troopers gallop into the glade and surround the house.

Had I still been seated there, I should have been caught in full khaki, and that would have been the end of me, but out here in the open my English tunic saved me, for the soldiers took me for one of their own men, and let me ride away. Seeing this, I went slowly until I was out of sight among the trees, and then rode all out to rouse the commando.

I crossed the ford, and, as I breasted the other bank, looked back to see that the English had discovered their mistake and were streaming behind me like hounds on a hot scent. My grey pony was equal to the occasion and I was able to keep well ahead of my pursuers, firing alarm shots as I went, for I knew that if all these troops came on our commando unprepared and off-saddled among the trees, with their horses out at graze, there might be a serious disaster.

I had still about six hundred yards to go, and when I rode in among our men I was relieved to find that they were rushing about the thorn trees bringing in their horses.

There was not a moment to lose, for, at the rate at which the English were approaching, they would be there long before the horses could be brought in and saddled. About fifteen or sixteen men, however, were mounted, having had their animals by them, and General Smuts called to them to ride forward and delay the oncoming enemy until the rest were ready.

With Commandant Bouwer at our head, we galloped back, but, before we had gone far, a hundred or more English horsemen came charging at us. We jumped to the ground and fired, upon which the troopers opened out and also dismounted, giving rapid fire and obliging us to fall back behind the wall of a small dam, that very opportunely stood dose by.

From here we were in a more favourable position to rake them, which we did so effectively that the men withdrew into denser bush, from which they fired heavily, but we kept our heads well down and had no casualties.

Thus far we had satisfactorily carried out our orders to hold up the enemy until the commando was collected, but we could see parties of English horsemen filtering round us through the bush in constantly increasing numbers, and, to make matters worse, they were unlimbering a field-gun on rising ground to our left. In a few moments shells were bursting overhead, against which the wall offered little or no protection, so Bouwer, boldly riding on to the crest of the dam, scanned the country to the rear, until he saw the commando move from the clearing where we had left them which meant that our task was accomplished. When he called out that the commando was making fast down the river to the south, we retreated at once. As soon as the English saw us go, they came in hot pursuit.

The sun was setting and the short twilight giving way to darkness, otherwise it would have gone harder with us than it did. The troops were on our heels, yelling and firing as they pounded behind, and, had there been more daylight, I think we should all have been captured.

My khaki uniform saved me for the second time that day, for a batch of troopers rode by in the dusk, and, mistaking me for one of their men, shouted that I was to hurry, but passed on without taking further notice.

Owing to the bush, both English and Boers got separated into smaller groups, and single horsemen and parties of twos and threes were galloping about. It was soon quite dark, and, to avoid being further accosted, as there were soldiers in front and behind me, I halted in a copse to let them through. I waited for a long time, until the hue and cry had died down and I could see camp fires springing up ahead, which showed that the English were halting for the night.

I could not tell how my companions had fared, but my own position was sufficiently difficult, for I was alone with the enemy across my path and the commando gone.

When I thought that the soldiers had settled down, I cautiously rode on, picking my way with difficulty through the bush, for it was a dark night. After an hour or two I had skirted round their camp, and was following the course of the river once more.

At length I saw the gleam of a lighted window, and, stealing up, peered in to see five of our rearguard party of that afternoon standing in conversation with the inmates of the house.

I joined them at once, eager to hear news of the rest of our band, but they knew nothing, nor did they know what had become of the commando. As it was useless trying to pick up the spoor on so dark a night, and as our horses were tired, we got some food, and went a little distance to sleep amongst the trees, confidently expecting to overhaul our men next day. Shortly before sunrise we saddled up and crossed the river towards a conical hill lying on the other side, from which we should be able to see over the plains.

As we rode on, we found two more of our men, who had escaped from last night's affair, and had also taken to the thickets on the banks. There were now eight of us, and, when we got to the foot of the hill, we left our horses and climbed up. As we reached the top the sun was rising, and, like sailors adrift in a boat, we anxiously scanned the horizon for a sign of the commando, but the country to the south lay open before us without a horseman in view.

General Smuts must have ridden all night, for although we could see for half a day's journey, he and his men had vanished, and difficult weeks were to elapse before we found them again.

23. A LONG TRAIL

For a long time we remained on the top, still hoping to see our men, but at last yesterday's English column came down the opposite bank of the river, so we made haste to get down to our horses and reach safer quarters. Searching out a less conspicuous hill, we left our animals to graze in a neighbouring hollow, while we lay amongst the boulders watching the progress of the enemy. Instead of trekking on, as we expected them to do, they went into camp at a farm three miles away. This was a misfortune, as our chief desire was to make a start towards picking up the trail, but, with the English halted by the river and their patrols scouring the plain in all directions, we dared not venture out into the open, and were obliged to let the valuable hours go by while our commando was getting farther and farther away.

They kept us until nearly sunset before moving off, and then went south, from which we inferred that they were starting on a night march after General Smuts. So we only waited until the last horseman was riding away before we went down to the farm to get information.

It was dark before we reached there, and the owner, a well-to-do Dutch farmer, named le Roux, quickly told us such news as he had gleaned from the officers and soldiers during the day.

In the first place he said that three or four of our delaying party had been captured, and that one of them, my friend Jack Baxter, had been executed that morning at an adjoining farm for wearing khaki.

We were thunderstruck. The inhabitants of the districts through which we had passed could not have known of the death penalty or they would surely have mentioned it to us, and it was only when le Roux produced a recent newspaper, containing Lord Kitchener's proclamation, that we understood the position. We learned, too, for the first time, that other men of ours had been shot for the same reason, although it was only later, as more newspapers came into our hands that we found out their names.

From what I could make out, the executions had been kept quiet, but now, for some reason or other, perhaps the killing of Captain Watson, the military authorities were giving them publicity. From a farm labourer who came in, we had details of Baxter's shooting, which brought home to me how narrowly I had on several occasions missed a similar fate, so I lost no time in changing the tunic I wore for a coat which I borrowed from our host, who also supplied such of my companions as were in khaki with whatever he had in the way of civilian dress.

As to the commando, le Roux said that General Smuts was believed to be heading for the Swartbergen, a great range whose peaks we had seen during the day, looming fifty or sixty miles to the south. We said good-bye and rode on all night, and for the next three days made our way across the plains that lie towards the mountains.

The local inhabitants gave us word that General Smuts had passed by, but there were several English columns moving between, and their patrols were so active that we had to go warily. Once at dawn we were hotly chased for many miles, so our progress was slow, and our chance of speedily overtaking the commando grew perceptibly less.

William Conradi, who was with us at the Kraal during the 17th Lancers fight, as the oldest and most experienced of our party, took charge. The others were: Albert von Rooyen, Albert Pienaar, Cornelius Brink, W. Pypers, W. van der Merwe and a boy named Michael du Preez, all Transvaalers, except Conradi, who came from the Western Cape, and all good, brave fellows. On the afternoon of the third day I was ahead to watch the doings of a small English force, when I saw a horseman detach himself from them and come riding up the road in my direction. I lay in wait for him behind some trees, and, as he passed, I leaped out and knocked him from the saddle with the butt of my rifle.

He turned out on closer inspection to be a Hottentot soldier, such as the English employed as scouts and dispatch-bearers. He was more terrified than hurt, and, when on the off chance I ordered him to hand over the message which I thought he might be carrying, he did actually produce one from his boot. When my companions came up we carefully studied this document, which was addressed to a Colonel Scobell, informing him that General Smuts had crossed the Swartbergen into the district of Oudtshoorn the night before. It added that he had been reinforced by nearly a hundred men, which was a mystery to us, but we found afterwards that a roving band of fifty men had joined him the day before. They were the remnant of a commando that had long been operating in these parts under Commandant Scheepers, who had recently been executed for train-wrecking. All was therefore well with the commando, and we were still on the right track, so we divested our prisoner of his horse, rifle and ammunition, and told him to clear off, a command he obeyed with a cheerful 'Dag, mij baasies', as he trotted up the road.

We were by now within fifteen or twenty miles of the Swartbergen, but a ragged tract of foothills had to be crossed before we could reach the bottom of the range itself, and it took us the whole of the ensuing night to get there, for the going was dreadfully rough. Towards morning we came to a beaten highway, which, from information previously received, we knew to be the approach to Meiring's Poort, a pass leading over the mountains near here. The pass was not for us, because it was held by a garrison, but we decided to make use of the road for a while, as preferable to the boulder-strewn country across which we had been toiling. This landed us in a mess, for we ran into a body of English horse-men. It was too dark to make out their strength, and we were so mixed up with them that no one could shoot. For a few seconds we were milling about, neither side quite certain whether we were dealing with friend or foe, and no one uttered a word for fear of precipitating trouble. Then we heard William Conradi shout to us in English to break away, so we disengaged ourselves and turned back into the rough, while the English clattered away along the road without a shot having been fired.

After this we went more carefully, and sunrise found us leading our horses up the street of a tiny village standing at the bottom of the pass. Dogs began to bark, and windows to open, and we saw soldiers running to a large building, so we mounted and rode hastily out.

Before us rose the Swartbergen, steep as a house, but we climbed it all day, dragging our leg-weary horses, until we reached the top at dusk. From here we could look south over more mountains and deep valleys, and far beyond lay a grey haze, which we took to be the sea.

Our ascent during the day had not been unreasonably difficult for the north face, up which we had come, though steep, was grass-covered and devoid of krantzes, but the slope down which we had now to go was fringed with high crags, so, with darkness coming on, we were obliged to halt for the night.

We had eaten nothing for twenty hours, as the presence of the troops the day before had prevented us from foraging, so we sat cold and hungry, looking down into the black depths below.

After a while there was a faint twinkle of a light, evidently a farmhouse in some valley, and, as Michael du Preez and I were the youngest and hungriest of the party, we prevailed on the others to let us go down the mountain. It was a bad climb, for we had to feel our way in the dark by cracks and crevices, to the bottom of the cliffs, and it took us the rest of the night to do the remainder. So it was not till well after sunrise that we reached the farm whose light we had seen in the evening. The owner, an Englishman named Holm, gave us a generous meal, including an omelette made from ostrich egg, to which we did full justice. After getting from him a further supply of food for our companions, and eliciting the information that General Smuts had passed down the valley the day before with enemy troops hanging on behind, Michael and I started up the mountain once more. We were desperately tired, having had no sleep for two nights running, so it took us seven hours to drag ourselves to where the others were waiting. They had, in the meanwhile succeeded in finding a practicable way down the cliff for the horses, and we found them considerably below the spot at which we had left them the night before. They were so famished that they had begun to look over the horses with a view to shooting the worst of them for food, but our arrival, each with a bag containing an ostrich egg, meat, and bread, made this unnecessary, and they fell to cooking a huge meal instead. When all had fin-ished, Conradi ordered an immediate start, for we had told him that General

Smuts was in the valley, and he was for not losing a moment in going after him, so Michael and I had to go along once more.

Climbing down was difficult, and in places we had to roll boulders into the torrent that rushed down the gorge we were descending, to form a bridge for the horses. Halfway down, we came on a cattle-path, which made progress easier, and we reached the foot of the mountain by ten or eleven that night. We halted in an orchard, and I was asleep almost as soon as I had the saddle off my horse.

We were now in the great valley that runs parallel to the Swartbergen towards the town of Oudtshoorn, and I well remember how oppressed we felt in this region of mountains, for we were accustomed to the open country and wide horizons of the north.

As we made our way down the valley all that day, we were comforted with news of General Smuts at every farm-house, and we were hopeful of coming up with him at any moment, for the commando tracks lay plain before us on the road. By nightfall we were so hot on the trail that we passed a homestead where our men had halted that afternoon, and a little farther on we were told that Edgar Duncker and Nicolas Swart had gone by on foot only an hour before. Their horses had been killed during the retreat at the Kareega River, and, like ourselves, they had been following the commando ever since.

We hurried on, intending to catch up before halting, but after dark we lost the tracks owing to stony soil, and could find no farmhouse at which to make inquiries, so we camped in a gully for the night, feeling sure that we should see the commando the first thing in the morning.

We were up at sunrise, eagerly gazing down the valley. Sure enough there rose a cloud of dust, and we could make out horsemen riding among the trees, and we saddled in haste, congratulating ourselves that our search was over.

But disappointment was in store, for, as we hurried down the road, a woman ran from a field with outstretched arms, to warn us that those men were English troops who lead come into the valley overnight, and indeed, before long, so many of them came riding from farm to farm in our direction that we had to go up one of the smaller lateral valleys to escape their attentions. We did not know what had become of our men, but from what the woman told us, General Smuts had evidently got wind of the English movements and had escaped under cover of darkness, but in which direction we were unable to discover - a sad blow, after having so nearly rejoined the commando.

We continued up the smaller valley, then climbed over a height and descended into another of the broad valleys that abound in these parts.

I had never been here before, but our family clan is a large one, some of whose branches have spread far from the older settlements around Table Bay, so I was not surprised that afternoon to come on a connection of mine named Rex, a lineal descendant of George Rex, the morganatic son of King George III by Hannah Lightfoot, the Quakeress. George Rex had been sent out to South Africa in 1775, and given a large tract of land at the Knysna, on condition that he did not again trouble his august parent. His descendants still live there, and one of them had married my mother's brother.

Rex and I spent an hour discussing family ties, and before I left he insisted upon giving me a pair of new boots, as mine were considerably the worse for wear. For this he was fined and imprisoned by the military, and I read in a newspaper that he was convicted of 'comforting the King's enemies', which amused me greatly, although I was sorry that I had landed him in trouble.

Soon after this the ubiquitous English patrols were once more in evidence, on a house-to-house visitation, so a local farmer accompanied us to where a path led into a narrow kloof, and, having put us on our way, slipped home again. This path ran between high crags, that sometimes almost met overhead, until at length it reached the side of a mountain up which it ran. We followed to the top, and got there long after sunset. We could not see the country beyond, but through the darkness shone a light from a farmhouse, and, as we were anxious to pick up the lost trail of the commando, Pypers and I went down to make inquiries. The slope was steep, but clear of rocks, and by midnight we were hammering at the door of a large homestead. It belonged to an Englishman named Guest, who, when he opened the door and saw who we were, exclaimed, 'My God! First come the Boers this morning and slaughter my sheep; then come the British, who kill more sheep instead of catching the Boers, and now I am hauled out of bed at this time of night by more Boers! ' We spoke to him pleasantly, and the old fellow cooled down enough to explain that General Smuts had camped on his farm at eleven that morning, and was followed by a pursuing English force, that had also halted here and made free of his live-stock, so he not unnaturally looked upon our arrival as the last straw in a distressful day. Becoming more affable, he roused the servants and gave us a good supper, during which he told us that Duncker and Nicolas Swart had caught up the commando here. Having eaten well, and obtained as much information as we could, we persuaded our host to give us enough food for our friends, and started back.

As we went off he doubtless heaved a sigh of relief at having got rid of us, but, had he known it, his troubles were only beginning.

Pypers and I reached the others shortly before daybreak, and as Conradi was not one to let the grass grow under his feet, he started us off at once. At the first dawn of what turned out to be a lively day, we began leading our horses down the mountain, and towards eight o'clock were nearing Guest's house, when there swung into view, round a bend of the valley, some two hundred English horsemen, riding hard for the farm. Our presence there during the night must have been reported to them, for they were riding like men with a set purpose, and on nearing the homestead they divided to right and left, to surround the buildings and orchards. Luckily we were able to hustle ourselves and our animals into a gully, without being seen, and from our hiding-place we watched the activities of the soldiers with considerable interest. When they drew a blank at the farm, they deployed along the foot of the slope on which we were, and, splitting into parties, began a systematic search. Soon on every knoll and hillock men stood scanning the mountain-side, as if they knew that we were somewhere about, but, although some of the troopers came within a hundred yards of us, we were not discovered.

We did not fire for we knew that if we did it would be all over with us, so we lay hidden, meaning only to shoot when there was no other alternative. A man on a white-faced Argentine came trotting up to within twenty yards of us. He dismounted to examine the path for hoof-marks, and was so close to us, that had one of our horses jingled a bit, he must have heard it. We held our breath until he got into the saddle again and rode away, little thinking on what a thread his life had hung, for we had him covered, and, had he seen us, he would have been a dead man, but we had no wish to precipitate a general battle against impossible odds, and we let him go.

After what seemed an age, the hunt died down and the soldiers gradually drifted back to the farmhouse, where they camped for two hours, during which we could not move. We saw the men flinging oat-sheaves from a loft, and chasing poultry, and I could not help feeling sorry for Mr. Guest, who was once more being put under the harrow - and not for the last time either, as it proved.

When the troops at length saddled and rode away, we waited barely long enough for the last man to be off the premises before we hurried to the house.

When Mr. Guest saw us appear, with the soldiers only just going through the garden beyond, he looked as if he had seen an apparition, and when we laid him under further contribution he seemed on the verge of a fit. However, he complied with our demands, grumbling and complaining at first, and then laughing at his ill luck. Having satisfied our requirements we rode up the valley a little distance, to where there was a pleasant orchard and a large cultivated field hedged round with high branches of thorn, in the manner customary in this area. This was the one error of judgment we made throughout our trip, for instead of making for the wider country lower down, we had entered a cul-de-sac.

We thought that the English were finally gone, and prepared a meal, after which I made a second mistake, for, while the others kept their horses by them, I turned my little Arab, all saddled as he was, into the field, and, thoroughly weary from having been up all night, sought out a shady spot in the lee of the thorn-fence and without telling the others where I was, fell sound asleep.

I was awakened, I do not know how long after, by the clash of rifle-fire near by, and, starting to my feet half dazed, saw a number of English soldiers standing before their horses and blazing away at my seven companions, who were riding down the valley for their lives. I had only myself to blame for being left behind, as they did not know where I was, and were in any case unable to wait. My chief hope of escape was my horse, but he was standing inside the field in full view of the firing soldiers. They had not yet noticed me, as I was screened by the fence, so I parted some of the branches to see what chance there was of getting at my pony. By great good luck he was standing on the other side, within a few yards of me. The firing had alarmed him, for he was restlessly tossing his head and sniffing the air, and I could see that in another moment he would bolt, so I called to quiet him, and, worming my way through a weak spot in the fence, ran up to where he stood quivering with excitement. Jumping into the saddle, I rode for a small gateway in the far corner, which was the only outlet. The soldiers saw me at once, and turned their fire upon me, in spite of which I managed to get through the opening, but, just as I was gathering speed beyond, a bullet brought my poor horse headlong to the ground and flung me yards over his head. Picking up my rifle I ran towards the homestead, thinking that my party might be making a stand there. The soldiers beyond the field kept firing at me as I appeared and disappeared amongst the trees, but I got within hail of the house unharmed. At the corner of a barn stood six or seven men, whom in my haste I took to be my friends, and I made straight for them. But as I came within thirty yards of them, one stepped forward, and, levelling his rifle, called on me to halt.

They were English soldiers, and not the only ones, for more came rushing round from the stables and out of the dwelling-house. Escape seemed impossible, but I made a bid for it. To my right was a small grove of poplars, and, swerving aside, I dashed for this cover before they could send more than a bullet or two after me.

Volleys came crashing through the trees as I ran, but I emerged safely on the other side into hummocky ground, where I twisted and turned to such good effect that, although the men came hurrying round to cut off my retreat, I got into a broken stretch with no more serious damage than a gash from a bullet, which ripped up the sole of my boot and made running difficult.

Breasting a knoll, I glanced back. The soldiers near the field had mounted their horses, and were coming after me. Of those around the homestead, some were running in my direction, and others were in the yard throwing saddles on their animals, and I had a final glimpse of Mr. Guest in his shirt-sleeves on the stoep wildly gesticulating, but whether he was urging on the men to my capture or protesting against the crowning disaster of a battle on his doorstep, there was no time to consider, for I was in a very tight corner.

There was no sign of my companions. The sharp ground was cutting my foot, the horsemen were close behind me, and already I could hear the men yelling at me to stop, and I was just deciding that I had better do so, when I came on a deep nullah running down the mountain-side. Here it flashed on me that if my pursuers saw me disappear over the bank, they would naturally think that I was making down its bed to the centre of the valley, or up towards the mountain. Looking aslant my shoulder, to make sure that they saw what I was doing, I went over the bank, but instead of trying to escape up or down the water-course, as they would expect, I found a spot on the opposite side, where the rains had washed out a shallow runnel, and, crawling up this, went flat on my face into the bushes beyond, which stood just high enough to conceal a prostrate man. Having left the nullah unperceived, I worked myself forward another fifty yards to a slightly denser patch, and stopped there.

The soldiers, seeing me jump into the spruit, did exactly what I anticipated. On reaching the spot where they had seen me vanish, they separated into two parties, one of which galloped up the mountain-side, and the other down towards the valley. I had a clear view of the search from where I lay, and after a while I could see, from the undecided way in which they were riding about, that they were completely nonplussed.

In the end they must have concluded that I had got away on the upperside, for they spread out along the mountain slope like beaters at a shoot, moving farther and farther from my hiding-place. I knew now that I was comparatively safe, for the sun was setting, and before long I heard them clattering back to the farm, where presently their camp fires shone out, indicating that Mr. Guest was once more to be an unwilling host.

I felt proud of my successful ruse, but there was little else pleasant to contemplate. I lay in the bracken like a hunted rabbit; my foot throbbed painfully; my companions were gone, and so was the commando; my horse was dead and my saddle and belongings were in the hands of the enemy.

As thinking did not mend matters, I rose at length, and limped off in the dark.

After about an hour, I heard the sound of a hymn and the wheeze of a harmonium, such as stands in almost every Dutch farmhouse, and knew that I was nearing friends. When I knocked at the door there was a hush at first, for in these disturbed times a visit late at night meant military requisition, but then I heard a shuffle of feet and the door opened.

A whole family was peering from within. When I told them who I was, they almost dragged me into the house, so eager were they to help. I must have looked very dishevelled, for the women wept with pity while removing the boot from my sore foot, and during the more painful process of extracting a thorn, nearly an inch long, that had run into the palm of my hand when I was thrown from my horse that afternoon. They fetched hot water and tore up clean linen for bandages; a meal was laid, with coffee, and the kindly people almost quarrelled for the right to serve me, so keen was their sympathy, although they knew that it might mean for them fines and imprisonment. Having attended to my wants, they took further counsel. It was agreed that I could not remain here, for even if the continuous patrols did not ferret me out for themselves, my presence was certain to be reported by the coloured farm labourers, who all over the Cape sided with the British. As I assured them that I was well able to walk, it was decided that I must continue westward on the off-chance of coming up with General Smuts, who might be held up somewhere. It seemed a forlorn hope, but as there was the risk of an enemy detachment coming by at any moment, I made ready to start as soon as my boot had been sufficiently repaired.

The head of the family, a patriarch of seventy, insisted on acting as my guide during the first stage of the journey and firmly refused to waive the right in favour of his sons, who offered themselves. A grain-bag was packed with food, and after an affecting leave-taking, the old man and I set out. We trudged along, hour after hour, until his strength gave out and I made him turn back, his voice shaking with emotion as he wished me God-speed. My foot scarcely hindered me, and now that I was alone I made good speed on the well-marked wagon-road upon which he had set me, until, towards three in the morning, it dipped down into a ravine. By the time I reached the bottom the moon was clear, and by its light I saw several fresh hoof marks on the ground. On examining these, I recognized the slightly malformed marks of Michael du Preez's pony, and closer investigation showed me the footprints of men which I knew at once as those of some, if not all, of my seven missing companions, who had crossed the road here on their way down the ravine. This providential discovery cheered me immensely, for I had known all along that my hopes of overtaking the commando by myself were slim, but it was pretty certain that I could catch up with the men who had passed here so recently, and I lost no time in following their spoor.

After some miles they had branched off into a smaller kloof, and I followed along this without difficulty, for the tracks lay clear in the dusty cattle-path. At last, as day was breaking, I heard the whicker of a horse and, going forward carefully, found all seven men fast asleep beneath the trees. They were astonished to see me, as they had made certain that I was either dead or taken. They themselves had been hard put to it to make their escape from the farm, and although not one of them had received a scratch, yet out of the nine horses we had possessed between us, no less than six had been killed, and, what was almost as serious, we had lost the bulk of our saddles, cooking-tins, and blankets. We agreed that the first thing to do was to replenish our equipment, so we continued along the gully, until a long march brought us into the thickly populated valley of the Caminassi River, where we heard many rumours about our commando, but no certain news, beyond the fact that General Smuts was making west with a strong force of cavalry closely pressing him. The people willingly supplied our wants, and, for the next three days, we slowly felt our way down the broad valley. Far ahead were tall pillars of dust, made, they told us, by General French with thousands of horsemen, engaged in a great drive behind our commando, and occasionally we heard the distant boom of guns. As five of us were on foot, we had to proceed with great caution, and repeatedly we had to hide for hours at a time, to avoid bodies of horsemen passing from the rear to join their advance-columns ahead.

The more we saw of the valley, crowded with columns on the march, the less we liked it. William Conradi, after watching for some time, said that he had a better plan. Instead of following the commando any longer, he proposed to turn north across the Swartbergen, back into the Karoo country from which we had come. He said that General Smuts was almost certainly heading for the Western Cape, and, if we got that mountain range between ourselves and the troops, we could travel unmolested and perhaps join him when the chase had died down. We agreed, and set off at once. For two days we worked our way through the intervening country, towards where the Swartbergen stood like a wall on the northern horizon. At a village called Armoed we had trouble, for a party of soldiers rode at us as we were leaving it, and only the falling dusk and our brisk reply to their firing enabled us to escape through the river, into the bush on the other side.

My foot gave me no pain, and we got along safely, thanks to the local farmers, who kept us well informed.

On the morning of the third day we reached the foot of the mountain chain, just east of the Seven Weeks Gorge. Into this poort ran the main road to the open Karoo, but the pass was garrisoned, and our only course lay up the flank of the

range. As there were English patrols riding about we began the ascent without
delay, toiling upward steadily, until we made the summit by evening. These were
the same mountains which we had crossed coming in the opposite direction days
before. At that crossing the Swartbergen had consisted of a single clear-cut
barrier, but here it forked out into numerous sierras, that looked like giving us
much trouble.

As it was getting dark, and heavy rain began to fall, we dropped some distance over the crest to seek shelter for the night. It was too cold to sleep and too
damp to light a fire, so we sat shivering until dawn, when we started to grope our
way down the mountain-side enveloped in a dense mist. Towards four in the
afternoon we were below the clouds, and could see a long narrow canyon lying at
our feet, its sides closed in by perpendicular cliffs. On the floor of the chasm, a
thousand feet below, we made out a cluster of huts, and, thinking to find natives
there to guide us, we went down in a body to investigate, leaving the horses in a
ravine to look after themselves. We climbed through a fissure in the crags, and
reached the bottom soon after sunset. As we approached the huts, a shaggy
giant in goat-skins appeared and spoke to us in strange outlandish Dutch. He
was a white man named Cordier, who lived here with his wife and a brood of
half-wild children, in complete isolation from the outside world. He knew all
about us, for one of his sons had been up the mountain that morning, and,
hearing the sound of men and horses in the mist, had stalked us and carefully
noted our number and the language we spoke, after which he had vanished over
the edge of the cliffs to warn his father.

We were received with uncouth but sincere hospitality, and we applied ourselves gratefully to the goats' meat, milk, and wild honey that were placed before
us. Cordier told us that no British troops had ever penetrated this fastness and
that we were the first Boers to do so. He had heard vaguely of the war, but his
knowledge of the events of the last two years was scanty.

We spent that night and the next day with this curious Swiss Family Robin-
son, and in the evening toiled up the cliffs again, accompanied by our host and
some of his colts, who stayed with us around our camp fires, and led us the
following morning across rugged mountains, until by dark we looked down at
last upon the northern plains. Our intention now was to descend to the open
country and, keeping the mountains well on our left, to strike west towards the
districts of the Cape lying along the Atlantic seaboard two hundred miles away,
where we hoped ultimately to get news of General Smuts.

We spent another night on the heights, and, parting from our guides at daybreak, climbed down the slopes to level ground and headed across the plains. We
were now in the 'Gough' Karoo, as the Hottentots call it, an arid, waterless
region, sparsely occupied by wandering herdsmen. By next day we crossed the
railway line that runs from Capetown to the north. There were no block-houses,
as in the Transvaal and Free State, so we had no difficulty, although we saw the
double-tiered watch-towers at either end of the bridge over the Dwyka River.

On the far side of the line lay country even less inhabited, and we suffered
severely from thirst and hunger, for water was to be had only by digging in the

dry gravel-courses with our bare hands, and for food we had to subsist on what we had brought with us.

About a week after passing the railway line, always going due west, a patrol of English soldiers appeared on the baking plain. They opened fire at us, and when we replied they made off, doubtless to report to some larger force in the neighbourhood.

The day after that we reached a prosperous-looking farmhouse, the first we had seen since crossing the Swartbergen. At this place we had a miniature battle, for while we were talking to the owner and his wife, twelve or fifteen troopers suddenly rode on to a ridge and fired on us. We told our friends to go indoors, and ran down into the spruit, from which we worked forward, thinking to get near enough to our opponents to dislodge them and capture their horses, but by the time we got within a hundred yards of the troopers they were pinning us down with such accurate shooting that we had to hug the earth, and were only too glad to crawl back out of harm's way after dark, and retrieve our three horses and belongings at the farm.

For the next two days we travelled slowly on, gradually approaching the more thickly settled district that lies towards Calvinia.

At every house at which we touched we made inquiries for General Smuts, but no word of him was known. However, a pleasant surprise was awaiting us. Early one morning, as we sat by our fire, we saw a diminutive cart come over the rise, drawn by two donkeys. On the seat was a grey-bearded old Dutch farmer of the poorer class and beside him a smart English sergeant. When we stopped this queerly assorted couple, we were astonished to learn that they had quitted General Smuts and his commando only an hour or two before. The soldier said that he had been captured the previous day while scouting, and after spending the night with our men, had been released that morning.

We were so delighted with this unexpected good news that we insisted on shaking hands with our informant, who could not at first understand our elation. When we explained, he said that for his part he had less cause for congratulation because, having been deprived of his horse, and having no mind to walk ninety-odd miles to the nearest military post, he had ordered his fellow-traveller in the King's name to provide him with transport.

As the only available conveyance was the one we saw, he was not looking forward to the journey, particularly as relations were strained with the driver. The farmer was glum and angry at having to drive a *verdomde rooinek* (as he called him) on a journey that would take him from home for the better part of a fortnight, and would subject him to the jeers of all his neighbours on his return, while the servant was no better pleased with his companion, who, he said, did not understand a word of English and only grunted when spoken to. We did not waste much time on the incongruous pair, and, after wishing them a pleasant journey, hurried on.

Tramping forward for seven or eight miles, we breasted a rise, and there, on the banks of a river below, was the welcome sight of many horses at graze and smoke rising from among the trees to show that our long quest was at an end. A mounted sentry rode out to see who we were, and, after shaking hands, galloped back to spread the news of our arrival. Soon the entire commando was running to meet us, and we were surrounded by a laughing, cheering crowd, all anxious to show their pleasure at our safe return. General Smuts was among the foremost to greet us. He said he had long given us up for lost, and warmly praised the way in which we had come through without losing a man.

Great indeed was our joy at getting back, but for me there was a fly in the ointment, for I found that the 'Rijk Section' was practically wiped out. First, there was Jack Borrius minus an eye, and still suffering from a swollen, festering hand; then there lay Ben Coetzee with a bullet in his leg; Nicolas Swart, with a shattered arm, the result of a revolver shot at close quarters; and Edgar Duncker, with a bullet through his thigh and three fingers of his right hand blown to pieces. In addition, my uncle Jan Mulder (he was really my step-uncle) and our inconspicuous but loyal companion, Jan van Zijl, had been captured, so that there was very little left of the old unit, Wyndell, Frits Balogh, and I being the only foundation members not incapacitated.

The total loss to the commando during our absence, apart from a dozen wounded who had come along, was not more than seven or eight men, in spite of heavy fighting all the way.

In the meanwhile, the other half of our force under van Deventer was not yet accounted for, but General Smuts fully expected that, under so experienced a leader, they would eventually turn up.

24. CALMER WATERS

From now onward, the circumstances of our expedition into the Cape radically altered for the better. Here in the far-west there were no railways, and the country was so difficult for large bodies of troops that we had reached comparative sanctuary. North, stretching towards the Orange River hundreds of miles away, lay a great territory practically free of the enemy, save for rare columns passing by, and a few garrisons scattered long distances apart so that we had the country almost to ourselves.

Small bands of local rebels had long been carrying on a desultory warfare of their own, between here and the coast, and General Smuts told us that he was going to reorganize these into larger commandos until he was strong enough to undertake big-scale operations, which he thought might ease the pressure in the two Republics. Thus we looked forward with fresh interest to the new stage of the war opening before us.

That same evening we moved off, still going west, our wounded now comfortably driven in carts, while those of us who had returned without horses were provided with temporary mounts, a welcome change after our long tramp. In a few days' time we reached Elandsvlei, an oasis with waving palms and running water, and here we halted for two whole days. This was the first time since crossing the Orange River into the Cape that we had stayed in one place for even a day and a night, and, needless to say, both man and beast revelled in the unaccustomed holiday. In the hills near by ran a troop of mules, and some friends and I, managed to catch half a dozen of them, mine being a powerful black, who squealed and bit and threw me several times before I mastered him. Then he was quite gentle and I rode him for many hundreds of miles during the next few months.

From Elandsvlei we went north-west via Biddow to place called Kobbee, a deep valley that reminded me of Dreadful Hollow in *Robbery Under Arms*, and here again we lay over for several days, feeding our animals on the plentiful crops. Thence we crossed the intervening mountains to the great plain that runs towards the Atlantic; sixty miles away. At the foot of these mountains lies the village of van Rijnsdorp. It had been recently garrisoned by the British, but

Commandant Maritz had swooped down and captured it. This Maritz was a policeman from Johannesburg, who, after many adventures, had established himself in these parts as a leader of various rebel bands.

He was a short, dark man, of enormous physical strength, crude and ruthless in his methods, but a splendid guerrilla leader, and according to his lights an ardent patriot, of whom I was to see more later on.

He had sacked the village and disappeared with his retainers, and we found the original civil population in peaceful occupation, the English having apparently abandoned the place for good.

As the 'Rijk Section' was now practically defunct, General Smuts ordered William Conradi and me to join his staff. This was in recognition of our late exploit, and was tantamount to military promotion. The rest of the 'Rijk Section' was absorbed into Commandant Bouwer's commando, with the exception of Ben Coetzee, who rode away, his leg still in splints, in search of Maritz, for they were old friends. This, then, was the end of that small company with whom I had come into the Cape. Like Isaac Malherbe's Corporalship and the 'A.C.C.', it, too, had been destroyed, but I am glad to have served with three such bodies of men.

I was now what might correspond to a staff officer in a regular army, although none of us on General Smuts's headquarters bore any distinguishing title, beyond the fact that the rest of the men in friendly derision referred to us as 'Kripvreters'—a Kripvreter being a stall-fed horse, as distinguished from one having to scratch for its own living on the veld.

On assuming my new duties, however, I soon found that, so far from being staffed, the members of the staff, in addition to having to fight and forage for themselves like the rest, were employed as dispatch-riders, and during the next few weeks our life was one continual round of weary rides in search of one portion or another of the commando, for General Smuts had now divided his force into smaller groups, often stationed days apart, to provide more easily for grazing and food.

In December (1901) he left the commando scattered along the banks of the Olifants River near van Rijnsdorp, and, with his staff, moved up the mountains to a spot called Willems River, where he began his work of collecting the various rebel bands into organized commandos. A large number of men from this area had either joined Maritz or were riding about on their own, sniping at British columns or waylaying convoys, and, in order to get into touch with these irregulars, we 'Kripvreters' were sent during the next few weeks on long rides, in the course of which we travelled unnumbered miles from south of the Olifants River to far beyond Calvinia and back, until we knew every inch of the country.

The inhabitants sympathised with us, and looked upon us as their champions, so we were welcomed wherever we went and, despite the long gruelling journeys on mule-back, I enjoyed myself, for I was not above feeling a pleasant glow when the womenfolk waved from before the farmhouses, and the men shouted greetings from the road-side.

On Christmas Day, returning from a hundred-mile errand beyond Calvinia, I saw mounted men camped in the distance, and making thither, found them to be

Commandant van Deventer's missing column. My unexpected appearance amongst them was hailed with joy, for this was their first word of us since we had parted below the Zuurbergen, and for a long time I was busy telling them how we had fared and listening to their experiences. They had only just arrived here, having been driven out of their course for several weeks, but they had done well, for they had captured several convoys and many prisoners, and they had more horses, rifles, and ammunition than they could use.

After a pleasant evening's talk around the camp-fires, I remained there for the night, and took the road again next day, getting back by the 28th to General Smuts, who was greatly pleased at my news.

My mule had unflinchingly trotted the better part of two hundred miles in five days, and the following morning I was off again in search of Maritz, whom I found eighty miles away in the neighbourhood of Tontelbos. This place was an important grain-growing centre, at which the British had posted a force of men, to prevent the crops from being carried away. Maritz attacked the garrison the day before I arrived, but was repulsed with heavy loss, he himself bring severely wounded. I found him seated on a chair in a farmhouse with two of his men dressing his wound, a terrible gash below the right armpit, exposing the lung, an injury that would have killed most men, but he was like a bull and seemed little the worse for it.

I saw the year 1902 in with them, and then started back, catching up General Smuts three days later at Nieuwoudsville on the escarpment. During all this time our main commando under Commandant Bouwer was lying down on the plains to the south, having occasional brushes with the English, but on the whole passing a quiet time. Some of our patrols went beyond Porterville, to within sight of Table Mountain, and my old companion Krige (the General's brother-in-law), with whom I had served in Isaac Malherbe's Corporalship, and who had been so badly wounded at Spion Kop, even penetrated as far as Malmesbury, and brought back a large sum of money for the use of the commando from General Smuts's father, who lived there.

During a visit which I paid at this time to our men along the Olifants River, I met my old Ladysmith tent-mate, Walter de Vos, who had likewise been wounded on Spion Kop, and whom I had last seen lying on the slope of that hill, on the day of the big fight two years before. He had latterly been in command of one of the local rebel bands, and we spent the morning talking over old times; but he was killed an hour after my going, in an outpost affair nearby.

Early in January General Smuts decided to go north to the Orange River, to organize the numerous rebel patrols that were under arms there. Our company consisted of himself and his staff only. It was a three-hundred-mile ride through desert country, and we went first of all to Tontelbos, now evacuated, as the crops were in. Maritz was here on a pallet of straw in an empty dwelling-house, but he made light of his wound and was well on the mend.

From Tontelbos we moved north through country thinly occupied by Nomad Boers (Trek Boers), who spend their lives going from one well to another with their flocks, like the old peoples in the Bible. They are a primitive patriarchal folk, knowing little of the outside world, but of a brave and sturdy stock, and many of them were under arms.

We travelled mostly at night to avoid the blazing heat of day, and at length reached Kakamas, a small irrigation colony founded by the Dutch Church on the south bank of the Orange River. The settlement was still in its infancy and the inhabitants lived in rude huts and shelters made of grass and reeds, but they had built a canal from the river, and had established fields and orchards so successfully that the place had become a supply depot for the surrounding districts. We spent a pleasant fortnight here, eating fruit and swimming in the river every day. As soon as General Smuts had completed his arrangements with the guerrilla bands, many of whom rode in from the desert to meet him, we returned south, reaching Tontelbos again towards the second week in February. Maritz was no longer here, but as the grazing was good in the cropped wheat-lands, we lay over a few days to rest our animals and ourselves.

General Smuts then decided to go eastwards in search of Commandant van Deventer. We did not know exactly where his commando was, but we travelled up along the Fish River, and after a day or two got word that he was thirty or forty miles away. We rode thither all that night, and towards daylight heard the sound of gun-fire and small-arms and saw a red glare in the sky. Quickening our pace, we reached a farmhouse called Middelpost at dawn, and found two or three men here in charge of a dozen wounded.

They told us that van Deventer was fighting close by with an English column on its way to Calvinia, so, after a few hurried questions, we rode to where we could see his men, lining the crest of some small kopjes, their horses tethered below. On higher ground away to the left were small parties of English troops, and a single field-piece stood in full view but out of rifle-range. The men at the farmhouse warned us to ride for it, as they said that the gunners had the distance to a yard, so we set off at a gallop. They were right, for when we had got about halfway, there was a flash at the gun, and a shell came tearing at us.

A local schoolmaster named Hugo, who had joined a few weeks before, was riding beside me. The shell burst on us with a roar, but although I was nearer the gun, neither my mule nor I received a scratch. But when the smoke cleared I saw that my companion was badly hit. He was swaying in his saddle with blood streaming from his chest. His rifle dropped to the ground, and he fell forward on the neck of his animal. Then he recovered himself and said he was not going to give the gunners the satisfaction of knowing that they had hit anyone, so raising himself he rode for cover of the hill. Other shells came after, but no one else was hit, and, having retrieved the fallen rifle, I rode on and found that Hugo had fainted and fallen from his horse, and that General Smuts and the others were trying to staunch his wound. It was at the base of his left lung, and I fished out the twisted buckle of his braces, and a cartridge-clip with five rounds of ammu-nition, all of which had been driven into the cavity, in addition to the shell-fragment which I could not recover. I thought that he had not ten minutes to live, but two months later he was in the saddle once more. We made him comfortable, and climbed up to where Commandant van Deventer and his men were holding the ridge above. This was the first time that General Smuts had come among them since the parting in Somerset East, and there were cheers and shouts of greeting when they saw him. Van Deventer himself hastened forward to welcome us, and in a few seconds we were in the firing-line. Looking down the forward side of the hill, we saw an interesting sight.

Immediately below, on the level ground by the banks of a spruit, stood some hundred and twenty English convoy-wagons, most of them burning fiercely to the crackle of exploding rifle ammunition, for every wagon seemed to carry several cases. Scattered among the blazing vehicles lay dead men and horses, and there were a large number of live troop-horses and mules, that had stampeded during the night, but had drifted back into the burring camp, where, in spite of the smoke and flames and the bursting cartridges, they were feeding on the seed oats and other fodder that our men had flung from the wagons during their hasty search for loot, before setting them on fire.

Van Deventer gave us a brief account of what had happened. A long convoy had approached the evening before, accompanied by a mounted column. He had disputed their way, whereupon the English troops parked their wagons beside the spruit, and took up covering positions, but during the night he and his men broke through the line on foot, and, entering the camp, set it on fire. In the dark the troops were unable effectively to hinder the work of destruction, and the position when we arrived was that van Deventer, having fired the wagons, had withdrawn before daylight, and the two sides were now facing one another with the convoy burning between them, neither side permitting the other to approach it. The bulk of the English soldiers had taken post at a farmhouse surrounded by a walled garden, about nine hundred yards away, from which they were maintaining a hot rifle-fire.

To the left, four hundred yards off, lay more of them on a stone hill, with their field-gun on a rise behind, and on the right in another kopje was an isolated detachment, so placed that they had anyone under short range who tried to enter the camp. Van Deventer told General Smuts that he was anxious to recover the animals feeding amongst the wagons, to which end he had a fewer minutes previously sent Field-Cornet Van der Berg with twenty-five men to clear the kopje overlooking the camp by a surprise attack from the rear. He had ordered them to ride round behind some other kopjes that screened the view.

I had now ridden my mule for upwards of a thousand miles. He was a willing animal, but with his shambling gait and long stride a mule at best makes a tiring mount, and I yearned for the easier seat of a horse. Another man in the staff, Martin Brink, had also been on a mule for months past, and was equally anxious for a change, so we decided to overtake the attacking party in the hope of getting a troop-horse or two. We ran down, and, mounting, followed the tracks made by Van der Berg's men as fast as we could go. He had led them with skill, for nowhere was their route visible from the kopje, and when, after a breathless gallop, we raced round the corner of a ridge into the open we found that he had taken the soldiers by surprise and that he and his men had reached the foot, and were climbing up under a ragged rifle-fire, without having sustained any visible loss. By the time we joined them the affair was as good as over. A shot or two was loosed, but in a few seconds the last of the soldiers stood up to surrender. It had, however, been an expensive little fight. Alouin Weber, an ex-Transvaal artillery officer, and two more men lay dead and Field-Cornet van der Berg and another were badly wounded, while several soldiers were killed and three or four wounded, out of the dozen or so who had been holding the post.

In any case, know that the kopje was in our hands, it was possible to make our way down to the spruit, on the opposite bank of which stood the burning wagons, so, leaving their friends to attend to the wounded, the rest of us lost no time in descending the slope and jumping into the spruit. We ran along the sandy bottom until we could peer over at the camp, a stone's throw away. Then we climbed out and rushed for the horses that were nosing the fodder-strewn ground. When the troops from the distant farm-house saw us running amongst the wagons, they opened fire, but we were not to be denied. My first effort was to insure myself against further mule-riding, and in three successive raids I brought away three good horses with saddles and holsters complete. I hurried each into the shelter of the spruit, and ran out again for the next. The other men were just as busy, and luckily no one was hit. As soon as I had secured my horses, I went back for other portable property, for several of the wagons and their loads were only half burnt, while some were scarcely damaged at all, and there was much useful loot still to be had. In dodging among the smouldering wagons I came on a fully laden scotch-cart that had been overlooked in the dark. It was quite intact, and, as the firing from the farmhouse was increasing, I seized a large portmanteau and shovelled into it all that I could find in the way of books, papers, boots and clothing, including some Bank of England notes, and then dragged it over the ground to the spruit.

I found that most of it belonged to Colonel Dorran, who had commanded the convoy, and that amongst his papers were the records of the Court Martial of Commandant Scheepers, at which he had presided. We had heard already that this well-known guerrilla leader had been captured and executed in the Midlands some months before for alleged train-wrecking.

After a hurried inspection of my new property, I distributed my haul evenly on my three horses and my mule, and rode back to General Smuts very pleased with the morning's work, for, no longer a ragged muleteer, I was now better horsed, shod, and equipped than at any time of the war.

Soon after this the English troops sent off their gun and began to retire southward, abandoning a large number of horses and mules that had broken away, and were roaming about the veld.

General Smuts and Commandant van Deventer decided not to pursue the retreating column, for, even if we captured them, we should only have to let them go again, and we had done so well in horseflesh that it did not seem worth while to go after them. We were now free to revisit the camp unmolested, and, in addition to hundreds of animals, the men recovered a considerable quantity of ammunition, saddlery, etc., and, most valuable of all, many cases of horse-shoes and nails. Five or six soldiers lay dead in the camp, and, when some of us rode up to the farmhouse where their main body had been, we found twenty or thirty wounded who had been left there in charge of a military doctor, several of them very badly injured. At the request of the Medical Officer I rode round to shoot the wounded horses and mules standing about the house, some with broken legs, others with blood dripping from their flanks, for, with no one to look after them, it was best to put them out of their misery. One of the horses I had taken from the camp was a beautiful little dark-grey Arab mare with a coat like velvet and nimble as a goat. I was mounted on her when I rode to the farmhouse, and here her former owner, a wounded officer named Chapman, lying on a stretcher outside, recognized her, and offered to buy her back from me for £65. He said her name was Ninny and that she was the best horse in the country. As money was of no use to me, and I knew a good horse when I saw one, I refused to sell, but I promised to look after her and treat her well.

The commando spent the night at the other little farm-house, where we had first found van Deventer's wounded, and here we buried our dead at sunrise next day. The bodies had been placed ready on a wagon, and, not knowing this, I spent the night under it, and, waking in the morning, found myself dotted with blood that had oozed through the planking overhead.

At the funeral General Smuts made a moving speech. He pointed out that among the dead were a Transvaaler, a Freestater, and a Colonial, all parts of South Africa being thus represented in the common sacrifice for liberty. When the ceremony was over I was ordered to ride to the place twenty miles away to which our wounded had been taken, to see that all was well. I found most of the men fairly comfortable, although there were several bad cases. One was a Colonial who had been shot through the stomach, and the woman of the house asked me to have a look at him as his side was inflamed. While she and I were examining the wound, he gave a deep groan and died without speaking. A wagon-driver helped me to bury him. We dug a hole beside the threshing-floor, and as we knew no funeral service, we simply carried him by the shoulders and knees, laid him in the grave, covered him with earth, and left him.

While I was at this farm we saw forty or fifty strange horsemen approaching from the north, and there was some alarm at first amongst the wounded, as we could not make out who they were. I fetched my horse and rifle and rode in their direction, until I was close enough to see that they were not British. They proved to be the survivors of a portion of the commando that General Smuts had left behind on his way through the Free State the year before, because their horses were too worn out to go on. He had placed Field-Comet Dreyer in charge, with orders to follow later, when the condition of their animals permitted, and the faithful band had carried out these instructions to the letter. As soon as possible they started south in our tracks, and, after many trials and dangers, this remnant had come through. Among them was the Reverend Mr. Kriel, with whom my brothers and I had quarrelled at Warm Baths in December, 1900.

In spite of his religious bigotry, he was a stout-hearted old man, whom I learned to respect. When they heard that General Smuts was in the district, they were so anxious to see him that they wanted to go off at once, but I told them to wait, as I knew that the General was coming our way, and he arrived that evening with van Deventer and his commando and there was great rejoicing on both sides.

Ever since General Smuts had gone to Kakamas in December, Commandant Bouwer with his commando had remained down on the plains near the Olifants River beyond van Rijnsdorp, and I was now sent to find them. I gave away my mule, but took all three of my newly acquired horses, loaded with my loot from the camp. I reached van Rijnsdorp in three days, going via Nieuwoudsville, and thence down the mountain pass to the country below. I found Bouwer in van Rijnsdorp, and most of his men camped along the True-true River not far off. They were the more pleased when I told them of van Deventer's success, because they had suffered an unpleasant reverse the previous morning.

A week before a Colonial named Lemuel Colaine had turned up amongst them with a tale that the English had put him in prison at Clan-William on a false charge of high treason. He said that he had escaped over the wall one night and had come in revenge to take up arms. Believing his story, they gave him a rifle and he joined the commando.

Colaine, however, was a spy in British pay, and, after collecting what information he could, he disappeared. No particular notice was taken of his absence, as the men were constantly riding off to visit farms, or look up friends at distant outposts, and it was thought that he had done the same; but the commando had a rude awakening when a body of English horse, with Colaine riding at their head, fell upon them at dawn, killing and wounding seventeen men, including my young friend Michael du Preez.

The attacking force took our men so completely by surprise that the troopers rode through the camp using their swords, and got away safely on the other side before our men could recover their wits. All were fierce in their denunciation of Colaine's treachery, and hoped that he would fall into their hands. And later Nemesis ran the right man to earth for once.

Meanwhile Bouwer was smarting under this setback, for not only had he lost good men, but the British were following up their success by an advance in force, with the object of retaking van Rijnsdorp, which we had come to regard as our headquarters, for it was the only town in South Africa still in Boer hands.

I remained with Bouwer overnight in the threatened village, and, as his scouts reported next morning that a strong column of English horsemen was pushing forward, he decided to retire northwards to the mountains until reinforcements could reach him.

I went out to watch the enemy movements with a party, among them being my old friends Nicolas Swart and Edgar Duncker, the former with his arm still in a sling, while the latter had his shattered hand in splints, and a pillow strapped to his saddle to ease his wounded thigh, for the sound of rifle-fire was an irresistible attraction to these two, and they refused to remain behind when they heard shots beyond the town. After going forward for a mile or two, we saw a long column of horsemen coming up from the direction of the Olifants River, their scouts thrown forward on a wide front, and we were soon engaged in a running fight, which continued until they pressed us back through the streets into the open country, where we took to our heels, to catch up with Bouwer's main body making for the mountains. In the course of one of these skirmishes, Duncker, riding beside me, was shot through the chest. We plugged the bullet-holes with pieces of his shirt, and he rode on with us for the fifteen-odd miles that we had to go before we overtook the commando. He was then sent to a farm among the foothills, and completely recovered in a few weeks. The English contented themselves with reoccupying our little capital and came no farther, so Bouwer did not retire up the mountains after all, but, determined to recover his lost ground, he sent me hurrying up the pass to ask General Smuts for help.

After riding hard for two days I came up with him near Calvinia, sixty miles off, and, when he heard that the troops were back in van Rijnsdorp, he ordered the commanders to gather. He sent word to van Deventer to bring his men to the head of the pass at Nieuwoudsville, where he would wait for him, while another messenger was sent to Bouwer, bidding him keep his men below until assistance came.

The various smaller local patrols were also ordered in, and General Smuts and his staff made for the appointed rendezvous at the edge of the berg.

The arrangements worked perfectly. In three days van Deventer arrived with his fighting-men, and we descended the mountains to Urion's Kraal on the plains, where Bouwer was eagerly awaiting us. This was the fist time that our entire original commando had been reunited since parting under the Zuurbergen, and there was great cheering and handshaking when we rode up. That night our whole force marched out, intending to attack van Rijnsdorp at daybreak, but when it grew light we found that the English troops had been withdrawn to a place called Windhoek, ten miles back, which was being turned into a fortified camp, so we lay over in the recovered village until dark. General Smuts had decided to attack Windhoek at dawn next morning, but I missed the fight, for I was not told of what was pending, and was sent off at sunset with a message to a post stationed towards the Olifants. I arrived after midnight, and spent the night with the picket. At dawn I was in the saddle on the return journey, and, as I rode towards van Rijnsdorp, I heard distant rifle-fire, and hurried towards it.

As I approached, the firing grew heavier for a while, and then died down altogether, so that I knew one side had been worsted. Then I came on Commandant van Deventer huddled on the ground before his horse, badly wounded and in great pain. Blood was pouring from a bullet-wound in his throat, and his tongue was so lacerated that he could not speak. Two men with him told me that the fight was over, and that the English camp at Windhoek had been captured. I galloped on, and met about a hundred disarmed soldiers, marching across the veld without their boots. They said our men had ordered them to find their way back to Clan-William, fifty miles away.

In a few seconds I reached the scene of action. General Smuts had surrounded the camp at daybreak, and, after a sharp fight, had overwhelmed it, killing and wounding many, and capturing the rest, about two hundred in number. He had not come off lightly either, having lost five men killed and sixteen wounded, but he had taken wagons, horses, arms and ammunition, and he head re-established his hold on these parts. As I rode through the camp I found Nicolas Swart lying on the ground apparently dead. A bullet had struck him in the chest and had traversed the length of his body, emerging at his left thigh, showing that he must have been bending forward when he was hit. His face was so pale that I thought him dead, so I went to one of the wagons in search of something to throw over his body, but when I came back his eyes were open, and he asked me in a whisper for a drink of water, which I gave him from my bottle. We carried him into the shade of a wagon, and roughly bandaged his wounds. As we could do nothing further for the moment, I left him, in order to look around the rest of the captured convoy now being ransacked by the men. It was parked around the dwelling-house in which the troops had made their last stand, and, seeing Wyndell of the 'Rijk Section', I went to tell him about Nicolas. He had shared in the attack, but did not know that Nick was wounded, and he said we must search the house for pillow-slips or sheeting for better bandages. As we went through the rooms, strewn with upturned chairs, etc., in the hand-to-hand fighting, we saw a man in civilian clothing crouched under the arched fireplace in the kitchen. I thought it was the owner of the farm, not yet recovered from his fright, but when I drew Wyndell's attention to him he exclaimed, 'By God! It's Colaine!' I did not know Colaine, but Wyndell dragged him from the house, shouting to the men outside to come and see who was here, and soon dozens of angry men were muttering threats and curses at the wretched spy. He was a man of about forty-five, in appearance a typical back-veld Boer, with flowing beard and corduroys. He was brave enough now, for when the men fiercely assured him of his certain fate he shrugged his shoulders, and showed no sign of fear. Commandant Bouwer came up while we were crowding round, and ordered two men to guard him until General Smuts was notified.

Wyndell and I, having found some linen, went back to look for Nicolas, but found him gone, and were told that he had been loaded on a mule-wagon with other casualties, for removal to another farm.

As I was well found in horses and equipment since the Middelpost affair, the present convoy did not much interest me, but I collected some newspapers and books, and, leaving the men at their looting, I prepared to ride down to the farm known as Aties, belonging to old Isaac van Zijl, the local member of Parliament, where General Smuts was said to be. But first I went to see who were killed, and was sad to find among them young Martin Wessels, a school-friend who had spent many of his holidays with my brothers and myself in the old Bloemfontein days. I had met him two days before, for the first time during the war, having come on him with one of the small rebel bands in the neighbourhood. He had been wounded and captured by the British a year ago, but with Cornelius Vermaas, now also dead, he had leaped the train in the Hex River Mountains to rejoin the commandos. When I entered the homestead at Aties, General Smuts was in the dining-room talking to the owner, Isaac van Zijl, whose wife and daughters were there, too, and before long Colaine, the spy, was ushered in by his guards, who wanted to know what to do with their prisoner. General Smuts had heard the whole story of by Colaine's treachery, and, after questioning the escort to make sure of the man's identity, he sentenced him to death without further formality. When the General said to the guards, 'Take him out and shoot him!' Colaine's nerve failed him, and, falling on his knees, he begged for mercy, while the women fled from the room in tears. General Smuts repeated his order, but as the condemned man was being led out, the Reverend Mr. Kriel came in, and asked leave to pray for the soul of this poor sinner. So Cocaine was taken to a little smithy behind the dwelling-house, and when I looked in a little later, I saw him and the clergyman kneeling side by side against a plough-tail, deep in prayer. After a while Andries de Wet of our staff was told to collect a firing party, and, as he disliked the job, he asked me to accompany him. We sent some Hottentot servants to dig a grave out of sight of the house, to spare the feelings of its inmates, and, ordering three men who had off-saddled in the garden to fetch their rifles, we went to the workshop door. Catching Mr. Kriel's eye, de Wet pointed to the prisoner, and the clergyman touched the kneeling man on the shoulder and said, 'Brother, be a man, your time has come.' Colaine took the news calmly; he rose from his knees, shook the parson by the hand, and bidding good-bye to the guards, said that he was ready. We led him to where the grave was being dug. On the way he spoke to us. He said he knew he deserved to die, but he was a poor man and had taken blood-money to keep his wife and children from starving. The Hottentots were just completing the grave when we came up, and the unfortunate man blanched when he looked into the shallow pit. Perhaps he had still hoped for a reprieve, until he saw it. Even now he tried to gain time, by appealing to us to send for Mr. Kriel, to say a final prayer with him. Then he turned to me, and asked me to fetch General Smuts, but we felt that the sooner it was over the better, so de Wet blindfolded him, and placed him at the head of the grave. Realizing that this was the end, Colaine held up his hands, and in a low tone recited the Lord's Prayer, while the firing party silently ranged themselves. As he came to the final 'Amen', they fired. With a convulsive jerk he pitched backward into the grave, and the frightened Hottentots quickly covered him with earth.

When we returned, we found that the wounded had been brought down from Windhoek, and were being placed in the main dwelling-house. Nicolas Swart was still alive, in fact the jolting seemed to have improved his condition, for he was conscious and able to speak. He was put in a room by himself, whilst the rest were laid on mattresses or on straw, wherever the mistress of the house and her daughters could find room for them. Nicolas was taken with a sick man's fancy that I should remain by his side. When I tried to leave him, he seized my hand and would not let me go, so General Smuts said I was to stay, and I sat by his side all that afternoon and all through the following night. At intervals I renewed the wad of damp cloth over the wound in his chest, doing this for close on twenty hours, and soon after daybreak he fell into an easy sleep. From then onward he began slowly to mend, and within a month was well again. Of the other wounded only one man died, the rest all making good progress, thanks to the care of the women and the wonderful climate.

The camp at Windhoek had cost us more men than it was worth, but the English were discouraged from further attempts to dislodge us and from the Olifants northwards we were left in possession of all area that we were beginning to regard as our peculiar property. So much was this the case that General Smuts once more broke up the commandos, and distributed the men in small patrols until he should need them for a fresh effort. This entailed much work for the members of the staff, who were kept riding backwards and forwards from one detachment to another, in order to maintain contact.

I, however, stayed behind at the farm, as Nicolas Swart would not hear of my leaving.

While I was here I had time to read the English newspapers that I had found in the Windhoek camp. I gathered from certain letters and articles that there were many people in England who thought the war unfair. I cut out one poem and have kept it ever since. It ran:

Peace On Earth, Goodwill To Man.
Christmas Day, 1901.

The story is too old: no more it thrills.
Pity is dead; peace is a paltry art.
How can a glory on Judean hills
Make glad my heart?

The mighty splendours of our state shall show
A worthier creed than decalogue or love,
Let death and vengeance, launched on every foe,
Our greatness prove.

Why mock us with the thoughts of Bethlehem
And glory humbled, and exalting grace?
Celestial music fits not with our theme
Our pride of race.

Dear God, forgive! Let other hearts be stone;
Christ's natal message shakes me like a reed.
Nor pride nor power nor country can condone,
The wild beast's creed?

At the end of ten days Nicolas was so much better that I was able to get away in search of General Smuts, whom I found on the banks of the Olifants River down towards the mouth. The sea lay only twenty-five miles from here and the day after my return he sent word to the units quartered within reach, that all who had never seen it were to be sent to him. Some sixty or seventy men arrived within the next forty-eight hours, and with these we set off for a small inlet on the coast called Fishwater. We rode via the Ebenezer Mission Station, and towards afternoon caught a glint of the sea through a gap in the dunes. It was amusing to watch the expression on the men's faces as the great expanse of ocean burst on their view, for few of them had seen anything bigger than the dam on their parents' farms, and, as we topped the last sand-hills, they looked in amazement on water that stretched beyond the horizon.

With one accord they reined in their horses in silence, and then, like the Greek soldiers, rushed forward in a body, crying, 'The sea! The sea!' -each wanting to be first on the beach.

Soon they were throwing off their clothes, and our trouble was, not to get them to enter the waves, but to prevent them from venturing in too deep, for they were pitching down their saddles and riding barebacked into the surf, shouting and laughing whenever a rider and his mount were thrown headlong by the breakers.

After a while General Smuts ordered three of us to ride along the shore towards some huts in the distance, to inquire whether any troops had been here of late. In doing so we had an amusing encounter with a Hottentot fisherman. He stared open-mouthed at sight of armed Boers patrolling the water-line, and, seeing his surprise, I halted my horse and ordered him in a peremptory tone to show me where the road went through. He said, 'What road, Baas?' Pretending to be angry, I replied, 'The road to England, you fool, and show me the way at once, for we are crossing tonight to capture London.' He looked at me for a moment, and then exclaimed, 'My God, Baas, don't do it; the water is over your head here, and you will all be drowned.'

When next I met Maritz and told him this story, he said that two of his men had recently ridden on to the beach at Lambert's Bay, where an English cruiser lay at anchor close in-shore. Dismounting, they opened fire. Their bullets pattered harmlessly against the armoured side of the warship, and when the crew turned a gun on them they made haste to disappear into the sand hills, but, on their return to their commando, they boasted that they had fought the only naval action of the war!

That night we camped in the dunes, sitting around great fires of driftwood, the men discussing what they had seen until far into the night, and telling each other of the things they would have to recount when they got home again.

We spent two more days here, boating on the estuary and helping the local fishermen to drag their nets. Then we returned along the Olifants River to our starting-place, proud of having ridden our horses into the sea.

25. THE LAST PHASE

General Smuts now made further plans.

To the north, one hundred and fifty miles away, lay the important copper-mining centre of O'Okiep, with its subsidiary villages of Springbok and Concordia. These places were held by British garrisons, and he decided to look them up. So far as I could gather, his intention was not so much to capture the towns, as to lure a relief expedition thither, for he calculated that, if he threatened them, the British would be compelled to hurry a force round by the sea to their assistance. He would then break away south, and make for the old settled districts around the Cape. Thus at any rate was the rumour current among us, and the men were enthusiastic at the thought of raiding down towards Table Bay. They even talked of taking Capetown itself, and we on the staff were cheered, as we rode to tell the outlying patrols and corporalships that they were to gather once more.

After a few days the whole commando was assembled, and we faced north on a long journey through the barren rugged country of Namaqualand.

Owing to difficulties of food-supply and water, we were, presently split into smaller parties, each with instructions to make for a point in the Kamiesbergen. General Smuts and his staff travelled by a separate route to the Leliefontein Mission Station, which we reached in six days.

We found the place sacked and gutted, and among the rocks beyond the burned houses lay twenty or thirty dead Hottentots, still clutching their anti-quated muzzle-loaders. This was Maritz's handiwork. He had ridden into the station with a few men, to interview the European missionaries, when he was set upon by armed Hottentots, he and his escort narrowly escaping with their lives. To avenge the insult, he returned next morning with a stronger force and wiped out the settlement, which seemed to many of us a ruthless and unjustifiable act. General Smuts said nothing, but I saw him walk past the boulders where the dead lay, and on his return he was moody and curt, as was his custom when displeased.

We lived in an atmosphere of rotting corpses for some days, for we bad to wait here for news that our forces had arrived within striking distance of the copper-mills; then we moved nearer. At Silverfountains we found Bouwer with his men, as well as Maritz and a considerable number of local rebels, but, as van Deventer's commando was still absent, I was sent in search of him.

I started at daybreak one morning on what was the longest unbroken spell of riding and fighting that I had during the war, for I did not rest or sleep for eighty hours. I rode all that day, continually changing horses (I had my two spare mounts alongside), and making inquiries from farmers and shepherds. With the help of a guide I located van Deventer by midnight, and on receipt of my message he took the road at once. I had to travel back with him through that night and for most of the next day until, towards sunset, we reached General Smuts and the rest of our force at Silverfountains. Having now been in the saddles for thirty-six hours, I hoped for a rest, but at dusk the whistles blew, and the commando started off for the villages of Springbok, thirty miles away. our course ran at first among rough hills, through which we made slow progress, and then across more open country, until, by four in the morning, we closed in on the village, the different sections moving round to prearranged posts, under the guidance of local farmers, who had volunteered to lead them.

Springbok lies about three miles from O'Okiep, which is the same distance from Concordia, and all three were held by mixed garrisons of British troops and Hottentot levies. Each place was to be attacked in turn, and Springbok came first. its defenders only numbered about one hundred and twenty, but they occupied three well-built forts on high ground, whose loopholes commanded all approaches, so that the disproportion of fighting strength (we had about four hundred men) was not so great as it seemed, particularly as we had to detach nearly half our men to watch Concordia and O'Okiep, in case of a sortie.

Whenever there was any fighting, the staff were re-absorbed into the ranks as ordinary privates, so I was now under Commandant Bouwer, with a detached party, whose instructions were to occupy a low neck over which the main road from O'Okiep crosses into Springbok.

Each contingent filed off quietly in the dark to its allotted post, our orders being to invest the place, but to make no frontal attack, as it was expected that the forts would surrender when they found themselves isolated.

No. 1 Fort, which we were to deal with, was a large round-house, standing on the slag-heap of a mine-shaft. It was heavily loopholed, and the approaches were obstructed by barbed-wire entanglements, so that although less than three dozen men were holding it, they had a clear sweep in all directions, and its capture would be by no means easy without our losing a number of men.

No. 2 Fort lay some hundreds of yards farther away on a low hill, and No. 3 was built on rock overlooking the streets and houses at the far side of the village.

Our party of about forty strong made its way to the neck under a guide, and halted to consult. The night was black, and, as none of us knew exactly where our fort lay, although the guide said it was close by, we decided to send a small patrol to investigate. There were two Irishmen with us, Lang and Gallagher, members of Bouwer's commando, and, with the Irish love of explosives, they had ferreted out a quantity of dynamite and fuses from some outlying mine the day before, with which they had made half a dozen hand-grenades. They were eager to try these, and volunteered to go forward with Edgar Duncker and myself. Leaving the rest behind the neck, we groped our way on until we could make out the dim outline of a wall, where-upon the Irishmen drew the blanket they had brought over their heads, and ignited the fuses of two of the bombs.

The moment the fuses took, the blanket was flung aside, and the projectiles went sizzling through the air, while we hugged the ground to await the result. The bombs blew up simultaneously with a crash and we rushed forward to find that they had exploded harmlessly in an empty cattle-kraal.

The noise, however, brought the enemy to life, for we heard a hoarse 'Halt! Who comes there?' out of the darkness ahead, followed by a crash of musketry, by the light of which we saw the fort, fifteen or twenty yards away, with every port-hole belching fire. One bullet struck the top of the kraal wall as I was looking over, and the fragments of lead and nickel splashed into my face. I thought at first that I was blinded, but I got off lightly, the punctures being only skin-deep, and I had the pieces of metal removed next day with a knife.

In the meanwhile, as the fire was heavy, we remained crouching under cover of the kraal, loosing an occasional shot, but making no attempt to advance on the fort, as we were already nearer than we liked. By now there was also fierce rifle-fire from the other forts, showing that there, too, our men had stirred up hornets' nests, and, when there was a slight lull on our front, we bolted back for the shelter of the neck behind which the others were halted.

General Smuts rode up out of the dark as we were discussing our next move, and, as it was clearing dawn, he ordered us to stay here and see that no one entered or left the fort during the coming day. Having given his instructions, he went off to visit the other posts, and our men distributed themselves amongst the rocks to watch for day-light, while I carried out a small operation of my own. Taking advantage of the still uncertain light, I slipped away, and crawled to a rise at the back of the fort. Here I searched out a convenient stone within forty yards of the enemy, and lay down to wait until the visibility was good enough for shooting. As soon as the sun was well up, I began putting bullets into the loopholes, until I had almost emptied my bandoliers.

The soldiers in the round-house tried hard to locate me, but there was a shrub screening my hiding-place, and, although an occasional bullet flattened itself close by, I lay undetected. When I had nearly finished my ammunition, I wormed my way from rock to rock until I was safe behind the slope and able to rejoin my companions, satisfied that I had given the occupants of the fort an unpleasant time. This was my birthday, the third I had spent in the war, and we passed the rest of the day making more hand-grenades, as we were determined to try again that night.

General Smuts paid us another visit, and, after watching our efforts, told us to send dynamite round to our men at the other two places, which he thought should also be bombed. As soon as it was dark we made ready. Commandant Bouwer came up with some more men, and it was arranged that a smaller party should again go forward to throw the dynamite, after which the others would make a dash at the fort.

Commandant Bouwer, the two Irishmen, and Duncker and I formed the advance-guard. Carrying our boots in our hands for greater silence, we felt our way to the foot of the mound on which the fort stood. Quietly scaling the slope, we reached the outer circle of wire entanglements, without an alarm being raised, and, as we could get no farther, we crouched below the rim, and each lit and threw a bomb. Nearly all of them burst on the roof, and there followed a second or two of dead silence, which we took to mean that the men inside were dead or stunned, but, as we were preparing to climb the wires, a roll of fire flashed along the loopholes and sent us tumbling pell-mell down for cover. The moment the explosions had taken place the balance of our party had rushed through the dark, in order to push home the attack, and they were scrambling up just as we came down, so that there was a collision, which brought us to the bottom in a heap, where we lay laughing helplessly, before we could disentangle ourselves. Despite the stream of bullets, General Smuts now came to us, and, after having climbed the embankment to look at the fort, told Bouwer to remain where he was, without making a direct assault, as the soldiers were bound to surrender sooner or later. Of this, however, there was no immediate sign, for, so far from surrendering, they were shouting strongly flavoured remarks at us, as an accompaniment to their rifle-fire, so we sat down below the rubble-heap to await developments.

During all this time there was firing from the other two forts, and after a while we heard a dull explosion at No. 2, followed by cheers from our men. Soon word was shouted that Albert van Rooyen, of our staff, had breached it with a single bomb that brought about the surrender of the defenders. From what we had seen of No. 3 in daylight, we judged it to be the most difficult of all, for it stood on a high rock, like a castle on the Rhine, and we had not much hope that it would be easily overcome. Before long, however, a bomb went off there too, and we heard the voice of Ben Coetzee calling out to the soldiers to give in. After a short interval there was more cheering, and No. 3 had also surrendered. We shouted to tell the men in No. 1 Fort, but they replied by jeers and volleys. We flung our remaining bombs at them, without apparent effect, and although, as we found afterwards, the steel girders of the roof were buckled, yet they braved it out.

As our stock of grenades was exhausted, General Smuts told me to make my way round the outside of the village to No 3, to bring back dynamite from Maritz, who must have plenty left. I slipped away into the dark, escaping the bullets, but, instead of going wide, I ran as fast as I could through the streets, past the darkened houses.

When I reached No. 3, I saw light shining through the loopholes above, so I climbed the narrow sandbagged stairway and got through the steel trap-door that gave access to the inside, and here I found Maritz and some of his men sorting out ammunition and firearms by lantern light.

The English had hit on the same idea as ourselves for making hand-grenades, and there were several dozen home-made bombs very similar to ours, only smaller. [8]

---

[8] *The Times History of the War; A curious feature (of the operations around O'Okiep) was the use, first by the Boers, and then in retaliation by the defenders, of dynamite bombs.*

Filling a bag with as many as I could carry I accompanied Maritz to where his prisoners were collected at an hotel near by. There were about thirty including the officer in command of the village. I asked him to give me a letter to No. 1 garrison advising them to lay down their arms. This he flatly refused to do. He told me that he had been obliged to surrender his own fort because part of it was built jutting over on wooden beams, and some of our men had got underneath it and were placing dynamite, so that resistance was useless, but he said that, if the men in No. 1 were able to hold out, then good luck to them.

The most I was able to get from him was a pencilled note, scribbled on the bar counter, and addressed to a Mr. Stewart who was in command there, to say that 2 and 3 had been taken, and that he must act according to circumstances.

With this and the bombs, I returned once more through the streets and reached No. 1 mound in safety. When I told general Smuts that I had a note for Mr. Stewart, he said I was to climb up and give it to him. This was more easily said than done, for, when I reached the top, the wire entanglements stopped me, and the soldiers, moreover, were still firing. However, I stood up, and called out, 'Mr. Stewart, Mr. Stewart, here is a letter for you'. At this there was silence, followed by a murmur of voices consulting within, and then a gruff voice asked what I wanted with Mr. Stewart. I said I wanted him to surrender, whereupon I was told to go to hell, and there was a renewed burst of firing, which I only escaped by leaping down.

As a matter of fact, although we did not know it, Mr. Stewart had been lying dead inside the round-house for many hours, and his men were holding out by themselves.

General Smuts, finding them resolute, ordered us to fling the bombs which I had brought. We did this, but they were too light, and only produced more sarcastic remarks and more firing, so he ordered Commandant Bouwer to withdraw his men to the neck, as thirst and hunger would subdue the garrison in the end. When the men slipped back I made off into the town again, for on my return journey through the streets I had heard the stamping of horses in a stable, and had decided to fetch them out.

After groping about the main street for some time, I found the stable, and, striking a match, saw two fine animals at a manger. While I was bringing them away I heard a horseman approaching in the dark. As he passed I seized his reins, and brought him to a standstill, at the same time digging the muzzle of my rifle into his side. He proved to be a British officer, a Lieutenant McIntire, who told me, when he had got over his surprise, that he had been away on a long patrol towards the Orange River for over a week.

He had heard the sound of firing as he neared Springbok, but did not know that the place had been surrounded.

I relieved him of his horse, a sporting Lee-Metford, and a Webley revolver (a weapon which I had long coveted), and, as the hotel at which Maritz and his men were celebrating was brilliantly lit up, I directed my prisoner thither, for I did not wish to be bothered with him. He pretended to go there, but I discovered afterwards that he had doubled back, and made his way past our men to O'Okiep, where I had word of him a few days later, when I went in to demand its surrender.

As for the rest of his patrol, I could hear by the jingling of bits and trampling of hoofs that they were waiting for their officer close by in the dark, so I yelled at them in Dutch and fired several shots, which sent them galloping back, and at sunrise our men rounded them up in a kopje a mile or two away, their horses being too done up to go farther.

I led my three captured horses along and as I went I stumbled on Edgar Duncker looking for a shop to loot. We joined hands and going along the street saw an open, lighted doorway. Here we found a room full of soldiers, with their rifles still in their hands. When we appeared some stood to attention, and one of them said that they were the defenders of No. 1 Fort, that had so stubbornly denied us. They had held out for as long as they could, but their water-supply had long since given out, and they had been forced by thirst to vacate the block-house. Finding that our men had gone from below, they had marched silently into the town, hoping to find a dwelling-house provided with water-tanks where they could carry on the fight. When we appeared, they realized how forlorn was their hope of further resistance, and, after Duncker and I had helped them to find some drinking water in a yard behind, we took them to join their fellows at the hotel.

We were anxious to see the inside of No. 1 Fort, so we got a lantern, and, taking one of the soldiers to lead the way, went to inspect it. The entrance was a zig-zag passage, built high with sandbags, and the doorway was so low that we had to crawl inside. From floor to roof stood a huge iron water-cistern, occupying most of the cramped space. It had been pierced by so many bullets that the water had run out, and in the end the men had been obliged to leave. On a sort of firing-platform lay several dead men. One was Mr. Stewart, and another was a young local volunteer named van Couvorden, son of a doctor from Holland. Both had been shot through the head, and our guide said that they had been killed by a sniper from a rock, which he pointed out to me, when it grew light. It was the very rock from which I had fired the morning before, and this left little doubt in my mind that these two men had fallen to my rifle.

The whole village was now in our hands. Certainly we had far outnumbered the soldiers, but nevertheless it was good work done, for we had captured over a hundred prisoners, and a large stock of rifles, ammunition, and supplies, without the loss of a single man killed or wounded and this against fortified works. General Smuts took up his quarters after daybreak in a large dwelling-house, and we members of the staff busied ourselves with collecting food-stuffs and stores for the use of our mess.

As I had gone for three full days and nights without sleep or rest, I now sought out a bed and turned in without removing my boots. I slept for twenty-four hours, and did not wake until the morning of the next day, when I found my friend Nicolas Swart sitting on the bed beside me. He was almost recovered from his wounds, and had just arrived from the south. He said that General Smuts had taken van Deventer's and Bouwer's men against the neighbouring town of

Concordia, but had left special instructions that I was not to be disturbed, so they had gone away without me. Nicolas promised to take care of my spare horses and other belongings, so I saddled my mare Jinny, and rode after them.

When I reached Concordia, five miles away, it had just surrendered. About one hundred and fifty prisoners were taken, a motley collection of volunteers and Hottentot levies, with many rifles, and an abundance of clothing and other supplies.

In view of this success, General Smuts sent P. Muller and myself to O'Okiep, the largest of the three mining places, with a letter demanding its surrender.

We set off at a gallop with a white cloth on a whipstick, and as the place lay only four miles away, we were soon approaching it. I saw at once that here was a harder nut to crack, for a ring of block-houses and wire entanglements stood all around the town, and inside the circle was a large central fort, flanked by a strong redoubt on a conical hill. As we rode up to the nearest block-house on the plain, half a dozen soldiers ran forward, and when I told them that we had a letter from our General demanding their surrender, one of them shipped the stock of his rifle and said, 'Surrender! Surrender be damned; we're Brummagem boys, we're waiting for ye,' which also seemed unpromising. As we sat our horses, an infuriated officer rushed up from the next block-house, and violently abused us. He was an officer, but no gentleman, for he blustered and swore, and at the point of his revolver ordered us to put up our hands, while he went through our pockets. When I protested that we were under the flag of truce, he violently told me to hold my tongue, and, blindfolding us, marched us into town on foot, to a running fire of angry comment at our effrontery in daring to demand their surrender. I answered him at intervals, until he clapped his revolver to my forehead, and threatened to blow my brains out if I uttered another word, when I began to suspect that we had to do with a madman, and held my tongue.

The climax came when his eyes fell on my horse, being led behind us. I had taken the saddle from lieutenant McIntyre, whose name was marked on the holsters, and the fact that I had come into their lines on a British saddle, and a horse marked with the British broad-arrow, threw him into a fresh paroxysm, and, bawling obscene oaths, he hustled and jostled us along as if we were common malefactors. He was the most disagreeable, in fact the only disagreeable, Englishman whom I met in the war, for, with this one exception, I had no unpleasant word from officer or private in all the time that we were out against them. At length we reached some sort of a camp, to judge by the sounds around us, and here we were left sulkily standing for about an hour, still subjected to abuse. Then a different stamp of man rode up, a superior officer, at whose approach our tormentor faded away, not to reappear. The newcomer was furious when he heard of our treatment, and he at once led us into a tent, and gave us each a cigar and a cooling drink. When, after some time, a reply arrived from Colonel Shelton, the officer in command of O'Okiep, our host personally helped us to mount our horses (for we were still blindfolded), and accompanied us to a point beyond the outer defences. There he uncovered our eyes and bade us a friendly good-bye.

The reply we brought from Colonel Shelton was couched in more elegant language than that received earlier in the morning from the Brummagem boys, but it was to much the same effect, for it said that he had plenty of men and munitions in the town, and that we could do as we liked.

When we handed this answer to General Smuts, he decided on a blockade. He said he did not very much care whether he took O'Okiep or not, as he had all the arms, ammunition, and horses that he wanted, but he was going to make a show of besieging the place, until a relief force arrived, after which he would decide what to do next.

In order to judge for himself how the land lay, he took a patrol out within half an hour of our return. We rode forward until we reached a line of hills overlooking the town. From here we could see troops paraded on an open space close to the main fort, and it seemed that they were being addressed by an officer. This was probably Colonel Shelton, for heliograph messages from him to the relief force, intercepted later, showed that he was given to oratory, and high-flown phrases about England's far-flung Empire and the upholding of the flag.

We opened fire at fifteen hundred yards, and, although we could not see that we had hit anyone, we cleared the parade ground in a few seconds, the soldiers running to their stations, and returning our fire from the blockhouses. If we did no damage below, I drew blood nearer at hand. A large flock of goats was coming up the slope of the hill from the direction of the town, in charge of a Hottentot herdboy. When the firing started, he turned the animals back towards the English lines, so I ran down to within shouting distance, and beckoned him to drive the goats up our way, but, instead of obeying, he, bravely enough, urged them back the faster. As it would have been foolish to allow so valuable a meat-supply to escape, I was obliged to shoot, but I aimed low, and brought him to earth with a bullet through his leg. Then I chased the flock to our side of the hill, with shots from the town spattering about. The wounded herdboy crawled down to the block-house fence, and was fetched in on a stretcher, and I daresay he recovered. As a result of his inspection General Smuts decided that it would be worth his while to bomb some of the defences. He said that by pressing we should force the authorities to dispatch reliefs round by sea from Capetown. Already there was a heliograph winking away towards Port Nolloth on the coast, no doubt asking for help, and his forecast ultimately proved correct in every particular, for in a few days we had word that ships were arriving with a considerable force.

We now returned to our headquarters at Concordia, and, as there was a supply of dynamite and fuses at the copper-mine, we once more set about making bombs.

That night a party of Maritz's men was sent against two block-houses that had been marked down during the day. One of them was the redoubt on a high sugar-loaf kopje, the other was to the right on a somewhat lower ridge.

The assaulting party consisted of twenty men, and as they were under Ben Coetzee, my old friend, I joined them when they met after dark. We started from Concordia, and, when we reached the spot from which we had watched the town that afternoon, we left our horses behind, and worked our way on foot over broken ground to the ridge on which the smaller block-house was situated. We crawled stealthily upward until we were challenged by a sentry, with his 'Halt! Who goes there?' Ben immediately lit and flung a bomb, timing it so well that it brought down a section of the block-house wall, out of which the garrison of ten men came tumbling. They belonged to the Warwickshire Regiment, and, although none of them were killed, all were shaken and dazed. We sent the prisoners, rifles and ammunition to the rear under escort, and then set out to look for the second work on the hill. It was so dark that we lost our bearings and presently found ourselves in the town's cemetery.

After yet more floundering we were challenged and fired at from Fort Shelton, the main stronghold of O'Okiep, situated in the village. We retreated, intending to make back for our horses, but as we went we were halted for the third time, a voice calling to us from somewhere high above our heads. Rifle shots followed, in the glare of which we made out the block-house for which we were looking. Ben Coetzee said we must climb up to it, and we did so unharmed, for the shooting was wild. As soon as we got under cover of the rock-capped summit, we lobbed our remaining bombs on to the roof and against the loopholed wall without making any visible impression, the soldiers within continuing to fire. Then we wormed our way down to our horses, and home to Concordia by midnight.

When General Smuts got our report in the morning, he ordered another raid against the same block-house for the next night. This time Commandant Bouwer supplied the bombers, and I went with them. We left our horses at the same place after dark, and again climbed up. We threw more than a dozen bombs, but in vain; the men within maintained an unceasing fire; the dynamite seemed ineffective, and we had to return empty-handed. Our efforts must have been anxiously followed by the rest of the O'Okiep garrison, for, as we scrambled down, there came a hail through the darkness, 'No. 4 Blockhouse, how are you, lads?' to which a voice replied, 'No. 4 Blockhouse is a-a-all right' and there was much cheering in the town below.

Next morning General Smuts said that the block-house was of no value to us, but that, as we had committed ourselves to taking it, we must carry the work, and he ordered Maritz to go in person. With him went the Marquis de Kersauson, a young French adventurer who had been his constant associate since the war began. I went too, and, as before, we were challenged, but reached the ledge in safety. The first thing Maritz did was to stand on another man's shoulders in order to calculate the throwing distance.

He then climbed down and fastened three bombs together, weighing about twenty pounds. No other man could have hoped to throw so heavy a missile that length, but standing precariously on the shoulders of one of his men, he lit the fuse and hurled the triple grenade right on the roof. The fuse flared and sizzled for a second or two, lighting up the scene for many yards around, and then there was a tremendous roar, and stones and sandbags went flying in all directions. Silence followed, and realizing that the defenders were dead or stunned, we helped each other on to the rocky platform and, crawling over and under the wire entanglements, rushed the entrance passage. From within we heard groans and a muffled voice, 'Stop throwing; stop throwing,' so we crowded in. Striking matches, we saw that the roof was blown down upon the soldiers. A few were dead, and the rest lay on the ground stunned. About half were Warwicks and the rest Hottentot levies. The sergeant in command, on recovering, told us they were the original garrison who had been there since our first attack, having specially asked to remain, and certainly they had acquitted themselves well. The dead and injured men were removed, also the arms and ammunition, and then we placed the remaining sticks of dynamite in the loopholes, and blew No. 4 Block-house into still further ruin before we returned to Concordia.

As the other works and block-houses around O'Okiep could only be approached over level ground bare of cover, General Smuts forbade any further bombing expeditions, and contented himself with investing the town, until such time as the relief force arrived. We had captured some two hundred prisoners in the other two villages and a large stock of supplies, so we could afford to rest for the present, and the next two weeks were spent quietly. I thoroughly enjoyed the lull, and commandeered a small cottage in Concordia to set up housekeeping with Duncker and Nicolas Swart, who was not yet completely recovered from his wounds and required attention. We pressed several Hottentot prisoners into our service as grooms and cook-boys, and as there was plenty of food in the military and mining depots, and sheep and goats in the hills to be had for the fetching, we lived well. General Smuts and the rest of the staff took another building in the village, while Bouwer and Maritz, with their men, lay camped in small parties in the hills around O'Okiep, and van Deventer's commando was posted twenty miles west astride the railway line that comes up from Port Nolloth, to watch the progress of the relief expedition which was now assembling. And so we waited quietly for the order to break away south, on what would have been the most dramatic stroke of the war.

26. THE LOST CAUSE

On the surface things looked prosperous. Five months ago we had come into this western country hunted like outlaws, and today we practically held the whole area from the Olifants to the Orange River four hundred miles away, save for small garrison towns here and there, whose occupants could not show themselves beyond the range of their forts without the risk of instant capture at the hands of the rebel patrols told off to watch them, while we roamed all the territory at will we had enjoyed a number of successes which the British probably regarded as minor incidents, but which our men looked upon as important victories and all this had greatly raised their spirits. Unfortunately, while matters stood thus well with us, the situation in the two Republics up north was far otherwise. Lord Kitchener's relentless policy of attrition was slowly breaking the hearts of the commandos. We had been out of touch with them for so long that we did not realize the desperate straits to which they had come, and our men judged the position from our own more favourable circumstances. Personally, I was not quite so sanguine, for, from such English newspapers as had come my way, I had learned something of the true state of affairs, but I hoped that all would yet be well and I kept my thoughts to myself.

Towards the end of April (1902) I rode out one afternoon with Duncker and Nicolas Swart to snipe at the English posts on the other side of O'Okiep, and, as we were returning to our horses, we saw a cart coming along the road from the south with a white flag waving over the hood. Galloping up, we found two British officers insides who said that they were the bearers of a dispatch from Lord Kitchener.

We took them to Concordia, our pickets amongst the hills riding down from all sides to hear what it was about, but the officers professed ignorance of the contents of their message, although I had an uneasy suspicion of the truth.

When we reached Concordia, General Smuts took them inside his house and remained closeted with them for some time, after which he came out and walked away into the veld by himself in deep thought. We knew then that there was grave news.

That evening he showed me the dispatch. It was a communication from Lord Kitchener to say that a meeting between the English and Boer leaders was to be held at Vereeniging, on the banks of the Vaal River, with a view to discussing peace terms, and he was summoned to attend. A safe-conduct was enclosed, under which he was to proceed through the English lines to Port Nolloth, where he would be taken by sea to Capetown, and from there by rail to the Transvaal.

All this was ominous, and he spoke forebodingly of the future, but, in spite of the shadow that hung over us, one item almost made me forget the darker side, for the safe-conduct provided for a Secretary and an Orderly, and he said that I was to go with him as one of these. I was so delighted at the prospect of going on a journey like this that for the time being I gave thought to little else.

The men were the real tragedy. They had endured against great odds, facing years of peril and hardship without pay or reward, and they still had so much faith in the cause for which they were fighting that, when the news trickled through next day that General Smuts was to go to a peace conference, they were convinced that the British were suing for terms and were ready to restore our country.

It was pitiful to listen to their talk, and to see their faces light up when they spoke of having won through at last, and I, for one, had not the heart to disillusion them, or even to hint at a result other than favourable, so steadfast was their trust.

General Smuts set to work at once. Next morning a messenger was sent into O'Okiep, to advise the garrison that both sides were to refrain front active military operations while the Congress lasted, and the two British officers went on ahead to Steinkopf, to warn the relief force collecting there that we were shortly passing through their-pickets.

The day after that the commando came in from the out-lying posts to say good-bye to their leader. The men paraded before the Court House, each man sitting his horse, rifle at thigh, while General Smuts addressed them. He briefly told them of the object of his going, and asked them to be prepared for disappointment if need be, but there were only cheers and shouts of courage, as they pressed from all sides to wish him farewell.

I steered through the throng to shake hands with such as I could reach, waving to others beyond, and in this way I saw the last of many good friends and companions.

We set off next day, escorted by a small patrol. I left my spare horses, rifle, and gear with Nicolas Swart and Edgar Duncker, my best friends, whom I have not met again. We reached van Deventer's commando that afternoon where they were watching the troops that had come up from the sea, and for the last time we spent a night around camp fires. In the morning we made ready to pass into the English lines. As we started, General Smuts told me that his brother-in-law, Krige, was the other man to accompany him, and he said we were to arrange amongst ourselves which was to be Secretary and which Orderly, so I chose to be Orderly, as I thought it meant an aide-de-camp, and left my companion to be Secretary. Soon after that we saddled our horses, said good-bye to van Deventer and his men, and rode down the valley towards the English lines. Far down we were met by Colonel Collins, who commanded the relief expedition. Here our escort took over our horses, and, after singing our Commando Hymn, and firing a farewell volley into the air, they wheeled round and galloped cheering away towards their own side, to the manifest interest of the English officers and troopers lined up beside the road. With them went the last of our free life and all that it had meant to us.

A cart was brought, in which General Smuts, Krige, and I were driven to a large camp standing beside the railway line, where a guard of honour was drawn up to receive us, behind which crowds of soldiers had gathered to see the Boer Emissaries. I now discovered that I had made a mistake, and that an Orderly was an officer's batman, whereas a Secretaryship carried commissioned rank. Krige was invited into Colonel Collins's tent with General Smuts, while I was led to the servants' mess, and when, an hour later, a train stood ready to take us to Port Nolloth he and General Smuts were ceremoniously ushered into a first-class compartment, whilst I was put aboard an open cattle-truck with the luggage. However, being in an enemy camp and travelling by rail for the first time for nearly two years was so exciting that it made no difference to me where I was, and Krige and I appreciated the humorous side of our respective positions. Whenever he looked out of the carriage window and saw me sitting in the truck behind, he roared with laughter, and so did I, at his having become an officer, and I a servant.

When the train drew up at the next station there was another guard of honour for General Smuts and his Secretary, who were taken in to a grand luncheon, whilst I forgathered with the batmen in the kitchen behind. At the next halting-place I underwent record promotion. There was an officer of the Hussars, Captain Barclay, who had been deputed to accompany us to the coast, and having seen me standing about, he asked General Smuts who I was. The General explained that on commando there were no social distinctions, but that he had brought me along because he thought my father might be at the Conference. Captain Barclay telephoned up the line to Colonel Collins, to say that a son of the Transvaal State Secretary was of the party as an orderly, and he presently came to me and said, 'Young man, you are Chief-of-Staff to General Smuts; come along and join us.' He jokingly assured me that the promotion from batman to field rank in the course of one morning was the quickest known in any army.

Towards evening we reached Port Nolloth, a dreary little seaport, where many troopships lay at anchor. One of these, the *Lake Erie*, was under steam, and even as the train ran into the station, a boat set out to fetch us.

This was the end of our long roving. We stood on the quayside, silently looking back on the way we had come, each busy with his own thoughts. I do not know what was in the minds of my companions, but perhaps they, too, were thinking of the long road we had travelled, of camp-fires on mountains and plains, and of the good men and splendid horses that were dead.

With heavy hearts we got into the boat that was to take us to the ship, and the moment we were on board they weighed anchor, and we sailed southward.

In spite of our mission, the voyage was one of great pleasure to me. After years of rough fare and hard living, we had luxurious cabins, with soft beds to lie on; a steward with coffee in the morning, a bath ready prepared and food such as I had almost forgotten the existence of. All this seemed like a dream, and I enjoyed every moment of it.

We reached Capetown in five days, and were transhipped to Simonstown on board the battleship *Monarch* with Captain Parkes, and here again we spent a week in comfort, for officers and men vied with each other in their efforts to welcome us. The British, with all their faults, are a generous nation, and not only on the man-of-war, but throughout the time that we were amongst them, there was no word said that could hurt our feelings or offend our pride, although they knew that we were on an errand of defeat.

At length orders came for us to go north. We were rowed ashore after dark to a landing-stage below the Simonstown railway station, and taken to a train that was standing ready. We were hurried through the suburbs of Capetown and then switched on to the main line at Salt River Junction, to find ourselves at Matjes-fontein in the Karoo next day. Here General French came to see us, a squat, ill-tempered man, whom we did not like, although he tried to be friendly. He sat talking to us for an hour or more trying to draw General Smuts, who had no difficulty in parrying his clumsy questions. When he made no head-way, he became more natural and spoke of his experiences during the war, in the course of which he told us how narrowly we had missed capturing him that night below the Stormbergen.

From Matjesfontein we continued our journey, travelling at night only, an armoured train puffing ahead all the way, its searchlight sweeping the veld. Each day we were side-tracked at some lonely spot till dark, and thus made slow progress. I have been told that we were purposely delayed lest, coming from the Cape where the outlook was brighter, we might persuade the Transvaalers that things were not so bad as they seemed. For this reason Lord Kitchener did not wish us to appear amongst them until matters had gone too far for them to turn back. However that may be, it took us the better part of a week to reach Kroon-stad in the Northern Free State, where Lord Kitchener was to meet us. Soon after our arrival he rode up to the station on a magnificent black charger, followed by a numerous suite, including turbaned Pathans, in Eastern costume with gold-mounted scimitars.

His retinue waited outside while he came into our compartment to talk. He was anxious to bring the war to a close, for he referred again and again to the hopelessness of our struggle, telling us that he had four hundred thousand troops in South Africa against our eighteen thousand. He said that he was prepared to let the burghers retain their horses and saddles in recognition or the fight that they had made, and that the British Government would help to rebuild the destroyed farmhouses, the burning of which he defended on military grounds.

General Smuts taxed him with having unfairly executed our men in the Cape, and this, too, he justified, on the plea that we had used khaki uniforms to decoy his soldiers.

Before going he told us that we were to proceed to the Eastern Transvaal, to find General Botha, and that the conference at Vereeniging would only take place after that.

Accordingly, from Kroonstad, still escorted by an armoured train, we crossed the Vaal River into the Transvaal. We went through Johannesburg at night, and here they turned us east on to the Natal line, until we came to the town of Standerton, where we left the train and travelled by cart along a block-house line that ran straight over the high veld. At intervals there were small English camps, at each of which the troops turned out and treated us with courtesy.

We journeyed for a day and-a-half, until we reached a point where a party of horsemen sent by General Botha was awaiting us. They had brought spare horses, so we left the cart with the troopers, and, striking across country, travelled for two days over bare and deserted plains, to the place where the Commandant-General was expecting us. Here about three hundred men were assembled. They were delegates from every commando in the Eastern Transvaal, come to elect representatives to the Peace Congress to be held at Vereeniging, and nothing could have proved more clearly how nearly the Boer cause was spent than these starving, ragged men, clad in skins or sacking, their bodies covered with sores, from lack of salt and food, and their appearance was a great shock to us, who came from the better-conditioned forces in the Cape. Their spirit was daunted, but they had reached the limit of physical was endurance, and we realized that, if these haggard, emaciated men were the pick of the Transvaal commandos, then the war must be irretrievably lost.

Food was so scarce that General Botha himself had only a five strips of leathery biltong to offer us, and he said that, but for the lucky chance of having raided a small herd of cattle from the British a fortnight before, he would have been unable to hold the meeting at all.

I inquired at once for news of my father and my three brothers. General Botha gave me word of my father. He told me that he was with one of the northern commandos, and would in all probability be at the coming Conference. He could tell me nothing of my brothers, but by asking among the men, I learned that my eldest brother, Hjalmar, had been captured by the Australians more than a year before, and that my second brother, Joubert, was taken prisoner whilst lying ill of malarial fever in the low country, apparently not long after I had last seen him at the Warm Baths, towards the end of 1900. I could find out nothing about my youngest brother Arnt.

Next day the elections were held. Even in adversity the Boer instinct for speeches and wordy wrangling asserted itself, and the time was passed in oratory, and with nominations and re-nominations of candidates, but by evening the complicated balloting was finished, and some thirty delegates elected.

Next morning the gathering dispersed, the men riding off on their hungry-looking horses to rejoin their distant units, while General Botha and the successful deputies started back for the English block-house line.

We arrived here by the following evening. The troops supplied us with food, for we were famishing, and we now returned along the block-houses to Standerton, the soldiers everywhere standing respectfully to attention as our tattered cavalcade went by. At Standerton we entrained for Vereeniging. This is a small mining village on the banks of the Vaal River, where, nearly two years before, I had watched the Irishmen burning the railway stores during the retreat from the south.

The British had prepared a large tented camp for our reception, and almost the first man I saw as we entered was my father, shaggy and unkempt, but strong and well, and our greeting after so long a parting was deep and heartfelt.

And now the delegates came in from the rest of the Transvaal and from the Free State. Every leader of note was there. General de la Rey, Christian de Wet, President Steyn, Beyers, Kemp, and many others, the best of the Boer fighting-men. We learned from General de Wet that my younger brother had been serving under him for more than a year, and that he was still safe and sound, so we were all accounted for. Although two were prisoners of war, we had been luckier than the majority of families, most of whom were mourning their dead, whereas all five of us were still alive.

I know little of the actual Peace Conference as I was not a delegate, but the outcome was a foregone conclusion. Every representative had the same disastrous tale to tell of starvation, lack of ammunitions horses, and clothing, and of how the great block-house system was strangling their efforts to carry on the war. Added to this was the heavy death-roll among the women and children, of whom twenty-five thousand had already died in the concentration camps, and the universal ruin that had overtaken the country. Every homestead was burned, all crops and live-stock destroyed, and there was nothing left but to bow to the inevitable.

After prolonged debates the Conference suspended its sittings for a day, whilst General Botha, my father, general de la Rey and others went to Pretoria to conclude the final treaty with Lord Kitchener and Lord Milner.

On their return peace was an accomplished fact.

Of the sting of defeat—I shall not speak, but there was no whining or irresponsible talk. All present accepted the verdict stoically, and the delegates returned quietly to their respective commandos, to make known the terms of surrender. I was spared the ordeal of returning to break the news to our men in the Cape, for my father insisted upon my remaining with him when General Smuts went south. When he came to take leave of me, he said that he dreaded the task of telling the men, and our hearts were heavy at he thought of the disappointment awaiting them. We shook hands for the last time, and then he, too, was gone.

My father was sent into the low country, to arrange for the bringing in of the commando with which he had been serving. We travelled by rail to Balmoral

Station on the Delagoa Bay line, and from there on horseback into the wild country through which my brother and I had ridden in search of General Beyers, earlier in the war. After two days hard going we found the camp, and my father had the unpleasant duty of telling the men that all was over. Most of them took it calmly, but some cursed and vowed hat they would never surrender. My father, although he had himself voted against peace at the Conference, pointed out to them that they should either submit to what had been done, or leave the country, as he intended doing. This quieted the more turbulent, and we started back next day for Balmoral, where the men were to hand in their rifles. this depressing ceremony was presided over by an English officer, seated at a table beneath the trees, with a regiment of troops in reserve close by. Despite his protests, our men fired away their ammunition into the air, smashed their rifle-butts and sullenly flung the broken weapons down, before putting their names to the undertaking which each man was called upon to sign, that he would abide by the peace terms.

When my father's turn came, he handed over his rifle to the officer in charge, but refused to sign. He said that although he was one of the signatories to the Peace Treaty, he had told Lord Milner at the time that he was setting his hand to the document in his official capacity as State Secretary of the Transvaal and not as a private individual, and Lord Milner had accepted his signature on that basis.

The officer pointed out that he would not be allowed to remain in the country, and my father agreed. I had no very strong convictions on the subject, but I had to stand by him, so I also refused to sign, and was told that I would be put across the border, which troubled me little, as I was eager to see more of the world.

When all was over, the men rode off on their different ways, to search for what remained of their families and ruined homes.

My father and I went to Balmoral Station, where a message had been received from Lord Milner confirming the order that we were to be deported, but qualifying it to the extent of allowing my father a fortnight in which to settle his affairs in Pretoria. And so we returned, after more than two years of wandering. We found our home in the possession of a British General with sentries outside who forbade approach. Our household goods had disappeared, and had it not been for the hospitality of a friend we should have gone roofless. During this time my younger brother came riding in from the Free State, six inches taller than when I last saw him, and none the worse for his long adventure. He, too, decided to go, and so, towards the end of June, we went into self-imposed exile.

As we were waiting on the border at Komati Poort, before passing into Portuguese territory, my father wrote on a piece of paper a verse which he gave me.

It ran:

SOUTH AFRICA,

> Whatever foreign shores my feet must tread,
> My hopes for thee are not yet dead.
> Thy freedom's sun may for a while be set,
> But not for ever, God does not forget,

and he said that until liberty came to his country he would not return.

He is now in America and my brother and I are under the French flag in Madagascar.

We have heard of my other two brothers. The eldest has reached Holland from his prison camp in India, and the other is still in Bermuda awaiting release.

Maritz and Robert de Kersauson are with us in Madagascar. We have been on an expedition far down into the Sakalave country, to see whether we could settle there.

General Gallieni provided us with riding-mules and a contingent of Senegalese soldiers, as those parts are still in a state of unrest. It was like going to war again, but all went quietly, and we saw much that was of interest - lakes and forests; swamps teeming with crocodiles, and great open plains grazed by herds of wild cattle. But for all its beauty the island repels one in some intangible manner, and in the end we shall not stay.

At present we are eking out a living convoying goods by ox-transport between Mahatsara on the East Coast and Antananarive, hard work in dank fever-stricken forests, and across mountains sodden with eternal rain; and in my spare time I have written this book.

Antananarive,
Madagascar.
1903.

Breinigsville, PA USA
04 August 2010
243068BV00004B/21/P